THE PITTSBURGH THEOLOGICAL MONOGRAPH SERIES

Dikran Y. Hadidian

General Editor

27

THE PERSONALIST CHALLENGE

INTERSUBJECTIVITY AND ONTOLOGY

THE PERSONALIST CHALLENGE

INTERSUBJECTIVITY AND ONTOLOGY

BY

Maurice Nédoncelle

Translated by
François C. Gérard and Francis F. Burch

PICKWICK PUBLICATIONS

Allison Park, Pennsylvania

1984

Originally published as *Intersubjectivité
et Ontologie: le defi personnaliste*.
© 1974 by Editions Nauwelaerts.
This translation consists of Chapters
I-XVII and the Final Remarks from
the original edition.

Copyright © 1984 by **Pickwick Publications**
4137 Timberlane Drive, Allison Park, PA 15101

Library of Congress Cataloging in Publication Data

Nédoncelle, Maurice.
    The personalist challenge.

    (The Pittsburgh theological monograph series ; 27)
    Translation of: Intersubjectivité et ontologie.
    1. Intersubjectivity. 2. Ontology. 3. Phenomenology.
4. Religion—Philosophy. I. Title. II. Series.
B824.18.N4313   1984   126   83-26293
ISBN 0-915138-29-8

CONTENTS

III. Religious Philosophy

INTRODUCTION

Here is the world, sound as a
nut, perfect, not the smallest
piece of chaos left, never a stitch
nor an end, not a mark of haste,
or botching, or second thought;
but the theory of the world is
a thing of shreds and patches.

--Ralph Waldo Emerson

Maurice Nédoncelle (1905-1976) was an important figure in the world of French intellect, his voice was heard at conferences and in symposia throughout the world, and he continues to be cited by leading authorities on a variety of philosophical and theological questions. Yet not all of his works have received the translations they deserve and beyond France he has not the audience he merits.

The Personalist Challenge, a version of Nédoncelle's last major publication, makes accessible a timely study. The philosopher hoped that this digest of his thoughts of a lifetime might help to give personalist philosophy a "second wind" in the face of a growing army of militant anti-personalists. He would not find that its numbers have diminished in the 1980's.

Personalist philosophies are not new, but Nédoncelle's personalism is an aggressive opposition to several modern efforts to restrict the traditional preserve of the philosopher. This larger question is really the heart of his corpus and sustains his personalist argument in the changing climate of French philosophy and politics. To appreciate his accomplishment, we need to be familiar with his circumstances. Philosophers react to what is in the air, but winds change. We can be left wondering what inspired or provoked them. A brief review of some forces that helped shape Nédoncelle's thought may be useful.

The Cartesian Tradition

Nédoncelle should be seen in the context of debate which was initiated in France by the confrontation between the Cartesians and scholastics. Descartes' method (especially his subjectivity, his starting point of universal doubt, and his insistence on clear and distinct ideas) has been an issue. So much philosophical discussion of the last three hundred years has concerned philosophical doubt, clarity, distinctions, the knowing subject.

Husserl's phenomenology is the more immediate basis of Nédoncelle's philosophy and a study of Husserl's sources quickly reveals this classic confrontation. Husserl's most influential professor in Vienna was a Thomist and an empiricist. Franz Brentano offered the scholastic tradition, but insisted on a method which held natural science for prototype. The Cartesian clarity and distinction of concepts and their articulation here received added support from Hume and from mathematically structured fields, the "hard" sciences.

Brentano was also a psychologist and in the forefront of his philosophy is the notion of intentionality, the notion that the basic structure of human existence is to be toward, that every intentional act refers to something. This subjective dynamism adds a new element to the scholastic-Cartesian discussion. We find in Husserl, from his early reflections on mathematics to his **Méditations Cartésiennes** (reworkings of his lectures at the Sorbonne in 1930), a very similar concept of intentionality.

Nédoncelle's "intersubjectivity" has clear traces of intentionality. He does more than repeat the ancient and medieval formulae for thought and existence. Phenomenological analysis which takes into account at once the one experiencing and what is experienced involves elements removed from Platonic ideas or Aristotelian natures or the scholastic attempts to bring the two into an objective cosmos.

The Debate Concerning Christian Philosophy

Nédoncelle's early intellectual evolution took place in a context which questioned the possibility of a Christian philosophy. In 1931, the Société Française de Philosophie launched a debate which drew upon such thinkers as Blondel and over the years engaged, among others, Maritain, de Lubac, Nédoncelle. The full sweep of this exchange reveals great complication and wide implications which cannot be considered here, but which were recently summed up with remarkable clarity in Henri de Lubac's **Recherches**

dans la Foi, (Paris, 1979). At bottom, it is an argument over what to include or exclude from "scientific" philosophy.

The marriage of nineteenth-century German rationalism and materialism produced one of those offspring that for better or worse exerted an influence well beyond its time and place. Observation and analysis of the material world, rigorous methodologies bounded by strict "reason," deep suspicion of any inferential step beyond material fact and of any other human faculty--"science" was redefined and "scientific" became the cachet of the "serious" scholar in all fields. Classical studies and history quickly adjusted, but with a growing consensus on general method and with a firm focus on fundamental research, the "scientists" envisioned disciplining every discipline, transforming every area of study into a "science" and every scholar into a "scientist."

The prodigious quantity and quality of Wissenschaft--much of it still supports some branches of study--sooner or later made suspect other approaches and goals. Many a fine intellect felt obliged to defend a method or to justify a stand, because it was at variance with the new scientism. Philosophy and theology were not immune; for the new textual, historical, and archeological explorations could not fail to yield information and to raise questions germane to traditional thought and religion.

From our present vantage, much of the general debate may appear ill-advised and ill-humored. To accept the postulates of nineteenth-century scientism was to be trapped with many of its conclusions. The attempt to fight it on its own ground and according to its own rules guaranteed at best a Pyrrhic victory and at worst a foregone disaster. Nevertheless, the controversy continued into our century and the milieu of the philosophico-religious conflict was influenced by "scientific" history, by "scientific" textual criticism, and by a prevailing sense that anything traditional was on the defensive, that earlier inquiries had attempted too much and achieved too little, that they were not methodologically sound. This intimidation continues to be felt in some quarters, well past the time when the serious scholar should submit to the narrow straights of outmoded concepts of both matter and reason, and when the limits of all methodologies have been the outspoken frustration of thinkers from a Malraux to an Einstein.

Still the achievements of the movement are not to be denied. Both philosophy and theology have profited from lexicography and critical texts. For example, the **Thesaurus Linguae Latinae** and the Tübingen editions are witness of meticulous devotion to the most minute detail, and they have provided a new confidence in fundamental terms and texts. But Nédoncelle saw equally real limitations. Sharper discrimination of elements and clearer control of materials are all to the good; the handicap appears when there is an unwillingness to accept anything beyond the confines of such method and matter. The failure to work with a critical edition of a text need not vitiate the project; facts and ideas whose evidence of origin and development is lost are not thereby invalidated. A study need not be value-free (as if that were possible) to be valuable. The old does not yield so easily to the new.

Definitions are of course part of the issue. History and philosophy are redefined. Herodotus and Tacitus certainly did not compose histories and the Bible is clearly not historical, if we confine history within the norms of nineteenth-century historicism. Strangely it took decades before the timid opposition found courage enough to insist that such ancient authors were indeed historians, that they were not naïve, that they wrote from premises and achieved goals quite other than those desired by their critics, and that there is nothing wrong with that. The search for the actual words of Pericles or for the "historical" Jesus is valuable, but it is not the only justifiable historical approach to evidence, especially to authors who did not intend to offer detail, but rather substance.

Philosophers on the whole resisted redefinition more ardently than historians, perhaps because they realized more clearly what was at stake. Behind the argument concerning the possibility of a Christian philosophy lies a question that is more fundamental than this partisan debate may suggest. Philosophers can be guilty of several faults. Two are particularly limiting. First, they may throw away some element discovered in analysis, because these do not accord with an hypothesis or fit into a synthesis. Second, philosophers can be guilty of considering elements in such isolation that they assume unjustified importance for very lack of competition, from a paucity of material; here such items take on meaning that would appear out of kilter with other elements in the broader context.

Nédoncelle struggles to avoid these pitfalls. His investigations from the 1930's on have all touched in some way on the relation of philosophy to theology or, more precisely, on the frequent interrelation of rational and religious experience. Finally, in 1956, he devoted an entire work to the question: **Existe-t-il une Philosophie Chrétienne**? At this point, he sides with the position of Maurice Blondel. A philosophy can be Christian and a Christian philosophy will be one which "by proclaiming the insufficiency of human nature to resolve the whole problem of man, discerns and in some sense marks out a supernatural gift which would resolve the problem but for which philosophy itself cannot substitute" (**Is There a Christian Philosophy?** New York, 1960, p. 149). This clarification should be kept in mind through Nédoncelle's consideration of the autonomy of philosophy. His own philosophy is in tension with theology.

Postwar Pessimism

While engaged in the struggle not to let slip from philosophy what they considered a significant part of human experience--
the sense of the divine--this line of French thinkers found itself
in an era of death and destruction. Many folk blamed the political
and economic situation on intellectuals. Whatever their position
on the question of a Christian philosophy, most European philosophers felt called to be militant, to withstand and force back the
anti-philosophical tide which followed Germany's collapse in the
1940's. This is not the place to dispute the thesis that history
is the working out of philosophy, but German disillusionment with
the thought that had led to disastrous consequences and indeed
a suspicion of all philosophy are too well known to require comment.

French pessimism was less, but it is clear enough in
Sartre and the early existentialists. Sartre returned from his studies
in Germany with plenty of ideas from Husserl and Heidegger.
"Dasein zum Tode" ("to be there toward death") and its miasma
of "Sorge" ("care") were pervasive. Indeed, much mid-century
existentialism now appears to have been an attempt to push aside
earlier optimism about what we know and how we should behave.
Atheistic and antisocial, the popular existentialist heroes of stage
and page in the 1940's and early 1950's were alone in the universe.
The mood would mellow, but for all his early activism, Sartre's
mature politics and ethics are late additions to his corpus. Camus'
socialized rebel is a good decade older than his isolated stranger.
The context of the intellectuals at this time is the subject of
Simone de Beauvoir's best-selling and prize-winning, **The Mandarins.**

Who are we? Where do we stand in the universe? Postwar
philosophy was much concerned with the notion of person. Whether
or not philosophy would have developed the same notion of person
without Christian revelation, historically it did not. The New Testament reveals God both as personal and as triune, and the Christian
amplification and extension of these two related ideas is not
unimportant in the evolution of our concept of personality. Analysis
of person in isolation is logically possible, but constitutes self-
imposed limitations and does violence to experience. Metaphysically,
our personal existence is inconceivable without interpersonal relations, and daily life and thought bear this out. Wish and try as
we may, we cannot avoid a network of interontic and interpersonal
relationships. For mortals and gods, nirvana is temporary: pain
or karma or samsara refuse to be extinguished. We are not alone
on earth, in heaven, or in hell.

The implications of limiting the person are perhaps most

obvious in considerations of freedom. The Greeks were late in the day when they struggled to reconcile the will of man with the will of the gods and Nédoncelle was not impressed by the attempts to constrict freedom in the exaltation of the forces of nature. He rejected a variety of determinisms which threaten the self: some are bio-chemical and psychological, others economic and political. From within and without, the individual is pulled to surrender to forces beyond human control. To do so is, in Nédoncelle's view, a betrayal of both experience and philosophy.

Intersubjectivity and liberty are at issue here, as in the debate over Christian philosophy. As the philosopher denies a place in his world to God or to his fellowmen, so he diminishes the person. If he views all that is personal in the great chain of being as no different from what is not, he diminishes the person. Nédoncelle is no stranger to otherness and Angst, and he recognizes the limitations on human freedom, but he argues against accepting radical alienation with or without a fight and he firmly rejects radical slavery to whatever matter or force. The fullness of personal experience involves freedom and relationships (autonomy and heteronomy). The philosopher who confines us to a solipsistic prison or reduces us to realities that we do indeed experience as other narrows our philosophical universe.

Structuralism

By the 1960's, new currents of thought were washing over traditional boundaries of academic and professional fields and early structuralism was branching into a variety of blends of modern anthropological, psychoanalytical, and linguistic ideas. The cultural anthropology of Claude Lévi-Strauss, the rethinking of the notion of the unconscious as by Jacques Derrida, Jacques Lacan's theoretical views of reading and practical interpretation of Freudian texts, these are some of the more obvious points of departure. But there is also an influence from the United States.

The "new criticism" was taken seriously. Even professors at the Sorbonne directed students toward Warren, Wellek, and Wimsatt. The basic book was Warren and Wellek's **Theory of Literature,** but the central doctrine was to be found in W. K. Wimsatt's 1946 essay on "The Intentional Fallacy." By the 1960's, Northrop Frye had become a popular voice for the movement. Lawrence Lipking's fine survey on "Literary Criticism" in the recent handbook of the Modern Language Association of America uses Frye as the leading edge of the doctrine: "We have to avoid of course the blunder that is called the intentional fallacy in criticism. The question 'What did the author mean by this?' is always illegitimate. First, we can never know; second, there is no reason to suppose that the author knew; third, the question confuses imaginative with discursive writing. The legitimate form of the question is: 'What does the text say?' " (See **Introduction to Scholarship in Modern Languages and Literatures,** ed. Joseph Gibaldi, New York, 1981, p. 79).

Nédoncelle had read Warren and Wellek and was well aware of the climate that was fostering the "new" novel of a Nathalie Sarraute or Alain Robbe-Grillet and the "new" literary criticism of a Roland Barthes or Ferdinand de Saussure, the theater of the absurd of an Ionesco, and the view of a Beckett that the text got some order in the mess of life. All of it gave witness to doubt about what we know or can know concerning the world or our thoughts and emotions. Much of it echoed the traditions of logical empiricism, the new conceptions of the inner self, and a variety of politico-economic theories of second generation Marxists. Most of it was anti-humanist, an elevation of structure, habit, or force to an autonomy which neglects and, in some cases, denies the person.

Nédoncelle bristled against this new hermeticism. He was not unimpressed with some of the new insights, but he cautioned against the myopia of methodological intolerance and was particularly critical of the erosion of the rich philosophical tradition of the person. He would have concurred with the ire of Denis Donoghue's **Ferocious Alphabets** (New York, 1981): "I detest the current ideology which refers, gloatingly, to the death of the author, the obsolescence of the self, the end of man, and so forth."

The English-reading audience will be familiar with the "new criticism" which flourished in American universities for a generation and will recall the emphasis on text which offered an important corrective to the use of literary works as points of departure for excursus on biography or history. They will also recall that the more rabid apostles of the "new criticism" soon insisted that the literary text had a life of its own and that biography and history were irrelevant and anathema, and rallied to Archibald MacLeish's slogan: "A poem should not mean, but be!" But the structuralist extension of the doctrine--the exaltation of textual autonomy to the detriment of its heteronomy (what the critics of the last century called its Sitz im Leben)--has been slow to gain popularity in British and American academic circles.

Now, as the French debate over structuralism is cooling, the Anglo-American debate is heating up. Paul de Man at Yale, the translations of and comments on the French forerunners offered by the Johns Hopkins University Press, the frequent visits of French structuralists to foreign universities--Jacques Derrida was one of the most popular--such forces must now be reckoned with. By 1981, one Oxford professor could charge that he had been denied a permanent position for his advocacy of structuralism and another would resign to protest faculty conservatism. In 1982, the storm broke at Cambridge where some students and young faculty insist that examination graders punish heretics who abandon traditional approaches to literary studies for structural analysis. Still, in many English-speaking universities, structuralism deconstructionism, and semiotics are fast becoming the accepted orthodoxy of literary and linguistic faculties. Structural analysis is also now a commonplace of scriptural publications and is making advances into patristic studies.

Nédoncelle's Stance

The career of this sometime dean and longtime professor of philosophy at the University of Strasbourg spans the periods of renewed interest in the Schoolmen, of modern existentialism, of structuralism; the main and tributary movements of the twentieth-century philosophical current provided him with a rich mixture of thought. The breadth of his reflections give witness to a knowledge of systematic scholasticism and an interest in the history of ideas, but he was not a mere historian of philosophy. He was a philosopher, cosmopolitan and ecumenical, who used the tools of modern through and engaged in the modern arguments.

His humanist philosophy was born in confrontation, strengthened by research, and matured in reflection. It is not ivory-tower thought. The focus on the person is the result of education, but also of those events which forced their way into the neat systems of the classroom and demanded a hearing. People and events challenged him each step of the way and he was drawn into a variety of discussions, but movement from the personalist center was usually an exploration of the interontic or interpersonal relations of the person and a chance to define his own position by evaluating it with respect to those of other thinkers. He always argued against those who would dissuade exploration of personal values, relations, and functions. Where we do not explore, we will not discover.

Nédoncelle's presentation is a delicate balance which shows that he is trying to avoid the extremes of materialism and idealism, determinism and libertarianism, in short, the gamut of absolutisms and reductionisms whether Darwinian, Marxist, Freudian. His meticulous phenomenological description grounds him so firmly in his experience that he will not deny their reality to accommodate any a priori principle or system. Less convinced than Husserl and more in line with Max Scheler and Henri Bergson, he never decided whether phenomenology was pre-metaphysical or metaphysical, but he was aware that limited experience limits philosophy and that many philosophers present defective microcosms for the macrocosm. He is suspicious of thinkers who would cut philosophy free from experience and he shows little enthusiam for systems which elevate method at the expense of the philosophical goal or focus on this content to the distortion or dismissal of that.

The notion of person to which he is pulled by both positive and negative argument is always the same. Not a species of philosophical being confined to the mind, not a determined entity whether elevated or victimized by elements or forces beyond human control, not an alienated creature in a hostile universe, not a material quiddity incompatible with spirit and the divine, but the full person, the center of a near-infinite complexus of relationships, who cannot surrender radical identity and autonomy to any other person, group, or government.

Beneath it all lies the eternal question: should the philosopher pursue transcendent unity or minimal clarity? Etienne Gilson describes this tension in his "Preface" to M. D. Chenu's **Nature, Man, and Society in the Twelfth Century** as he reflects on Thomism:

> Those whose allegiances are to other traditions have difficulty grasping the extent to which the theology of St. Thomas concentrates within itself all the responses which one and the same mind can experience on all levels of man's intellectual life . . . "Thomism" is integrally and indivisibly a philosophy, a theology, a spirituality, and a mysticism born in its entirety from the word of God, nourishing itself on that word and illuminating it in turn with its own light. But that which is one in life necessarily becomes divided in teaching and, too often, becomes fragmented in history . . . To permit it [the unity of Thomistic theology] to be resolved into separate disciplines is to permit its destruction. In fact the theology of St. Thomas is not a constellation of diverse disciplines. Rather, it eminently embraces them all within its transcendent unity. (Chicago, 1957, p. xi).

We need not be Thomists to recognize the full range of human experience and to appreciate efforts at full articulation of reality. Nor need we share Gilson's or Chenu's position in the debate concerning Christian philosophy to recognize that philosophies which deal with only part of experience are only partial philosophies. And we can have no doubt that Nédoncelle would opt for wisdom (sapientia) over knowledge (scientia) and certainly over definitions. Even when this personalist phenomenologist is struggling with Descartes' cogito and Husserl's intentionality in the midst of existentialists and structuralists, he is still the philosopher in the root sense of the word; for he is, after all, the lover of sophia-- wisdom.

This Translation

Collections of papers have the virtues and defects of compilations. Considered as a single work, this volume reveals the central concerns of the philosopher and his commitment to explore the fullest range of reality. But composed over several years and originally intended for a variety of audiences, the individual studies show differences of style: subtle changes in viewpoint occur as we move from section to section, details and even digressions, interesting enough in themselves, do not always contribute to the main thrust of the investigation. Some sections are heavy with documentation, others were intended for a more popular audience and are not footnoted; some are easy introductions to a topic, others are hard going. In short, the line of development does not here appear as sharply etched as it does in works which Nédoncelle composed as single studies or which are more limited in scope, witness La Réciprocité des Consciences (1943) and Explorations Personnalistes (1970).

What we have is an intellectual autobiography not unlike Montaigne's **Essays.** Nédoncelle's series of attempts are not a quest for full thought or formal perfection, nor are they intended as final statements. They preserve a series of insights and represent repeated struggle to organize thought. Here, more clearly than in his previous books, we see how his mind works. Earlier volumes are the product of a process made more manifest in these pages. We get closer to the philosopher as a contemplative being and become aware of the distinction between contemplation and composition as we progress from his phenomenology, through his metaphysics, to his religious philosophy--the three sections of the English edition of **The Personalist Challenge.**

The French original has an historical section which is here omitted, not because it is without insights, but because the personalist tradition has often been detailed in modern histories of philosophy. Frederick Copleston's well-known **History of Philosophy** does not neglect the idea of person as it moves through the centuries. Also, Nédoncelle's historical studies constitute an argument from authority which has already been presented in the earlier sections where frequent references to the origin and development of western philosophy sketch an ample map for those who would pursue the history of such ideas beyond this work.

The Personalist Challenge: Intersubjectivity and Ontology is as close as we shall get to Nédoncelle's **Summa.**

Francis F. Burch
"Buena Vista"
15 May 1983

PHENOMENOLOGY

Chapter I

RELATIONSHIPS: A Few Examples [1]

I. A Privileged Relationship

Let us begin with an example: the baby and his mother. The tie linking them to each other is extraordinarily profound, at the physical level and at the psychological level as well. The infant is in a situation of complete dependence on the mother who represents to him a sort of providential total good.

The baby knows when his mother enters the nursery and leaves. Pediatricians recognize the importance of the presence of the mother for the infant, more particularly in the eighth month of his life, but even before. The mother herself experiences in her inner self the reactions of her child, his joys and pains. The relationship is uniquely precocious for the child; on both sides it expresses itself through a feeling of extreme acuity. Once a mother confided to me her astonishment at such an experience. "It is," she said, "something one doesn't experience with one's husband."

1. Although spontaneous and reciprocal, the relationship between mother and infant is obviously complex. The nature of the relation in the parental tie is different from that of the filial tie, which will go through many variations as the child grows up. These two people who at first seemed to be one only are irrevocably separated; as the child detaches himself from the mother he gains independence. In the same manner, having admired his father, he will probably withdraw to judge him.

One day, also, he will come back to his parents, thus closing the circle of his relationship. Consequently, the parents will experience a diversity of emotions. The continuity and reciprocity of the relationship do not prevent the diversity of perspectives, the parents' and the childs', nor do they rule out diversity in the history of the relationship.

2. Let us go back to the very beginning. The level of consciousness of the child is quite different from that of the mother. The baby is almost unconscious; thus, we commonly speak of his instinct or intuition. The mother, on the contrary, consciously goes to her child; she actually goes to him on purpose as well as with spontaniety. This difference in levels of consciousness between the two is at the same time moving and tragic: the suffering baby cannot speak, the mother cannot question him. One sees, therefore, a paradox: the vital sympathy of the parent cannot express itself in explanations intellectually understandable. Comprehension itself is strangely divided; immediate and intimate in some aspects, it is also weak and deprived of means of self-expression. Hence it is the experience of a unique relationship and at the same time a phenomenon of strangeness between two persons.

3. Finally, there is a difference in values. What are the anticipated goals of the relationship? On the one hand, they are food, care, and affection the child needs. On the other hand, we find the protection and love the infant requires for growth and well-being. What values does the relationship itself create? The child looks at the mother as a means to an end, the mother looks at her child as an end in itself. Later on, those values might change. The innocent egocentricity of the child will yield either to open egotism or to calculated generosity: the natural altruism of the mother will be transformed in jealous and authoritarian vigilance or in silent and heroic self-sacrifice, etc. . .

We, therefore, discover in a very elementary example that relating to another person is never simple and we should speak of it as a pluralistic experience. We are going to re-examine those points in a more general analysis.

II. Analysis of Relationship

1. First let us examine the forms. In the example above, we dealt with the "I - Thou" relationship. It is what we called a "dyade." It is the same relation in the experience of friendship and conjugal love; we find it also in the rapport between a doctor or a nurse and their patients. It is a bilateral relation, regardless of the fact that the reciprocity which characterizes friendship is not necessarily found in each case.

There are, however, altruistic relationships which are at the same time dyadic and asymmetrical. Such is the relation of a doctor or nurse to a seriously ill person going into a coma.

Besides the "I - Thou" relationship exists the "I - You (collective)" type. Examples are numerous: the father to his children, the professor to his students, the speaker to his audience, the priest at the altar, the industrialist, the statesman, etc. . .

Here we should notice that the "I - Thou" relationship is free from the tendency of being institutionalized, which is not the case of the collective type of relationship. The hinge of the relation is found in the family: dyadic situations flourish there, although each family unit is an institution; members may leave one by one but the family remains. It is different from the bond between a couple of friends who are not affected by any juridical structures because their association is freely agreed upon and revocable.

2. Let us move on now to the examination of the levels of relationship. In the first example we observed a case of maximal distance: a mother looking at her baby in a crib. Let us consider now the degree of reciprocity and draw a curve.

A minimum degree of reciprocity corresponds to a maximum degree of separatedness at the level of consciousness. Even a minimum of reciprocity, however, is not negligible. The vision of a face is a self-revealing reality. Consciously or not, the individual is a person present to the world. All encounters are irreplacable, and I am indebted for what they give me; the modification of my conscience is a response to the beneficial influence they exercise on me.

Reciprocity develops when the other person perceives my plan of action even when it is not well defined. The sick, for example, may be aware of his being treated without discerning the nature of treatment. He may fight it and yet, in his weakness, discern only vaguely people around him; however, the idea or picture of what is forced upon him maintains the reality of his family circle.

Next comes the case of the person who identifies my plan of action as really mine. In this case, there is co-operation and we reach a higher degree of reciprocity. Who could deny it? When the sick person co-operates with the efforts made on his behalf, he takes a decisive step toward his recovery. Such co-operation is essential to the success of a work team, for a collective enterprise would remain half paralyzed if it were not for the agreement between the members of that team, whatever their routes and functions. It is not required that such co-operation be blind and deprived of 'esprit critique'; on the contrary, the initiative of each one strengthens the unity of the group, provided it be intelligent and contribute to a greater responsiveness of the whole crew. Co-operation thus becomes a means of benefiting from someone's work and gives a stronger and richer presence to our individuality.

Co-operation, however, is not to be entirely and perfectly identified with reciprocity. The latter occurs only when the "I" seeks the development of the "Thou" for his own sake, receiving in return some tangible benefits. We have considered so far a partial agreement, the object of which was either the enrichment of the ego or the success of some objective, separated from both the "I" and "Thou." It was motivated by the desire of achieving something. When the objective is centered on one of the partners (as in the case of the therapeutic treatment of the sick), the self-dedication is admirable and yet remains unilateral. On the other hand, when the gift (as in the case of friendship) is returned to the giver, sometimes in a new and unforseen form, love is mutual and reciprocity reaches its maximum degree of intersubjective communion.

3. This happy result is not constant, not even frequent in human relationships. A combination of positive and negative values constitutes a strange experience. We have assumed, so far, that the final object of our analysis is love; indeed, this is what it should be. We must, however, broaden our inquiry and consider the various and most disconcerting aspects of that relationship: no longer love in its degrees of realization, but indifference and hostility.

Let us observe the importance of the element of anonymity in the "I - Thou" collective relationship; this from the very moment it is institutionalized and becomes an "I - They" type of relationship. One would be tempted to confuse such transformation with the appearance of an element of indifference or hostility. This, however, would be going to far!

Anonymity is not without reason. It becomes indispensable in our earthly situation to let someone's being develop, give it universality and share with it the benefit of our knowledge of things. This is why anonymity can find its way even into the "I - Thou" relationship and benefit it. For example, the nurse must assess the reactions of her patient on the basis of the impersonal data of medical and pharmaceutical experience. All her scientific knowledge will incorporate itself in the dyadic relation. It is also true of the relation existing between the individual self and the group of people one wants to inform, co-operate with or more generally serve in one way or another.

In the "I - They" relationship everything has to be geared to the benefit of each participant in the relationship. This is the aim not only of the head of the department, for example, but also of each employee; should the latter do nothing but punch tickets, he should do it in such a way as to be a useful person. And this is not the only reason. The relationship is further institutionalized by providing one group with a set of guidelines for action in order to caution individuals against all sorts of short-comings and more particularly against the intermittent character of human love. Continuity of self-dedication must be won. [2]

What the love-relation, however, may gain through the reciprocity of anonymity can be lost be undermining the spontaneity of individuals. The anonymous objectivity of a well-regulated institution inevitably leads to indifference, discontent or even hostility. The danger increases proportionally to the development of the science of communications and social organization. Conditions are created which threaten the survival of all inter-personal ties: the increasing number of participants, the cold proliferation of knowledge, the complexity of the law. In the long run, intimate contacts between people in our society creates a disengagement of consciences; solidarity runs against intimacy and becomes inhuman.

Thus the threefold possible orientation of an inter-relation between persons, namely: love, indifference and hatred, the last two attitudes are re-inforced although they already have deep roots in our biological nature and in our sinful conscience. It is unfortunately very common that our neighbor does not appeal to us but rather disturbs us or, at least, leaves us indifferent. And since mediocrity or weakness are commonly shared, the individual has plausible reasons for not trusting his neighbor. The encounter, then, is no longer joyful but suspicious, and the very nature of reciprocity changes: whereas at one time it was loving, it is now mutual distrust. The picture is so banal that it is not necessary to stress it. . .

In a manner of conclusion, let us say that the moral aspect of all good and bad values has a definite bearing on relationships. It will complicate the psychological make-up, the evolution of feelings and the unfolding of those Hybrids which explain the complexity of a relationship.

III. What is the Highest Common Denominator of all Relationships?

Are we facing an incoherent mass of relationships or is there one which is more fundamental than any other? Many philosophers subscribe to the latter. They are divided, however, into two groups: those who base their understanding on the possession-instinct and those who opt for the love-instinct.

In the first group we find Sartre. Looking at the other is, for him a threat. Being seen is being deprived of one's self; it is the beginning of alienation and destruction. Or, conversely, looking at someone is to spy on him and rob him of his very being. One knows the favorite saying: "L'enfer, c'est les autres" ("People are hell"). Love is impossible; it is an exercise in sadism and masochism because its object is beyond reach. Its aim is to possess someone's freedom or condition it through a process of identification; it turns a subject into an object. Neither he who imposes the game of love nor the recipient can play without illusion, failure and suffering.

I shall not surprise anybody by confessing that I personally belong to the other group of philosophers. For me, relating to another person is essentially a matter of reciprocity in the building up of two personalities. It is absurd in my own opinion to begin with hatred or indifference for these feelings are obviously negative and metaphysically secondary.

This affirmation presupposes the consideration of the initial motion of the intellect and will, in the relation process. What do we discover there? Initially, a surprise at the novelty and sometimes a feeling of distrust and antipathy. This psychological re-action, however, is not as important as it would appear. Emotions must rise from a first encounter. Or the very first contact is of altruistic nature. Perception, indeed, is by definition an outward motion recognizing another being; without it, acquaintance would be impossible. But it is possible that having taken that step we might selfishly exploit the response given to us and turn the encounter into a self-destructive experience, seeking to undermine or destroy the other person. Wickedness, however, is always a second step, preceded by a goodness or kindness conjointly with the first meeting of two personalities. At the root of the inter-subjective liaison, we find an element of understanding and decision which necessarily unfolds its object, affecting at the same time the subject itself. Perception, therefore, is a double promotion.

This ontological goodness, so to speak, is reciprocal due to the fact that the very existence in the world of the other person signifies his willingness to share his being and existence, as we have said already when speaking of the minimum level of reciprocity of consciousness. The human Dasein, therefore, rests on a basis of harmony and allows the recognition of the fundamental identity of relation and mutual love. There is an inevitable encounter of the "pour soi" and "pour l'autre" in the rising "nous" (a convergence of the "I" and "he" in the new "we").

Hence, we conclude that there is no rise and development of a personality in isolation. Each one of us has his inter-subjective heritage; he has been formed by his parents and environment; he has received what he is. In that sense, each owes to others what he becomes. His heritage grows as he receives more of his environment and contributes to it. In all aspects, inter-relations between people are a phenomenon of reciprocity in which each person creates his own self by contributing to someone else's being and receiving from him.

We need, now to demonstrate that those forms of relationships born of some initial mutuality and almost forced upon us, find their ultimate meaning in the clear reciprocity of a fully conscious love; in other words, love alone can unify relationships.

The thesis might seem to be a paradox. It is, however, inevitable if one observed the following points: a disposition to indifference or hatred cannot give love and has no synthetic quality to fully unify a personality; indifference or hatred, however, cannot reach their end without turning against themselves. If indifference wants to materialize its objective it demands of the "I" to grow, to strengthen itself against opposite forces; to be complete, however, the development of one "I" requires a recognition of the "Thou." Any attempt to withdraw would be self-defeating, for it would amount to self-denial. This is even more true of hatred which to materialize itself depends on the existence of the "Thou" whose perfection becomes the object of a more total hatred often disguised under the semblance of generous love. In other words, hatred, in that case, has to change its appearance to realize itself. One discovers, therefore, that the most synthetic relationship which rationally controls the development of all subsequent relations is the love-relationship.

This difficult analysis, however, does not lead us to deny the fact that the spectrum of empirical relations contrary to the encounter of love is very large, although of secondary importance. It is very important to stress the ontological priority of love. It would be utopian and disastrous to minimize the opposition love has to face in daily life and our difficulties in meeting its challenge. This is why we now should ask ourselves what dangers threaten a loving relationship, particularly at the present time.

IV. Threats to Our Relationship to the Other Person

The first danger is that a relationship to another person might decrease in scope as the result of a general depersonalization process. Technology and organization, once hypertrophied, lead not only to scientific and technological progress but also to psychic uniformity, social conditioning, all necessary because of the increase in world population. The paradox is that in our overpopulated world one finds it increasingly more difficult to meet one's neighbor. Encounters become sporadic, superficial, anonymous. They lose in depth what they gain in number. Automation often replaces individual presence. Metropolises are deserted; mass media insert between messages and their reception a series of distorting prisms which change the original messages or even erase them while pretending to communicate them. In the social game in which messages are passed on from mouth to ear with numerous transformations, one finds an amusing diversity which has a note of individuality. Each time a story is repeated an individual reveals some characteristic traits about himself in the very manner he has changed the message. In mass-media communication, on the other hand, everything is reduced to a series of signals which level attitudes and automatize the receivers.

The second danger is to see the relationship turning one person, who at one time was both source and end of the encounter, into some form of instrument or object. Certainly, practical egotism has always existed, but it is aggravated by civilization. Plato stigmatized it by gently making fun of physicians who treat the sick as impersonal objects, not allowing people to speak, asking no questions and depriving their art of all psychosomatic psychology, bragging about what is, in fact, a vain, mechanical science. (The Laws, 85 F, c-d). In our contemporary world, far more intoxicated than antiquity by our technical achievements, this injurious spirit not only affects technocrats but pervades public life, sowing a potential panic. For example, the insecurity created by the secret fear of the atomic bomb forces us to live in the here and now, rejecting permanent commitments, fragmenting our relationships into momentary services and short-lived contracts. It is a true case of infantile regression, the result of which is not long to come: a generalized distrust between human beings. Everybody protests against everybody. Discontent and aggressiveness inevitably follow the loss of sensitivity to neighbor and those values we should respect in him.

The above remarks can be verified in the areas of health and hospitalization. A French philosopher, Armand Cuvillier, who fought all his life on behalf of social causes, and whose testimony is above all suspicion, expressed in a booklet, no longer in print, his disillusion and bitterness that his late wife, stricken by the Hodgkin's disease, had been subjected to several confinement periods in a clinic. [3] Certainly the sick woman was often the object of care and devotion by both the medical and administrative staffs. There happened, however, many incredible incidents which revealed a complete lack of compassion and generosity on the part of a few people. When the author sought to determine the causes of such inhuman acts he was confronted by the financial restrictions which condition many hospitals. More often than not, however, he faced a mentality narrowly egocentric and selfish. The author, an old syndicalist, is humiliated as he discovers that unions, which in so many ways are useful, can be guilty of unforgivable inhumanity.

The third danger we must stigmatize comes from the same source: the transformation of people into means to an end often leads to the substitution of our desire to reality. We project on the other person the image corresponding to what we dream about him, remaking him for the satisfaction of our instinct of domination and pleasure. We have of him an illusory and selfish representation which we try to impose upon his person. This process is at the bottom of most misunderstanding in friendship and love. To put oneself into somebody else's place is one of the most difficult undertakings. To succeed one needs either natural imagination, or that imagination born of a loving concern or of a sense of practical justice (true justice is concrete and all comprehensive). Let us recognize the obstacle does not always arise from our bad moral dispositions, but often from the diversity of personalities. The alert individual who depends on first impressions does not understand easily people who keep inside and constantly rehearse old impressions often at a price for their whole existence. This is a well known distinction in psychology between "primary" and "secondary" characters. One should add to that the functional restriction the employee does not understand the employer's viewpoint and vice versa; both, however, are convinced that they understand everything; and yet a vague notion is not the equivalent of real experience.

The fourth and last danger occurs less frequently: it is the tendency of being overwhelmed by a relationship to the point of losing one's privacy and communion with God. In fact, such deviation happens only to exceptional people. One finds it in those professions which demand self-dedication. There are priests, doctors, nurses, teachers and even businessmen who are caught by their work to the point of neglecting the necessary development of knowledge and unwisely using their strength at the risk of self-destruction. Illusion in this case is to assume more resources than one has in reality, to imagine oneself as inexhaustible as God himself. One ceases to grow intellectually and spiritually for the sake of serving other people, when in fact they are being deprived of qualified and good help.

In reality, relationship to the other person, to be truly meaningful, must include a definite search for competence and inner balance. I would say further that the relationship, to be worth the effort, must also refrain from being exclusive and idolatrous. The second commandment which is to love one's neighbor, is observed in subordination to the first: to love God. Distortions of self-dedication by extremes are rare, however, as we have said already. As we confront inevitable tensions, it is clear that the real danger is to withdraw and neglect other people.

When such attitude is generalized social encounters include an enormous amount of sufferings, misunderstandings, failures, hurts of all kinds. True love is conditional to the development of the personality and inter-personal relations; its full realization, however, is rare. It is like a fragile plant, whose flowers too often wither. The roots, however, never die and its destiny is immutable.

V. God and One's Neighbor

In this brief report, I had to limit myself to the inter-human relationship without going into the religious implications of human life. I do not want to conclude, however, without raising my insights to the sublime level where one sees a relation to God as upholding all human inter-relationships.

It would seem to any superficial examination that communing with God is without analogy in human relations and any attempt at lumping them together would be mutually destructive. For example, is it possible to think of our union with God in the likeness of the "I - Thou" or even "I - He" relationship? God cannot be comprehended within the world. The disappearance of earthly reference is not as essential to the being of the Divine as the existence of the world is to inter-human communications and communions. Furthermore, do we need an element of transcendence for earthly associations? Is it not true that any reference to a heavenly partner is unnecessary to true development of our natural inter-subjectivity? Or, are we turning God into a means to promote our humanity, which is unworthy of him and us? Should we not, in fact, reject the divine as a rival interfering with our dyades and destroying its intimacy?

Actually those difficulties derive from the same fundamental error, which consists in limiting God as if He could not find his way into the very fiber of our experiences, that is the intimate act by which the "I" is affirmed, this in conformity with the will of the Creator. In the same way, God would be part of the affirmation of the "Thou", the progression of the "we" which brings people together since the divine dynamism creates all the "I" terms of human relations. And God himself creates that relation through which we introduce him in the world as one of us. If there is a God why should he not be omnipresent? and if God is omnipresent, why should he not be immanent to our limitations, events, symbols, without losing his transcendence? The disconcerting image of this world could give a sign of divine diversity. God is not somewhere; he would be nowhere if he were not everywhere as thought of our thoughts and will of our wills. He embraces all relationships. He is not a psychological perfection of the same. He is more and better than that. He initiates our relationship to another person; he comprehends it, frees it by giving it its norm and as the Infinite God gives it an unlimited scope. We must say of God that He is the ultimate end of our self and at the same time the "Other."

Any fear, therefore, that God might artificially interfere, as an enemy of one's selfness and reciprocity of conscious relations, is unfounded. He is the absolute supporting us. He counteracts only man's apathy and selfishness.

We discover now another error in the argumentation we are presently criticizing. One thinks that people are atoms caught in isolation, incapable of unselfcentered love, real interaction, and even creativeness, just because human creatures are not in harmonious relationship with the Creator. Having reduced the inter-relation to an artifical encounter of physical phenomena one no longer understands the uniqueness and living complexity of an inter-personal rapport in progress. In fact, if God appears at the end of all our journeys it is not to downgrade them or turn them into dead-end experiences, but rather to raise them to the level of a higher relationship which finds in him alone its real substance. The philosopher apprehends here what the theologian calls grace and Trinity.

The conclusion is that our worship of God is the corollary of the calling he gives us. In his presence and representation he is far less our image than we are his. Whatever the overflowing immensity of his attributes God is eminently in himself and for us a personal God. What distinguishes him from man is that he makes our relationship to people possible as our creator, in his creative relation to us; not as an archetype we should imitate, but as the almighty power which associates us to his creativity and does not hesitate to destroy the images of our ego-centeredness.

The objection, therefore, is overcome, which suggested that intersubjectivity is possible only in the presence of a third party (i.e., a world both alienated and close) always in the view of the "I" and "Thou." One should say that the persistence of the third party is, rather, the sign that the "I" and "Thou" are not yet entirely what they are meant to be. The hope of the perfect fulfillment of the "we", even at the interhuman level, finally rests on the absolute "Thou" of God and our union with him. He converts the separated third person into a "socius" and erases the estrangement of the world. The disappearance of the "he" in a clearly defined "we" is the permanent possibility of a heaven of people, prefigured in the realm of earthly mediation. [4]

NOTES

1. This text gives the substance of a lecture given October 17th, 1970, to the "Association Nationale Catholique du Nursing", during a workshop on Human relationships in a technological society.

2. Other relationships such as "I - we", "We - you", "We - they" should be examined; however, we do not have time to go into a more complex analysis.

14

3. A. Culvillier, **Le Scandale des Hôpitaux Publics en France**, Paris, 1964.

4. We have here an allusion to the Christian Trinity; the role of the Holy Spirit as love of the Father and Son not only secures the unity of the Trinity but also the intersubjective unity of God and his creatures and of creatures between themselves. This leads us to reabsorb the earthly concept of essence into concept of the intersubjectivity of the "we."

Chapter II

CONFRONTATION AND ENCOUNTER
The Initial Confrontation in the Encounter Between People

The language describing the interpersonal encounter remains vague; the expression "We met," for example, completely changes in meaning according to its context. It can signify:

1. Indifference to the other person, only slightly affected by occasional proximity in time and space, (We met by accident on the street or at a third person's);

2. A physical or moral clash (our bodies or our spirits have met in a more or less violent confrontation);

3. A communion of ideas or feelings suddenly revealing affinities (in such circumstances one often uses the expression or exclamation: "So, we finally meet.")

The notion of an initial confrontation is as vague as the meaning of the verb "to meet." Fichte thought that the "Anstoß" is a secondary element of the self and at the same time conditional to its fruitfulness or fecundity; it was also, for the philosopher, a negative infringement of the impersonal on the personal. Our analysis will develop in a different light; it will deal with the encounter of the "Thou" which is not necessarily a negation of the "I" subject, for the "Thou" can be the source of the "I" or the positive expression of its role, to the point that the latter becomes reciprocal.

We shall limit ourselves, however, to that aspect of the encounter which seems to be negative, namely, the initial confrontation of persons. What form does it take? Is it a constant fact? Understanding the phenomenology of the "Anstoß" will help us to clarify our experience affecting our personal lives and in the process discover the destiny of the person.

Confrontation as a Surprise

1. Becoming aware of another person is both a novelty and a surprise. Even if banality spoils many of our encounters, some spark of originality, a new call, may save a perception of the other from the damper of insignificance; if it were not for that originality, there would be no encounter, but a monotonous association of interchangeable individuals. There are cases where surprise--"admiration" in the XVII century meaning of the word--is so intense that it justifies its classification as a form of confrontation--hurt. The functioning of consciousness is affected; everything else is stopped or pushed aside by the new experience, by that temporary absorption in the other person. Through face and voice a new, enigmatic inaccessable center of being imposes its new reality. Confrontation comes precisely from the fact that a new being is facing ours and demands our attention to all its manifestations.

2. Furthermore, confrontation occurs in the area of those values which identify a person, at the moment they enter the scope of our experience. Banality may mitigate the shock of the confrontation, which remains, however, undeniable and in some extreme cases, violent; the exceptional beauty or ugliness of an individual, for example, may take us by complete surprise; so does his demonic perversity or moral virtue, or even, at a higher degree, the sacred "aura" which envelops the face of a saint. Artists and mystics have the aptitude of always experimenting --surprise in facing another person, even when that person may appear very ordinary and unassuming to the perspicacious and naive eyes of a third party.

3. What is, in fact, the shock of novelty? We are dissociated from the total reality of the world as we conceived it. A particular element is subjectively and objectively added to our knowledge and human experience. The birth of a child, for example, is the best illustration of that phenomenon; but all inter-personal relationships are also in their own different way a happening. The other person not only adds to the number of our relations and qualifies their nature, but the encounter frees us from our self-sufficiency and forces us out of the circle of our habits and initiatives. Someone came and relations between people changed.

4. The surprise is not necessarily tragic; for the encounter which ends my insularity answers the need to be part of the world. To live is to accept the "Dasein." If the "Dasein" confronts me in a destructive encounter, it also provides favorable answers to my needs. There are "good" surprises. The arrival of a challenger is a good surprise for the wrestler; this is also true of the experience of friendship and love, at first sight or not. The meeting

of a need and its solution, the co-incidence of two needs or the complemental nature of their solutions, all constitute good surprises. A psychological paradox often slips into whatever affinity brings together persons otherwise different in their primary or secondary characteristic traits or in the more mysterious areas of the mind and spirit, such as the sympathy of the saint for the sinner and the moral attraction they may have for each other. One easily imagines the concrete cases which might illustrate the above point. The surprise of a new inter-personal relationship can, in fact, assume many forms from a pleasant and beneficial shock to a dangerous and fatal confrontation.

5. There are many ways to minimize the negative risks of the encounter and increase the positive ones, real or not. Let us mention two kinds:

First, there is the convenient use of masks, "Larvatus prodeo." Individual relations benefit from some insurance against accidents, and almost everybody is willing to underwrite it. The premium to pay is the constraint of politeness. Confrontations are then attenuated because the inner self of the person is still hiding behind the surprise of the encounter, which at first tends to be a casual impersonal meeting. Then true love appears, which with its generosity is the opposite of the masks game. Love alone can tear down the walls of misunderstanding erected by nature, culture, life itself and thoughts.

Confrontation as an Obstacle

6. Boundaries between surprised consciousness and opposed consciousness are sometimes difficult to draw. We can, however, distinguish the confrontations of astonishment from that of opposition. The obstacle with which the "I" comes into collision derives from the spatial element of the encounter. The suggestion that two psyches may come into one space seems senseless since the psyche has no space dimension. Space, however, separates the eyes and when two consciousnesses first meet, it is in some physical reference: I see your body and you see mine; we look together at the same object from that accepted perspective created by the body of our partner. Spatial diversity, therefore, is always inherent in the encounter of people on earth and cannot be overcome until such time as mental reciprocity occurs under the impact of intellect and love. What we have just said about the visual encounter would apply also to the other senses (touch, hearing) through which we communicate with people. Bodies always identify the flux of consciousness; this is why there are obstacles between people.

7. In the same manner there is a temporal gap which hinders the initial communion of consciousness. One is ahead or behind the other; such is the condition of perceptiveness as differentiated from pure intuition. It is only at the end of a common development that two partners reach an identical rhythm of their becoming seen in their bodies through activity and quasi-simultaneity of behavior.

The spatial-temporal obstacle, always present at the beginning of the encounter, inevitably erects a barrier. Each one of us is aware, unconsciously at least, of this personal trait which isolates him and suffers because of it, as if he were an abandoned child, tempted to ignore those universal ties which, in fact, make of him a privileged person.

8. Parallel to the element of surprise and its values we could show how the elemental obstacle once erected has a divisive effect. When a man says to another; "You have hurt me," he means that one's convictions are incompatible, or he reacts against any questioning of his sincerity and signs of threat to his dignity and "raison d'être." In other words, their sets of values, openly or not, are in contradiction with each other. When the plaintiff feels that he is misunderstood, he also assumes that the offender is malicious, a reaction showing how far apart they are from one another. Their opposition can go beyond superficial evaluations to reveal deeper differences, such as the recognition of other gods. In that case inner relations to ultimate values are being questioned.

9. There are, however, two kinds of obstacles: one can be overcome, the other not. It is a well known fact among observers and novelists that at the origin of a great love one often finds a quarrel or at least a painful misunderstanding. Everything happens as if one confrontation had been the cause of a less superficial attention to the other person leading to a progressive appreciation, even before the end of the contest. The confrontation is therapeutic if it leads the individual to self-understanding and reform.

Some psychologists look for a different explanation. They observe in the initial hostile attitude a defensive movement against a new sympathy, at first unconfessed, but powerful enough to carry them away. In some extreme cases it could be an instinctive reaction against any bewitching which might subjugate one person or enslave the two to each other, like lovers under a spell. The temporary confrontation would be, therefore, a sign of freedom protesting its own disappearance.

It is, however, permissible, to see the confrontation as an initial and temporary stimulant for two wills which, taken out of their isolation, learn to join their soaring and free themselves from all fetters. Their encounter, good in the long run, started poorly to emphasize the potential good of the new relationship. Such awareness gives a feeling of liberation at least when the encounter is truly good--when bad it has a note of fatalism. Love cannot want confrontation for its own sake; it must create and maintain a central trust between people. Sometimes an imperative necessity demands of love to show a certain hardness to keep a right level of communion of hearts. This seems paradoxical and yet it demonstrates the dignity a confrontation of personalities can reach.

10. The shock of the initial encounter cannot always be overcome. "I do not want to see you again" is a rather sinister sentence, and yet it is not always hyperbolic. The least curable hatred is perhaps the one succeeding a passionate but disappointed attraction. We then have a case which is the exact reverse of the last one: there is nothing worse than the tragic end of something which initially was good. Profound incompatibilities, however, often appear early in a relationship. Each one detects a certain boredom or strangeness which rules out the possibility of a real communion. The "AnstoB" which then occurs, re-examines past and present because the shock of the encounter is destructive of self-acceptance; it also manifests the impossibility of a common future; it leaves only the possibility of relating to one another within the sphere of the "Dasein" or presence to the world. The latter relation cannot be destroyed even by death itself, since both parties have shared in the same humanity.

11. The last remark shows the insurmountable boundary which prevents an absolute split between two human beings. Even in the case of a murderer and his victim it is as profound as an indelible stigma. We also see another insurmountable limitation which prevents immediate and necessary communion at the level of sensorial perception. Such limitation is due to the fact that we live as if in a transitory reality; life constantly oscillates with changeable intensity between extremes and cannot reach its fulfillment in such variation. Is this strange law presiding over human encounters due to a leveling of spirits or to an incomplete evolution of matter? It is not our purpose to speculate on such a question: we should, however, note its importance.

The Confrontation as a Play

12. The analysis of the two forms of shock, surprise and confrontation, leads us to the discovery of a third kind of encounter: the play.

It is a transformation of the confrontation by its element of surprise, or perhaps an effort to transcend both to the benefit of freedom. This is what the musician does in the interplay of perfect chords and dissonances. The "ego" does the same while going its own way in the midst of other "egos," providing, of course, that the impact of the human circle be not too oppressive and stifling. The ego considers even the spontaneous shock of those encounters as a kind of challenge to achieve its own essence and that of the other person. Perhaps one person will detest the ideas of others but not necessarily at the expense of love. The confrontation teaches that the "we" and its components are imperfect; neither the "I" nor "Thou" perfectly know their inner self and what good or bad they contribute to each other. The irony of the play is that the shock of the confrontation is a living contribution to the common act. Such irony may assume different colorations: musical for the humanist, cynical for the politician; it may become beneficent creativity for the saint. The play, accepted by all as a chain of unforeseen events controlled by a certain rule of behavior, becomes a universal, "a priori" which transcends the particular event without suppressing it.

13. One must recognize that the confrontation as a play soon either leaves the area of initial encounters or transposes them to a higher level, that of a dialogue of consciousness. Empirically, as we have already noticed, reciprocity is a conquest. In order to develop bilaterally, as it should normally, the play must reach beyond its biological causes to be maintained by the harmony of wills. At that point, and only then, the confrontation assumes its real nature, a definite and sufficient reason for being.

14. In the interpersonal dialogue, which does very seldom happen, the representation of the other person becomes a presence. Overcoming their differences and oppositions, or at least ordering them, the two consciousnesses arrange their new rapport using them as a basis. They achieve that by refraining from talking for the sake of listening. The art of listening, with willingness to vulnerability, is not an end in itself but provides the necessary norm to the development and promotion of the two subjects and their endeavors.

The novelty of the common act and the test of freedom gives the two persons the direction which the first impressions of surprise and confrontation would have denied. At its conclusion the experience or play depends on a "Verbum"--Word which determines it. Since the confrontation just happens (as Fichte understood it so well), one must ask now if the initial fact is not indeed the encounter without hurt; this contrary to what we had first thought. Communion would happen at the very beginning as necessary to the comprehension of the confrontation and the encounterability which would not separate but presupposes a component of dissociated parts. We move now from the spatial-temporal type of encounters to the type which conditions us eternally; from the shock which underlines a phenomenon of duality we go back to its source which is unity.

16. This inference does not express a sentimental nostalgia or paint a parallel project; it is the outcome of the mind's inability to understand any encounter between men without referring to the immanence of the Word who dominates man. The Word is neither a Platonist archetype nor a maker of archetypes, but a presence which explains encounters and remedies absences. He assumes all surprises and obstacles into a play which gives them ideal purpose and already partial realization. He is himself a surprise par excellence, when we discover Him in us and between us and other people. He is also at the same time an obstacle, in the sense that we cannot substitute ourselves for Him who rules us. Finally, He is the play which determines all play between humans and denounces all abuses of the rules. He is all that, however, in a unique manner. He preceeds, goes with and brings to completion. He dominates all perspectives, but is not their grand total, nor is He the simple outcome of our human encounters and hurts. In Him undoubtedly resides the only hope that human encounters might achieve ultimate meaning, ratifying and co-ordinating everything in them which is good and transforming everything unjust or disharmonious.

Chapter III

MASK AND PERSON: From Theater to Life

What is the relationship between the mask and the person?

In terms of etymology, it is a relation of identity or at least continuity. "Person" comes from he Latin "persona" and the proper meaning of the word "persona" is "mask." A later Latin author, Aulus Gellius, assumed that there was a relation between the noun "persona" (Mask) and the verb "persono" (I make resound, reverberate or ring). However, let us not believe that; philologically it is only amusing. Linguists agree that "persona" has a totally different origin; it would come from the Etruc: Phersu.

In the tomb of the augurs of Corneto-Tarquinia this word Phersu is attached to a masked character wearing a pointed hat in a ritualistic scene. Moving from such an enigmatic designation, learned inductions rapidly developed; but I have no intention of enumerating them because the tracing from "phersu" to "persona" remains obscure. Let it suffice to remark that by the time of the Second Punic War, "persona" would mean: i) a theater mask; ii) the character of a play; iii) probably a part in a play; iv) and perhaps "person," already in our grammatical sense. With Cicero we have the proof that "persona" can also mean person as commonly used to refer to a human subject. From the theater, the word shifted to the areas of social life, law and psychology. Cicero even used the word to designate the philosophical notion of human individuality. And since a similar semantic evolution occurred in the usage of the area word "prosopon," we are tempted to conclude that being oneself is to play one's part in the human comedy and that, after all, our person is only a mask or a series of masks.

I

Is not the mask, however, the exact opposite of our intimacy? Of course, I do not refer only to those molds made

23

of wood or gypsum--plaster-of-Paris--which the actors of antiquity wore on their faces to impersonate a character. Pollox described for us a robing room which had seventy-six pieces of that kind (twenty-eight for tragedies, forty-four for comedies, and a few others for satirical dramas). I refer rather to the psychic mask which the actor wears prior to any other; a mask which even if custom-made and with nothing artificial, conceals, however, as much as it reveals the deep personality of the individual. And since it is from the theater that I have borrowed my introduction, it is also from it that I shall ask for a proof of the existing gap between the ego and the mask. I shall do that by examining a somewhat forgotten play by Euripides, the title of which is Helen.

In Homer, Helen was the "femme fatale," who by her adultery had caused the Trojan War. Confined in Ilium with her abductor, she kept an admirable moral awareness and despised herself to a certain degree. Euripides followed a different tradition, wrapped in mythology and stamped with his own originality. Helen is after all a faithful wife. She has not been truly kidnapped by Paris; it is a phantom, a mask in the likeness of the Queen which has been transported to Troy, and Paris has embraced nothing but a myth blown by the wind, while Hermes was taking the real Helen to Egypt, to the court of King Proteus, where she waited for the return of her husband Menelaus. Proteus is a real gentleman, who unfortunately dies, and his son Theoclymenes does not have the scruples of his father. He falls in love with the beautiful Helen and begs her to marry him. He orders also that all Greeks attempting to enter his palace be put to death. Helen, the true Helen, desperately resists the royal pretender. One tells her that Menelaus is dead; but she knows that in fact he is alive, thanks to the revelations of Theoclymenes' sister, who is a prophetess. Euripides calls her Theonoe, "divinely intelligent," while her brother --Theoclymenes--is only "divinely famous." The Menelaus who in the plunder of Troy had captured the false Helen, arrives; but only after a shipwreck which has left him in rags. He thought he had left his wife in a cave, then he suddenly is in her presence in a palace which he had foolishly entered. The scene in which man and wife recognize each other is one of the most admirable of Euripides theater. At first, Menelaus is reluctant to be convinced and responds with some reservations to his wife's affection. It is not difficult to understand. How could he immediately forget that, for all appearances, he has been humiliated, then led by some divine plot to a ten-year war? Finally, he lets his emotions rise and the couple re-discover their former happiness. Now they must escape. Menelaus is ready to fight, and, if necessary, to comtemplate a double suicide. Helen, much wiser, thinks of a deceit worthy of Ulysses. She pretends to consent to Theoclymenes' marriage proposal. She tells him that a Greek shipwrecked sailor-- who is in fact Menelaus--has just broken to her the news of Mene- laus' death. It is good news which pleases the heart of the Egyptian, who not only forgives the Greek, but also grants Helen permission to pay her last respects to a deceased husband. According to ancient custom of Hellenic worship, a funeral ceremony is held at sea. A boat is ready. The couple get on board, and Theoclymenes will never see them again. The end of the play tries supernatural means to appease his anger toward his sister, the prophetess, whom he accuses with some reason, of complicity in their incredible escape.

It is often said that the reunion scene is brilliant and that the rest of the act is padding. It is not true. **Helen** is neither tragedy nor comedy. It is a fairy-like play of Shakespeare's **"Tempest"** kind; it is admirably constructed; one's interest is kept alert and the drama yields many lessons. What I also discover in it is a two-fold concept of the mask. In the first part, we see that the false Helen is the victim of a jealous goddess, and victim of the passions which she stirs in spite of herself on earth.

Helen to the Chorus:

> "Friends, what is my inescapable fate? Has my mother conceived me to be a scandal to the human race? Yes, my birth, my life and everything in me rouse astonishment. I owe that to Hera and my beauty as well. I wish my face were smeared like a half-crazed drawing!"

Helen to Menelaus:

> "And I, the rejected one, cursed by the gods, far from my country, from my town, and separated from you because a god forced me into a humiliating union from which I deserted--without really deserting--my palace and my conjugal bed." [1]

In the second part, on the contrary, the mask is freely chosen, and deliberately accepted. It is a matter of wearing a mask to deceive Theoclymenes and respond to his unjust demands by making him the victim of well-deserved illusion. Helen rejects an indiscreet man, but her mask smiles out to him. Menelaus is a triumphant and vengeful husband; his mask, however, is that of a messenger in rags who announces the death of Menelaus. Helen and Menelaus renew their wedlock with joy and thank their protective gods; but their common mask is one of sadness; they sacrifice a bull and offer libations to a pseudo-deceased. To the magic of appearances in human behavior is substituted clever calculation for the sake of freedom.

Does it mean that Euripides' humanism is free of all transcendence? Not at all. The gods are difficult to understand, but easy to feel; if it had not been for their mysterious rivalry, the Trojan War would not have happened; but without their consent the flight from Egypt would have failed. Our nature, which they control, is a first mask which precedes our cunning, and the latter is a second mask which uses our nature. Both, however, and the gods themselves are dominated by fate beyond their reach; a fate which knowingly mixes necessity and freedom, appearance and reality.

And as far as Helen is concerned, where is she? She does not recognize herself in the adventures which happened to her and Theoclymenes does not recognize her in the schemes she has fabricated. Menelaus fights for a long time a most strange "quiproque." He is wondering if he is losing his mind and the reunion scene is one which in Ancient Theater most resembles a page of Pirandello. I concede that Helen's alibis are convenient and even suspect; I further concede that she becomes the accomplice of her own scheming. Euripides knew that very well, but his play stresses to a maximum the gap between the mask and the person. Helen, where is she? Divided in her inner self, buried under the events of her life in the narrow space which separates what she must bear from what she fabricates, she is imperceptible and yet totally herself. Have the Greeks not said it many times: the individual is ineffable. One of their poets remarked that if one could assemble three times ten thousand foxes, one would see one nature only shared by all of them, whereas in the human species, one finds as many different persons as people; [2] in other words, as many enigmas to decipher or leave untouched.

II

Euripides has led us from theater to life; let us try, therefore, to analyze the contrast of the mask and the person in real life.

1. First of all, there is the general appearance of the mask. I am referring here to the attitude we have, often unknowingly, towards other people. It is made of two opposite elements: on the one hand the glow of our personality perceptible through the body and, on the other hand, that series of qualities (in the philosophical meaning of the term) which are attached, so to speak, to the body without reflecting anything of the inner-self. One image can have two different meanings: goodness, for example, written on the face of the person and with it a real expression of the inner dispositions emanating unconsciously from the person; in other cases, the image can be like a natural varnish, hiding what is in fact indifference or wickedness. The appearance is, therefore, misleading; this is why it is unwise to judge people by their faces. Our intuition about other people is never immediately correct.

Of those two different images, the first expresses a real intention of the subject; it is general, however, coming from the body like light from a generator, but not focusing on any particular object. Joy, for example, emanates from a young person revealing his soul to the eyes of all, although it is not directed to any particular observer; furthermore, it is artless; at first the child does not try to impress.

Physical and psychic expressions which reflect a certain attitude without necessarily revealing the real self are responsible for most misunderstanding in the perception of the other person. The appearance is not only parallel to the real self, but often opposed to it. At first, neither observer nor subject is aware of that; a kind smile may hide a cruel soul; a soft gesture of the hand may mask a determination made of steel. Disillusions in love come from a failure to see reality under appearances, or from the wrong assumption that reality itself could be altered by appearances. And such a mistake may take place without any attempt by the loved one to deceive. In our youth particularly, do we not show signs of qualities which are not truly integrated into our person? Is it not true that we do not even know that we have them?

True or false appearances change. Marcel Proust has ruthlessly described their succession. In the second part of **Temps Retrouve,** he shows the deterioration with time of a human being and the impossibility of repairing him through artificial means. "Those faces made up in the course of time, even unwillingly, cannot be unmade by magic . . . " The change is not purely biological. It affects the character of the person. "The skinny, fragile, young girl had turned into a huge, lenient matron; in a social and moral sense it could be said that she was a different person." For this example, the new appearance supercedes all old ones; it can also recapitulate them all. Here we must quote Rembrandt for he has shown in the most striking fashion the past of a person in his present appearance: in the "Prodigal Son," it is a simple matter of looking at the kneeling son, the welcoming father and the older brother reluctant to step forward, to guess the long and sad story; it is no longer necessary to read the Gospel narration. Finally, there are prophetic appearances which foreshadow in the child, the adult and old man yet to be; it is, in a sense, a cruel game to make predictions, as Lorenzo Lotto's painting "Trois Âges de la Vie" did. His work can be found in the Pitti Gallery, in Florence.

2. Appearance is not a mask in the specific sense of the word; the latter is created when I become conscious of projecting an appearance to the eyes of other people. This representation for others of my being affects my behavior and helps me to use it as a means of influencing them. Something similar exists

even in the animal world. The young of mammifers can draw their parent's attention by mimics which could not be classified as pure reflexes. The beginnings of reflection, the ability to put oneself in somebody else's position have their biological roots probably in those weak individuals who are forced to use guile when dealing with stronger people. In man, this process has an enormous importance and conditions the whole area of inter-psychology. We know that we are visible, audible, touchable; we observe all changes of attitude in any personal contact either because our faces are spontaneously expressive or because of a change in gestures and manners. Our own image, however, is not seen in the other person as if it were reflected in a mirror; if I am angry, I do not see that my face is turning red and my eyes are full of passion, but I can feel the burning fire of my fury and I know that the other person is also affected by my sudden change in appearance. It is, therefore, from inside that I create my mimic and control the external mask to fit the varia-tions of my psychological play and the other person's reactions to it. The same processes take place in my partner, hence a correla-tion of masks: I affect his mask and he affects mine in the exact measure of the reciprocity of our appearances. The body, therefore, forces the inner self to exteriorize itself to become at times the victim, at times the aggressor.

A mask, however, is not necessarily physical. We create symbols which extend and complicate our psychic expression: in that manner, the hairdo and make-up constitute a strange intermedi-ary between the immovable physical mask and the removable clothing. Furthermore, we have speech, another extremely subtle kind of mask. Clothing and speech can detach themselves from the subject; they are the most mobile artificial symbols. Speech has an extreme mobility of its own; a word spoken is lost (verba volant . . . words fly). Speech is a mask which can mask itself, almost indefinably and in many different ways. Thoughts fly with words and words with thoughts. What are grammar and words, style and rhetoric, if not a systematic study of the anatomy and physiology of those masks? What are literary schools: classicism and romanticism, if not different manners of conceding the use of the same masks?

I stress here the inherent paradox of the physical mask. The first element of the paradox is the bringing together of appear-ance and reality since I chose one aspect of my appearance to express my true self! the other element of the same paradox dissociates appearance from reality by creating a protective distance between the two.

All masquerade, therefore, is ambiguous.

Sometimes I hide behind my mask and pretend to be what I am not; at other times, I change my appearance to reveal a greater reality of my being. Both objectives, however, are self-destructive, which demonstrates that deceiving cannot be the basis of a human relationship. The mask hides the true self. But how could the mask be identified as such without revealing something of the real person? It has often been noticed that costume balls cast a light on the secret and repressed dispositions of the guests. At the theater, not all actors are made to play the same part [3] In life, if I play the role of a rich lord, I betray my taste for luxury; if I put myself down, I show in fact my pride; if I change faces with all my interlocutors, I publicly demonstrate that I am nothing but a comedian.

On the other hand, the mask is meant to affect the other person's attitude; but the player is the victim of his own game. We end by becoming what we wanted to look like or appear. A frightened mother may become courageous by reassuring her child, an unfriendly storekeeper may end by being amiable: the demands of good business have changed him. The external mask, therefore, can neither isolate without betraying, nor direct towards the world without re-emphasizing the inner self.

That play of mirrors, which creates a variation of images of both subjects, can take several possible directions.

1. I can try to hide from myself by hiding from others, turning my back to my partner as well as ignoring my true self. This is, for example, the attitude of the ostrich--hiding one's head in the sand--or the attitude of the love-game meant to be a double illusion, or even the attitude of the starry-eyed which Labiche describes so well in a remarkable comedy.

2. I can also try to unmask a person by assuming an appropriate mask. Of all human relationship, this is the most common: a good example is found in the medieval tournament--each armed knight is trying to reach the weak point of his opponent's armor. Such strategies and tactics, however, are not necessarily used for aggression only: they can also serve some paternalistic intentions or a rugged friendship. One thinks also of the relationship between doctor and patient, between the spiritual counsellor and his advisee.

3. I can try to unmask myself by hiding from the other person; a rather unusual attitude. This is found in the case of either naive simplicity or ridiculous trust. There are people who take pleasure in being victimized. Nevertheless, such an attitude can be rewarding; in giving the best of one's self one should close his eyes to the other person's shortcomings in the hope of teaching him to become the kind of person he could be. One can also be motivated by a sense of self-esteem. It was the case of Saint Anselm who, warned by a friend against the lies of a third party,

proudly replied: "If I am right, the liar will be dishonored. If I am wrong, I will have lost my honor by making a false judgment."

4. Finally, it is possible to unmask oneself and the other person at the same time. This happens in those circumstances where all masks fall under the pressure of exasperation, discouragement or often hatred. It is also, thank God, what happens in a situation of complete trust and love--what Pierre-Henri Simon calls "L'histoire d'un Bonheur"--a story of happiness. Whenever masks re-appear in such happy experience, it is to play a game; because of mutual trust, masks no longer deceive. Everything is transparent.

III

We have just examined the mask as a perfection of a certain image of oneself. There is an external mask and an inner one, the latter being the image the self has of itself for its own sake. The self imagines its own identity to modify it. In this process, one self may borrow from outside some components. When a child dreams of becoming a sailor, he can do so because he has actually seen sailors; he dreams of being one of them and he looks at himself in that particular role. Components, however, and ultimate form may arise from inside. Each one of us has a multitude of potential identities; [4] it is simply a matter of choosing from one's recollections and desires, "alter-egos," some noble, others mediocre. The inner mask can seriously change a life; and it is a rather dangerous freedom which exercises itself in the intimate laboratory of the heart. In the crucial hours of a moral crisis, salvation often comes from an image of our past, or from a representation of our ideal self which maintains our stability at its highest level. Pluralism will undoubtedly manifest itself not only through multiple and often unrelated choices (one can be poetic in the morning and earthly in the afternoon), but also by the intensity we put in a choice, even a definite one, to express the variety of our inner dispositions, real or rejected. The inner mask manifests the incompleteness of our unity. Our personality is like a promise and our character is its visible trace, the product of a double movement psychic and intentional. It can be either: crystallized, it can confine the person, on the other hand, when more flexible, it can liberate. In the long run, however, the character is an intermediary between two extremes which are deadly determination and living unity as, indeed, the inner mask is also situated between two extremes: pure intimacy and absolute estrangement. The character demonstrates the fact that we never reach the end of our adventure; we never fully realize ourselves, we are constantly searching for our identity.

Here we should turn the whole issue around. We have, so far, opposed mask and person. Is it not true, however, that we have gradually resolved that the mask affects our inner self and our future has a tendency to be absorbed by the complexity of our inner experience? "I am" means that I move and search without ever taking hold of myself. Now, a new question suddenly arises: "Is it clear that there is something hidden to understand?" Are we anything more than a series of images, an accumulation of events, a pseudo-personality, a heap of sand which the wind blows or the pick levels down, and nothing more? This impermanency is often recognized by the philosophy of the East. David Hume, an eighteenth-century Scottish philosopher introduced it to the West. If we concede that he was right, we also mean that our first assumption in linguistics was true: persona means mask and mask, persona . . . Everything permanent in us is imaginary; it is the assumed character. The theater had led us to life, life is bringing us back to the theater.

Since I mentioned earlier the name of Pirandello, is it not he who will say the last word on this enigma? Let us read again a page of his essay on the birth of character:

> With complete lucidity the very substance of our daily life, as if hanging in the vacuum of our inner silence, appears in its ugliness, its impossible and mysterious coarseness; all our artifical relationships, their feelings and images collapse under it. The inner emptiness widens beyond our physical limitations to encircle our total being; a strange emptiness, indeed, made of suspended time and silence, a mysterious abyss. It takes an enormous effort to recapture a normal consciousness of things, to re-order our thoughts, to feel alive again in a usual way. But in this normal consciousness, however, we no longer believe; nor do we trust our well-ordered thoughts, or our ordinary sense of existence. We know, now, that they are illusions only; we have made them out of our instinct for survival; behind them, however, there is something else which man cannot see, except in death or madness. [5]

As you may have noticed, especially in the last sentence, Pirandello, haunted by the contrast between form and life, is a phenomenologist in appearance only. He strongly insists on man's inability both to know himself and to reach out. We live in a "feu de glaces"--distorting mirrors. Beyond our game, however, there is something which cannot be fully grasped. We find the same conviction shared by many mystics, Fenelon, for example. It causes the anxiety of Pirandello; it is also the most striking element of his message. Man is an exile. To be exiled, however, one must believe in the reality of a distant beloved country. We would have no trouble if we supposed that the person could be reduced to external reflections. The problem, however, is here, always reappearing: what is the true nature of the human person? What are we looking for when we try to unmask the conscience of the individual to reach his inner self?

Some Fathers of the Church, combining Plato and the Bible, look at man as a soul in need of liberation; for it is buried under a thick layer of skin like a number of tunics, multiplied and made heavier by sin. Muslim writers compare the self to an onion with many layers of skin, which must be peeled one by one. But, will the process ever end? Is there any reason why our intentions would not always be incompletely representative of our true self, a secret mask even partial and transitory?

To conclude, I should like now to take some comparisons from music. Each one of us is an irreplaceable theme, hidden under innumerable variations. The latter can be more or less perfect, they nevertheless express the theme which is our unique vocation. The list of my choices is necessarily dependent on some initial value [6] which is not mine or anybody else's, not even a force of nature but that of the creative will of God in me. I always find this value before me whenever I am trying to take hold of myself; it is like a call giving its particular style to all my efforts. My vocation to wholeness demands that I be unique and, conversely, my uniqueness demands that I be whole. It follows, therefore, that each new step I take will appear to me either like a mask or like a true expression of the very substance of my being, depending on whether I will put the stress on vocation or realization. I exist, however, in both aspects, and the depth of my being is in their coming together.

Consequently, there are acts which will more fully express that I am in harmony with the essence of my being: those are the acts which call for my perfect freedom. There are acts which will reveal my true being through the masks and others will make it more opaque to my consciousness. And among those acts capable of realizing a greater harmony between questions and answers about myself, I must give a special place to the acts of love. Indifference is good in appearance only, capable of supporting a more academic interest. Explosions of hatred, unilateral or reciprocal, reveal only the weak points of the personality. Cold discernment can be very sharp; it always lacks in scope and paralyzes individuals in molds, depriving them of hope. Love alone, in spite of all counterfeits, can embrace the whole being of the individual and respect his destiny. Every time I turn to others to love them, I unite and expand the world of consciousness as well. I enlighten my relationship to my own ego; I relate the mask to the person. I further establish a clear liaison between the internal and external masks and between the loving person and the loved one. For to love is to direct mental and inter-mental activities in such a way that they are both in the same straight line. Masks divide when left alone, but when trust and generosity replace calculation, life and its expression are brought together. Communion between people takes place, and persons relate to each other in the wisdom of the Creator.

NOTES

1. **Euripides' Theater,** from the French translation by H. Berguin and G. Duclos, Book II, Paris, Garnier, 1954, pp. 222-223, 241.

2. See the fragment attributed to Philémon in K. Freeman, **The Greek Way,** an anthology, London, 1947, p. 123.

3. What it limits--by the way--according to the words of Diderot: "The tears of a comedian descend from his head, but those of a sensible person, ascend from his heart."

4. One day, to a friend complaining that there were two persons in him, Bremond said rather humorously: "You have only two? I have at least a dozen!" The more genial one is, the greater number . . .

5. The French was quoted from G. Dumas' Pirandello, Paris, 1935, p. 57.

6. Initial--and final--in the metaphysical sense, but not necessarily separate in chronological order. It is like the theme given to a pianist as the beginning of a fugue. The personal theme is given with its potential variations.

Chapter IV

THE PERSON AND THE GROUP

If it is true, as Plato suggested, that the philosopher is a "synoptic man," nobody will object to my consideration of the group from a wider perspective than that of sciences such as psychology and sociology. My choice does not imply that I distrust those sciences; on the contrary. I shall indeed often refer to their finds; but I shall also proceed with a clear understanding of all potential dangers. All philosophical reflection must aim at universality, moving from elementary observations to reach, if possible, the most difficult problems of the reflective method.

To start from the bottom means, here, the examination of the animal base of the group. To reach the top, on the other hand, will imply the scrutinizing of the nature of the "transindividual" subject and asking whether it can be substituted for a "transcendental" subject. Between the animal and the transindividual, it will be possible to examine the specification and functions of human groups; and of course take a look at those informal groups which are the object of our study.

Living species are not usually found in one area only and they are not constituted of perfectly identical subjects. Each can be divided in groups and sub-groups consisting of different individuals, among whom are distributed hereditary characteristics, either predominating or in recession. Competition occurs not only between individuals but also between groups. For a group constitutes a pool of chromosomic genes, different from other types. Inequality among groups of dissimilar individuals, becomes, according to some biologists, the instrument of natural auto-selection by the species. This first selection is not to be confused with that selection based on external factors which attracted the attention of Darwinism. A herd of baboons, for example, is attacked: some members of the group fight vigorously at the risk of their life; they defend themselves better than others. Do we not have here one of the keys to the understanding of the evolution processes?

> Populations with a greater impulse to be on the alert undoubtedly possessed a greater aptitude for survival. A quality which, at first, was a characteristic of a few has spread through competition within the group to eventually become the characteristic of the species.

> Society is the group where the sharing of genes is tested. With complete unconcern for the fate of individuals, natural selection must seek to determine through group competition the phenotype and the processes of genetic variations. It is somewhat frightening to think of the cruelty of fate; and yet as we re-examine the phenomenon it becomes possible to see in it some reflection of immortality.

The lines I have just quoted are taken from a very popular book in the Anglo-Saxon world. [1] The author, Robert Ardrey, is a zoologist of great learning, a clear thinker, rather bitter, and versed in passionistic humor. Although he vulgarizes science very well, he can generalize also with some imprudence. He knows that some of his concepts are not always well defined; for example, his concept of the group at times designates a localized and well structured cluster of individuals; at other times, it is an unstructured group, amorphous like a grouping of unrelated city-dwellers.

The observations of the zoologist are interesting, in so far as they provide information on the animal base of human society. Let me quote one more text on the human species.

One can remark that the author and his non-conformist colleagues offer many different suggestions:

> Language is, generally speaking, the most serious barrier between populations of the human species. Linguistic boundaries therefore constitute also national boundaries. In the same manner, political boundaries which group together several linguistic families tend to be non-peaceful. Furthermore, even in the midst of populations of the same racial and linguistic origins, religion, geography and obligations of customs and work as well as economic and educational differences tend to undermine the possibilities of encounter and alliances. Therefore, the smallest group of individuals with equal opportunities for togetherness is known by the term: "dème" or "isolat." Dobzhansky has proposed the thesis that among people, even today, the "isolats" number in the hundreds, sometimes in the thousands, at the most. Matrimonial statistics in France

reveal the paradox that in mountainous regions isolats
may reach an average of 1,100 people in a certain population; while in Paris where a large mixing of populations
would be expected, isolats number only 900.77. [2]

Similar numbers would be found among seals in Alaska and elephants
in Tanzania.

The thought provoking and correct idea behind those
hypotheses on details and venturous statistics seems to be the
following: the human species keeps its animal substratum, always
ready to re-emerge at the level of our human behavior. We, too,
are divided in competitive groups of reproduction and defense.
We, too, are capable of descriptive communication within our
group, while incapable of relating or communing with others;
in comparison with animals, however, we have an additional dividing
factor which is language, a source of real hatred for the foreigner.
Such attractions and repulsions are often tied to these territorial
possessions which determine collective survival. When a mob is
moved by some descriptive symbol--"symbole signaletique"--it
renounces even its human language; the mob is then a monster
without a neocortex, destroying any individual who has openly
kept his rationality. The human group which abdicates humanity
reassumes--at its worst degree--the condition of excited monkeys.
For such group society no longer serves the individual, but the
latter is sacrificed to the ends of the former.

Human societies have invented what Ardrey calls the
individual; what I would prefer to call the person. Or rather it
is the person who, laboriously emerging from the chromosomic
pool of the hominoid group [3] produces a civilization. The human
realm then separates itself from the purely animal realm. Human
equilibrium is the result of a compromise. On the one hand, society
must recognize that the person is the only source of all scientific,
artistic or political civilization; and on the other hand, the person,
separated from the crowd, must confess that men are created
unequal and cannot escape the particularism of geography, hierar-
chies, competitions and zenophobia.

Deep inside each man is a reptile. The idea is evident
to the point of being commonplace. Ardrey, however, has another
idea which is more disturbing and less common. He is astonished
by the survival in human groups of some biological characteristics
of other superior vertebrates; the association of mobs and the
instinctive grouping of individuals of the same age, particularly
the young.

His guess is that the monogamous family group, assembling
in harmonious unity individuals of different sex and age, is only
a late and fragile evolution in the phylum of the primates from

which we originate. He asks whether the sub-group of young males, in the contemporary crises, do not prepare for such a deep altering that its consequences for our mores and institutions are incalculable. Accepting as a point of departure that the three fundamental desires of any human being are selfawareness, stimulation in life and enjoyment of real security, Ardrey does not believe at all that they are easy to satisfy simultaneously. He has a limited hope only in the future of our species: he is suspicious of egalitarian utopias and feminist mystics which hide our real situation and increase the risks of imbalance, violence and moral decay.

Once again, I should say that Ardrey's complex work fails to provide convincing proofs, only hypotheses for reflection on group-selection from the data of genetics are offered. Nothing is easier than criticizing some of his affirmations, used as a means of bringing together numerous but disparate facts. One cannot deny, however, that he has cast an interesting light on the reality of our animal base.

The Human Superstructure

The pre-personal grouping is spontaneous: it is an affective "Gemeinschaft" only epidermic or more profound, but free of artificiality and partly determined by the spatial-temporal proximity of its members. There is among them a community of impulsions and tastes in spite of individual differences. But it is not this primitive and concrete group which constitutes the originality of the human group in the zoological context.

At the extreme opposite, the group can be defined in purely abstract terms as an intellectual category such as that of things and people. It is then a matter of cataloging those diverse phenomena which have common characteristics. Round pebbles on the beach, books of the same size on library shelves, the bald heads of curates constitute such groups. It is evident, however, that creating intellectual categories in the course of a study does not imply being subject to classification; that does not constitute the originality of a human group.

What is, then, the superstructure which man adds to the animal substratum and logical definitions? It is certainly a conscious and intentional phenomenon, a free association of persons created, at least at the beginning, by their own self-determination. We cannot, however, reduce the group to a bond between two persons as is the case between friends, or a couple in love. Goals and means, as well as the type of participation, are different in the dyad and in the social group. The group exists only when a collective reality is found beyond a dual-intersubjectivity and a complex rapport beyond the dyadic one. The social "we" supposes not only the "I" and "thou" but also the plurality of the "thou", that is, the "you", as well as the emergence at the level of consciousness of the "he", often appearing at the weak point of an "I-thou" relationship. But the "they" can coexist at the strongest point of the "I-you" rapport. In other words, there is a human group whenever an individual consciousness wants to be in relation to others to discover among them some "thou's" whose complementarity will establish a resemblance. Each member realizes in the representation of the group egocentric at first a certain decentralization to the benefit of other individuals. This capacity is not only imaginative and pragmatic, as it is in the case of lower vertebrates, but also rational because it is joined to a concern for truth and justice. Speech makes the group possible and manifests the gift of reason. A wider perspective is possible for each member of the group. This is due to the linguistic ability of the speaker who can recapitulate everything topically as well as chronologically. At that time a linear and objective description is comprehended without any fundamental misunderstanding by the whole group. [4]

The total consciousness, or, if one prefers, the "we" of the group is not, as we have already said, identical to the "we" of the dyadic communion. It is because an element of distance interferes in the experience of time and space; even in a marginal degree, it is part of the very contexture of a social relationship, and this for several reasons.

First of all, the group embraces persons whose presence cannot be at the same time action and perception, for no other reason than that the becoming of each person is very complex. Even when closely knit a cultural, professional or even familial group is affected by spatial separation, poor information, and lack of simultaneity in interaction.

Furthermore, the group is not only inclusive, it is also included. The awareness each member has of the group is not the experience of being away from a large crowd or of the whole human family. We always conceive of our group as part of a larger whole. Hence the element of distance or rupture, because the boundaries of the group overlap the boundaries of our attention and information. The country beyond is at the same time indispensable and unknown, or foreign.

Finally, a third kind of distance affects the group. It is situated at the very center of the "we"; that is the rapport between the person and the community, because the "we" is not at first a real interpersonal communion, but simply a vocal communication, bringing the members into a group without constituting it. It is an object, a goal, as well as a method; it is more or less fluctuating. It could be compared to a tapestry, woven by several hands; it has a stable texture and frame: the essential or conventional norms of the group. It also has a pattern combining threads and colors: the individual contributions which constitute the history of the group. When intellectuality has the upper hand on the animal base, the "Gesellschaft" chills the "Gemeinschaft" (whatever the latter's origin, biological or spiritual). One then notices a triumph of ideology. The language underlines the difference: one no longer speaks in terms of a "group" but "grouping"--or consciously participating group.

From this analysis, we conclude that the human superstructure of the group makes possible a lasting choice, and with it the association of the persons' freedom with a permanent encounter. It is also evident that such possibility is limited in every aspect. It is limited quantitatively because the group subdivides itself to be incorporated in a larger whole. The smaller the number of participants in the group the higher its potential for renewal, hence the formation of many sub-groups to prevent the apathy and smothering of the common soul's vitality. In terms of number, it is normal that the group tend to remain small. [5] If it becomes too large, it loses its identity: it is then a crowd, a mass of people, a movement, a party, a church, a nation, a state, etc. . . with all the differences implied in them. In a large group, the amount of time allocated to its life is necessarily restricted; as a result, it deteriorates and dies, or worse, becomes an institution. All that leads to the understanding that the group is one of many; there is no group which, potentially at least, does not include several other groups or anti-groups.

To these quantitative limits some qualitative ones can be added: the prestige and leadership of the founder of the group and his successor, the influence of prominent members creates a "dominant" climate more or less subject to change. From such influences come ideas, images and regulations which affect the life of the group. The impact is often exercised with a certain creative fidelity in the process of change. It can happen, however, that this enthusiastic collaboration of an early period yields to a dull uniformity, members are only passive subjects of a vocal leaderhip, or repetitious propaganda. The group is not only conditioned from the outside, in essense it is contingent and even mortal.

The Fulfillment of the Person and the Mediation of the Group

To ask oneself whether the group fulfills the person or not is in fact trying to assess the functions of the group vis-a-vis the person. Obviously, they are many. Let me give a very incomplete list for the simple purpose of initiating some reflection on the subject.

1. The group may function as a mirror for the benefit

of its members. Each one projects on the whole group something of his real or ideal self; and a certain fusion takes place whenever membership in the group implies the formation of an effective and functional "we." Shifting away from the contemplation of the individual and collective self can contribute to the formation of persons and yet it also can be part of their deterioration. To look at oneself in a mirror is useful for shaving and combing one's hair. It is even more useful to look at the traffic in the car's rearview mirror, at the radar-screen of a plane to maintain a safe course. But what a catastrophe to yield to Narcissist imprudence! "Esprit de corps"--corporate feeling--can be a form of self-contemplation, like looking in a mirror. Depending on its intensity, it might be the strength or weakness of those in the group.

2. The same twofold mediation can be seen in another function of the group: to separate and sort out personal images. It is what I call the prismatic function. The group is, then, an analyst and selector; it does not create anything, but it operates a transformation of persons by registering the variations of their contribution to the group. The prismatic function changes us without our knowing, like air affects those who breathe. Whereas, however, the air mixes together all kinds of emanations, the group assimilates certain contributions only. It is also more selective of those activities directed towards the outside. It is sensitive to the prestige of some persons and to the influence of ideas as well as to the mechanics of communication.

Special attention must be given to professional activity, which is for the individual a means of fulfilling his personality, giving to that end additional features to social contacts. The physician, for example, sees the patient as a person. The group of his colleagues and patients forces him to sort out those images of himself and other people in the light of his particular work. The impression of the character on the person is very profound; it leads to an edification of self by virtue of specialized experiences. It does not start, however, by an additional measure of intra- or extra-consciousness. It begins with a subtraction of a certain strength of consciousness and a definite choice of relations to others.

3. Do we confer on the group a more creative role by comparing it to a crucible? Not really. This new image implies more than a selection process. A combination of personal contributions, a synthesis affecting all subjects, takes place. One does not find in the crucible, however, the creative power of ideas and initiatives; the latter is to be found in the nature of the ingredients put into it; and they come from the persons themselves. The crucible is nothing but a place of encounter for those elements which either can be harmonized or are in conflict. Everything new in the influence of the group for both the good and bad of

its participants and their cause, comes in the last analysis from the members. It is the mutual influence between people which is creative. In the group, however, influence may remain anonymous, without necessarily being impersonal. It expresses ideas and acts born in the individual consciousness. The mediation of the group provides the norms of the encounter. It is its only lasting being.

4. In other words, we could say that the dynamic function of the group identifies it as a regulator of possible pressures. As a matter of principle, participation in a group reduces conflicts between persons and creates a solidarity among participants. Union, however, which strengthens the group, can also harden its members in their relationship to people outside. If the group is exclusive, it becomes isolated and indifferent to the environment; if it is open, it welcomes ideas as well as people and integrates them to the dominant concerns contributing to its very life. For the latter case, however, the group may be even more antagonistic vis-a-vis all anti-groups. Opposition may even creep in among members and create dissident sub-groups. In any case, a group is always more or less a pressure-group. Pressures can be classified under sympathy, indifference, antipathy, affecting people either from the inside or outside. Once again, we remark that there is nothing creative in the proper sense of the word; and yet the group is not a simple vehicle operating on the basis of its own rules; it is also an amplifier of interpersonal influences; and the amplification benefits those individual's contributions, which multiply with time.

Mirror, prism, crucible, regulator: all those analogies point to the method of mediation. The thesis one can suggest is clear: human groups do not create anything personal or hyper-personal, but transmit something personal to persons, whose condition is to live in spatial-temporal isolation. The purpose of the group is to overcome distance but without renouncing axiological neutrality. The value of what it gives to the members is not in the act of transmission itself. The group detects and amplifies, like broadcasting stations, emissions independent of the transmitter in their scientific, esthetic or moral qualities. The mediation of the group does not invent, its simply communicates; eventually, it can deteriorate. One could find in the thesis I am defending here a vague application of the Neo-platonic emanation.

It is not enough to label certain functions to understand them. Mediation is a word which can be conceived in many ways. It oscillates between two forms. Sometimes, it is the act of mediation itself which makes it possible for the two opposites to communicate without fusion; and the act of mediation subsists independently. In other circumstances, it is a movement both reconciling those opposites and becoming part of their unity. A simple tool can be a mediator of some kind; a living organism is one of another kind. The mediation of the group and language includes both kinds. Let us take a simple example to illustrate this concept. In a football game, the sub-group of each time constitutes a "nous-ensemble"--a we-togetherness--which co-ordinates the members of the squad for the purpose of winning the game. The group of two antagonistic teams, however, creates a "we" far more independent of the individual players because it is divided; its mediator role is simply that of a tool. It has flaws; hence the necessity of a referee to reconcile the two teams and avoid a total disintegration of the "we" which must function for the good of the game.

This example indicates that the mediation of the group takes place not only between persons but also between persons and values; the rules of the game, the ideal of sports have a bearing on the game itself and mediation occurs at the level of that agreement reached by the members of the association.

To conclude, the group, the players and the values of the game become mediators; they co-operate without losing their identity. But the center of all mediating activity is in the persons involved. The consciousness of the group proceeds from there at different levels. One cannot pre-determine the factor of evolution and how it will affect the mediation of the group because by nature it is not stable or foreseeable.

The Informal Group

The instability we were just mentioning is characteristic of informal groups. It is perhaps a redundancy to use such an expression; because the group has to start. With time, it either consolidates itself or becomes institutionalized, or even disbands and disappears. In both hypotheses it is gone. In the history of societies, it seems that the group is a juvenile manifestation; a characteristic which the adjective "informal" underlines. It is born of a project of friends; it would like to be free of such structures as division of work and hierarchy; more often than not, however, it fails! The graveyard of such associations is full. When they survive and seem to prosper, it is not for long; they soon move inward and become clanish!

Nowadays, the success of so-called informal groups could not be explained, if there were not some explorable reality under an awkward appearance. The informal group is seldom a pure invention without ancestry; its goal is not completely original; and its expression is not without aggressiveness. It usually finds its place in the structure of traditional societies; but it contrasts with the cold and inefficient performance of the same. The group is, therefore, a secessionist and almost always dissident. The group, however, is not a "band" freed of all obligations toward institutions.

The informal group personifies a need for reform; it ignores norms of action but rejects reality. It pretends to give the latter more flexibility and make it easier to handle. It expresses the euphoria of rediscovered springs. It has no sense of being saturated.

It is not rapidly assimilated; it goes through the nemesis of accumulations; the number of participants will automatically destroy any possible equality among its promoters. [6] The formulation of its ideals will add to the complexity of its structure and paralyze exchanges. In these conditions, how would new requests for membership not be rejected? The group must metamorphose itself into an institution, if it does not want to mutilate the conscience of the members and provide them with nothing but fanaticism, no outlet but anarchy. It would be madness to manage a large department store as one would keep a boutique. The law of social biology is merciless: the faster the growth of an informal group, the shorter its existence as an informal group. The "numerus clausus" of adherents and ideas would be for the group another way to die; for then, it would become a secret society which by definition would not be informal but rather hyperformal.

Do we imply here that the role of the informal group is void? Not at all. It is very important, but vague. Of course, the informal group acts as mediator. Will it mediate, however, life or death to the institutions it wants to reform and to the values it intends to promote? A negative attitude toward established order almost always hides a danger of "Schadenfreude" at the beginning of the group. Will it give new sap to old trees? Will it change programs to win new positions and perform better than preceding teams? Or, will it accelerate the processes of disintegration of a society without promoting new realities except false charisma? Any philosophical reflection should have the courage to formulate a moral warning. We have just denounced the danger of negativism. It is not the worst, however; particularly if a negative position is experienced as suffering and accepted as a means to an end. The worst is someone's pretention to genius or the tyrannical dogmatism of unqualified theoreticians. The very existence of informal groups brings hope. When they do proliferate too much, however, and invade all fields of action, they become a matter of concern both to the moralist who sees there a lack of moderation and the historian and sociologist who can discern the symptoms of a society in an "impasse", if not a proof of decay.

The person may find in the informal character of the group a great opportunity for its development, thanks to new ideologies and the enthusiasm of co-operation. The person can also find a refuge in the group against the abuse of power or the pressure of mass-media. It can also be the victim of a mirage all the more destructive because more subtle than any other collective mediations.

From the Transindividual Subject to the Logos

As we reach to last part of this account, I would like to express some regrets and give credit to someone. I should acknowledge, here, the contribution of Lucien Goldmann, who died recently. He studied at great length the questions of the transindividual subject and transcendental subject. My regret is that I was unable to accept his invitation, some years ago, to discuss these matters with him. If, today, I disagree with him in some areas, my gratitude for his stimulating work remains the same.

A few months before his death, he addressed "La Société française de philosophie" on this subject in the following terms:

> The central concept of positive dialectic thought is that of the collective or transindividual subject.
>
> In a scientific perspective, this concept has the advantage of explaining many empirical data by a study of pre-structural genetics of the life of society and of the historical processes. In the special case of cultural work--particularly in literature where we have in the text itself, by and large, some direct facts--the concept allows the creation of relatively simple models for the understanding of the entirety of the text, or part of it at least, at a depth which cannot be reached by any other method of interpretation.
>
> From the philosophical point of view, the same concept makes all ideas of a transcendental subject superfluous and eliminates the possibility of false alternatives: subject-object, factual judgment--judgment of values, continuity-discontinuity, explication-interpretation, procession-structure, mechanism-idealism, theory-action, science-philosophy. [7]

Let us go back to the main points of the above quotation. According to Mr. Goldmann, the person can be explained in two different ways. On the one hand, there are organic characteristics, what he calls the individual and libidinous aspects. On the other hand, what a person does in co-operation with other people is important; it is part of his work and development. This leads us to the examination of several groups: family, profession, culture, etc.

Those groups are transindividual; they help people to relate to each other within the collectivity without forcing identification with it. Subjects mingle and yet retain their originality. They contribute to the rise of civilizations and define the intellectual categories through which we understand social relations.

For example, to understand Pascal or Racine, one must know the idiosyncrasies of those authors, because they reflect the groups they belong to. The analysis of their work, however, must go beyond those groupings of individuals to include a study of Jansenism, the "noblesse robe", etc. . . . without which the deep meaning of their writings would remain quasi-nonintelligible. Among all transindividual groups, there is one more privileged: the social class. It is the only group which is oriented toward the global society by virtue of its praxis. The weakness of many philosophies of the personality is to neglect the structure of historical phenomena; and the weakness of structuralism is to neglect functional factors. The dialectic of the transindividual subject controls the dualism of those systems and allows a better examination of social and, more particularly, cultural data with only a small margin of error.

In spite of our differences both in language and thought, I am inclined to agree with several of those affirmations. It seems evident that the person is not a "monad" without openings on the world; in fact, he exists only in a network of other persons; hence, he is basically social. Social relationships are part of the person. I am afraid, however, that Mr. Goldmann's analysis might minimize the role of the "I," to the benefit of the non-dyadic group, where communion (already difficult and irregular in the dyad) degenerates into a form of communication even when the group succeeds in rising above its animal basis. The debate goes on to determine whether great men explain society or society, great men. The debate often goes in circles and is fruitless. But it remains true that a great man alone, however dependent he may be on those groups which helped his development and provide him with check and balance, has this spark of creative genius which transcends its sources and opens new horizons. If Mozart had lived during the neolithic era, he would not have composed a concerto for flute, harp and orchestra; however, he would have created a new form of music. Even more so, Homer or Racine would not have been less important because of a transposition in time, because a poet does not need sophisticated forms to bare his soul.

Mr. Goldmann, like Durkheimian sociologists, is forced to recognize the existence of the unique gift of a person as essential and superior to all techniques and heritages. He is willing to call it "une virtualité que le sujet collectif élabore" (a potential arising from the collectivity), [p. 102.] I would rather say that we discover our true self by being exposed to the surrounding society; and by doing that, we renew the tie of intersubjectivity. Furthermore, one can speak of transindividual subjectivity but not of transindividual subject.

One more remark should deal with the so-called privilege

of the social class including those transindividual subjects. It is debatable that it would better explain the dialectic of society as a whole. Example: the miseries of the "noblesse de la robe" cannot fully explain Jansenism, since nobles of the same class could be found elsewhere, among the Jesuits and Libertins, etc. . . . In the same manner, the fact that Pascal embraces the spirituality of Christ's Passion shows that his deep faith is rooted in an experience which the categories of his time would not have understood. For we deal here with a transcendent world. There are so many "I-thou" relationships: that of man with his God has certain dimensions so different from the reality of man's relation to his class.

This leads us to the most difficult part of Mr. Goldmann's thesis: he believes that the existence of the transindividual subject rules out the existence of the transcendental subject. He criticizes Brunschwieg for having escaped from dualism, thanks to an impersonal "cogito", which cannot be perceived in the context of a positive experience. It is not my intention here to speak of Descartes and Husserl; nor is it my wish to explain my reasons for preferring a "transcendent subject" to a "transcendental subject." I would claim, however, for the philosopher the right not to see his task as completed when he has examined the transindividual subject of the sociologist. How could the unco-ordinated variety of empirical groups constitute a coherent whole? How could intellectual categories, the discovery of truth and error, the norms of progress and decline become absolutes when emerging from a brutal succession of events? And yet if those things do not depend on an absolute which transcends historical events, then history is nothing but a blind thrust making slaves of men.

However, conscience is not a slave. It sweeps over and judges whatever could affect it. It has a universal perspective. The uniqueness of its personal vocation liberates the subjects from their possible orientation within the group and establishes the basis for a hypersocial "we."

The simple fact that we are now interrogating outselves and the world suffices to relate us to a "logos" which binds us in our quest. The metaphysics of the logos is easier to forget than refute; for even those who ignore it cannot live without it. Within and beyond the group which creates it, the person discovers in himself a community no longer earthly, a transcendence of his being, an act which illuminates his behavior, a gift which confers freedom.

NOTES

1. Robert Ardrey, **The Social Contract,** London, 1970, p. 78-79, (translated from the author's French).

2. _Ibid._, p. 52.

3. The evolution from ape to man is recognized by Ardrey without any reservation. He gives great importance to the emergence of speech, and to the nature of hunting to explain the hominization as well as the fabrication of weapons, such as bow and arrow. His considerations, however, are weak and often beg the question; sometimes they resemble wild dreams.

4. I refer the reader here to E. Benveniste, "Le Langage et l'Expérience Humaine," in **Problèmes du langage,** Paris, 1966, p. 9-11.

5. Financial groups, press groups, etc. . . can organize powerful structures assembling many people. Is it an exception to the usual connotation of the word "group"? It is not certain. A corporation may bring together a small number of large companies. Furthermore, the public generally assumed that decisions are made at the top by a few directors, aloof from the larger visible organization and the complex machines of those companies. One must confess, however, that the word remains vague. With the connotation of "Elan," smallness may be in the quantity of holdings, not in the number of the owners. A "blood group" may assemble millions of people, but it can be characterized by a simple property, for example, preventing agglutination of red blood corpuscles at the time of blood transfusion.

6. The informal group, like all groups, has a father or founder. The father soon seeks the co-operation of co-founders. Their responsibility is to create an egalitarian brotherhood, which can be materialized asymptomatically for a short time only and between a few people only. Inequality is in the nature of societies.

7. "Pensée dialectique et sujet transindividuel," in Bulletin de la Société française de philosophie, 4th year, No. 3 (July-Sept.), 1970, p. 73-74.

Chapter V

TRANSMISSION OF EVIDENCE

Communication and Interpretation of Evidence

1. Material things often have the ability of communicating evidence as if they had the power of speech. Tape recorders are all witnesses of some kind. Another example, the simplest, perhaps, is the small piece of thread taped across the edge of a closet door to discover if some indiscreet person has searched the place in the owner's absence. "I placed a thread," the person will say, "and it was not there when I came back; it is proof that my home was searched." In that case, the object used for the purpose can provide irrefutable information. Once its function has been fulfilled, it can be set aside for further use or simply discarded; its only purpose was to detect an intrusion.

Sometimes, it is not necessary to fabricate that kind of device, for a natural sign suffices: finger prints, blood stains, and other clues of the same kind will be collected during the investigation, and once again the function of the mark will be limited to providing some information. Once the latter has been secured, the sign is no longer interesting, even less so than the piece of paper or the thread, because the natural clue is spontaneously tied to the event which cannot be repeated.

The situation is different when one deals with clocks, time-recorders and other recording-machines. The mechanism is permanent; it must be carefully kept in good repair if we want to use it indefinitely, whatever the temporary usefulness of a given recording.

2. The communication of evidence is mechanical in these examples, the list of which could be long, and their study interesting. The interpretation is also mechanical, at least in most cases. E. Castelli, however, reminds us that Pascal's thought introduced a new perspective when he said that, "Nature is such that it records the presence of a lost god in man and around him." [1] Let us put aside human nature to consider that marginal aspect of Pascal's concept of nature which we best understand today: our surrounding universe. Is it true that the very life of

the cosmos bears witness to the loss of a god? And does it communicate that information with the accuracy of a tape-recorder, leaving no room for interpretation? There is something more subtle in Pascal's thought. He does not refer to something similar to the experience one could have in the ruins of Pompeii, where a baker's shop was excavated and a petrified dog was found, clearly showing the nature of the catastrophe of the eruption of Vesuvius, two thousand years ago. Pascal suggests that nature, affected by the loss of a god, seeks revenge against those who refused to listen to her. Hence, his analysis of the misery where man without God finds himself.

3. All the cases we have just mentioned have some elements in common, which we want now to single out.

a. Some data are witnesses only in a metaphorical sense, because they would be nothing if it were not for the mind which gives them their auxiliary usefulness. It took the anxiety of a person to insert a tell-tale thread in the closet; it took the disarray of a distracted attention, confused by the diversity of rhythmical experiences to invent and use the clock; it took the uncertainty of shipwrecked Robinson Crusoe to notice and interpret the <u>footprints of the savages on the sand</u>; it took the philosophical and religious quest of Pascal to discover that nature itself was asking many questions. Even if the intra-human universe groans, it is a witness in a minor sense only; it gives evidence by association to personal beings which assimilate and use it. Either the Creator reveals himself in the sighs of nature or man hears and remembers them.

b. We can speak of the witness of things (Pascal prudently uses the word: mark) only by giving them the gift of memory or a resemblance of the same. They cannot keep in themselves the contacts they have received; to do that they need the help of a conscience. Their usefulness is to subsist between two experiences as if in a state of slumber; by doing so, it is not completely lost.

c. On the other hand, if we lend things, something more than their bare materiality, raising them to the level of witnesses, is it not because we submit them to a value higher than them and us? When I appeal to things and say that they do not lie, I assume that truth as a value exists and is threatened. Indeed, certain facts can be ignored by a conscience; or the latter can be obscured or confused by the former. Facts, then, can fall outside the scope of truth, which is contradictory and unacceptable, at least for a sensitive conscience. To avoid this crisis, the conscience must have recourse to matter in order to save the value of what exists. It is true, therefore, that the transmission of truth from deep to superficial consciousness is achieved through contact with matter. In other words, matter touched by man becomes a guarantee of authenticity in the recording of human history. The machinery for collecting clues contributes to intellectual discernment; furthermore, it is useful for the preservation of truth by correcting the deviations of a free mind.

We witness here the birth of a "sacramentalité naturelle"--natural sacramentalism. It works independently but only after it has been impregnated inside by an act of consciousness. This co-operation presupposes that the conscience cannot deny itself radically but can err, partially at least, if it refuses the help of the material world in determining its course.

Correlatively, we can see the whole complex concept of the "timographic material"--material witness--assume a new strength in its tie with other concepts such as that of "proof by witness" and "intellectual evidence", both arising in the con-sciousness with the help of matter. This is very well expressed in the meaning of the English word, evidence.

4. The core of witnessing is personal; but where does it come from? What is its nature? It is an obscure subject; we cannot throw any light on the communication of evidence without referring to an inner experience which helps us to understand the nature of our witnessing. The best way to deal with this question is to look at those unique moments of the experience of conscious-ness. [2]

Those moments of vision may come freely and suddenly. At that moment, whole new aspects of life are being discovered; although a long period of preparation may have taken place. In esthetic terms, these visions are often simple details being trans-formed as if the artist needed them to see the total reality. They offer an unexpected shorter and easier way to reach out and con-template the beauty of the world. An astonishing and somewhat baroque example is found in a poem of Yeats:

> I would find by the edge of that water
> The collar-bone of a hare
> Worn thin by the lapping of water
> And pierce it through with a gimlet and stare
> At the old bitter world where they marry in churches.

We cannot detach ourselves from that hare's collar-bone, abandoned by a stream, worn thin by erosion, which the poet pierced with a gimlet to look through at the bitter view of the world. . .

As Sir Kenneth Clark says, "The collar-bone of the hare has made the poem." [3] If communication, however, can be established between the poet and us with such a force, it is because of his ability to detach himself from this transfigured piece of bone. What happened exactly? The poet witnesses to a reality which has first affirmed itself in him. He has received such reality in the inner sanctuary of his self, as if by grace; at the same time, he experienced the bitter reality of nature where streams flow, animals die and people get married.

5. We reach now a series of conclusions:

a. Conscience reaches out from its own depth and at the same time is touched by the deep reality of another being.

b. It reaches those two realms of reality by a motion of grace which precedes it both chronologically and ontologically.

c. This grace can be defined as an illumination of the mind; its source is in a giving nature which is similar and yet superior to the receiving nature of the mind.

d. It is a witness to us and in us, although detached from us. It affirms the reality of a being more profound than the reality of pragmatic appearances; and it claims to reach this truth against all possible denegation.

e. We receive the evidence in a communion of our mind with the reality it discovers and with the grace which reveals it to it(self).

f. This communion is not a communication which would represent both a loss and a recovery, but rather a rising experience and some kind of unique harmony.

g. For the same reasons, such communion is not a projection of our "self" and its objects, but the advent of consciousness and of the reality which precedes all forms of projection.

h. Finally, the communion makes of us witnesses to the reality which is an immediate coalescence of being into oneness.

6. Yeats' image attracts our attention by its strangeness. It is quite possible that all is not pure in the interest it creates. It has the merit, however, of illustrating the fragmentary character of the "artistic perceptum", in relation to the intermittant nature and object of the corresponding "perception." In simpler terms, let us say that inspiration is not constant. The image, however, offers in some selected details a series of harmonies which go beyond those details.

These unique moments which rise from the moral and

religious consciousness as well as from interhuman relationships show all the same fundamental characteristics; unicity of content, unusual aspects of commonplace knowledge, union of inter-related components and the radiance which creates a kind of rainbow between subject and world.

These moments of vision, however, often seem to be insignificant to outside spectators. This is why it is so difficult, for example, to understand love or conversion when we are not the lover or convert. This makes us suddenly aware of an unevenness in witnessing. The inner witnessing of the mind has made of us witnesses; this first communication is the most original and the purest of all the phases which follow the experience of communion. Should we infer that even near the source of information, we are witnesses at the same level as the mind which has just witnessed to our inner self? Do we not enter here in the area of possible misunderstandings? Does not the human witness act at two different levels: internal and external?

7. To answer this question, we must go back to the initial stage of the adventure of the subject. We witness to everything we live. At that level witnessing and the motion of consciousness are one and the same act. Is it not, indeed, the privilege of the "cognito" to be and act without dissociation of the two functions? Furthermore, as we have already remarked, consciousness rises in a light which transcends it. It allows the subject to be translucid and to discover in its own transparence the depth of the realities to which it is invited. The trinity of the cognito, cogitatum and the Word, which makes them co-effective, is then permanent. This indivisibility makes of us a necessary witness: the conscience by its very existence confirms the witness.

8. But the witnessing of the inner conscience, which cannot be separated from the witness himself, follows a difficult course with many heterogenous moments. The importance of certain events distinguishes them from all others and demands that we look at them; it is as if a veil was torn, revealing a new horizon. These are instances of special significance. They are, however, psychologically ambiguous; they introduce us to the most intimate center of a being and give us a presentiment of some unknown recesses; their excellent quality contrasts with the lethargy of our spiritual experience and invites us to dissociate ourselves from our witnessing. It is so because we project our privileged life against our daily life; we pass from a witnessing truly experienced to a witnessing simply spoken. Without expressing it, we make a difference between two levels of consciousness and we set up an exchange--hence a communion--between the two. From now on, our witnessing is subject symbolically to a reflection of lights between appearance and reality. We constantly search for, but cannot recapture, our original experience since it has been transposed to the category of images.

9. The experience of the outside world is only at its first stage when it rises within us with no other language than that of an inner symbolism. Then the witnessing is externalized as the outcome of an inner impulse to radiate. This original impulse, however, leaves it fragile and enigmatic. It also breaks existing ties between subjects. Reaching out to the other person, it attempts to bridge a gap. Depending, however, for its existence on the use of speech, it is different from it because of a lack of continuity with both personal consciousness and inner symbolism. Something external is forced between two subjects and interrupts their communion. It leaves room for some refreshing communication only; an experience far less pure and dependable than the original communication received at the deep level of consciousness where it identifies itself with the person without isolating it from the universe.

In the spoken witnessing to the other person, the potential of the sacred and its openness to the universe subsist, but in a state of nostalgia not as a dynamic force since the witness, as such, is isolated and finds it difficult to pull out of his alienation.

10. Language, of course, functions at different levels and can use one level as a springboard to reach a higher one. It can also hide one level of performance from the other, as if it were a mask. There are sincere communications which are obscure and hidden behind a cryptic language. In confidence, true language often hides behind conventional forms, which it controls. [4] A noble testimony is often expressed in a conventional language which frequently contradicts true emotions, and yet is necessary to provide some kind of protection. The best illustration of that truth is given by E. Castelli: a man confesses to a murder which he has not committed, to spare his fellow-citizens from enemy retaliation; and the enemy officer pretends to believe the lie that he too might save the population. Real communication is transmitted through a lie that both interlocutors accept in an admirable, silent complicity. The best part of the language is unspeakable, although it uses words. [5]

This would apply to the language of action. Velasques, in his **Reddition de Breda** depicts feelings of greater quality than the official attitudes of the victor, who receives the keys of the defeated city from its defender. One would expect arrogance, desire to humiliate, but one discovers instead goodness without weakness, and confidence without meanness. The two men join in a human experience higher than the unpredictability of circumstances.

11. The witness, as we said, is isolated in many ways. What he is witnessing to is usually in the past, alive through memory and only for an instant. The witness is further isolated from the

source of existence which makes the event true. There is then the distance from the witness to those who listen to him. Finally, one may speak of the distance between the language itself and the conscience using it to express itself. Even when language is not in the form of speech, but expresses itself in gestures or emotions, there is a discordance between the real experience and its manifestation, and between the true intention and its expression. Example: "You were the witness to that car accident. You must, therefore, give us your report." Who does not see that, between the initial perception of the event and the deposition of the witness, all kinds of interpretations and deformation can creep in?

12. This is why the very act of witnessing is always threatened, even in the case where a divine witness strengthens the human one. It is that threat, in fact, which gives to the testimony, or supports it, that sacred quality which transcends it. The human witness, whose testimony is as much received as it is communicated, is implicitly antagonistic to his enemies. Those are numerous. He himself can be an enemy of the truth. He can be unwillingly mistaken; or he may lie out of weakness or malice. Another enemy is time, which erodes the memory. Still another enemy is the language, even written; interpretation will be difficult because of the many intermediaries between the message and its decipherment. Finally, false witnesses may attack the true deposition from outside by their ridicule and lies.

13. It is remarkable that even the true witness expresses only what he has experienced in his inner self. He tries to overcome the many ambiguities interfering with the proclamation of truth. And when he decides to be a false witness, he must still assume the appearance of trustworthiness, or, in other words, he must mimic what he betrays. In doing so, however, he aggravates his isolation and alienation under the cover of a faithful communication. It is this specious lie which obligates those who receive a testimony to take all legal precautions, such as the rule: "Testis unus, testis nullus." The probing by an impartial judge must test point by point the guile of a corrupt witness. The oath can serve both good and bad, creating at times a vicious circle; this is, perhaps, the reason why the gospel forbids taking oaths. When testimonies are made publicly there is a greater willingness to take an oath, which casts a kind of sinister shadow on the morality of collectivity.

14. We have just examined the possible deteriorations of a testimony in the process of being communicated. We must also mention human freedom with its contingency and vulnerability; and this is good. The historicity of certain choices, and the dignity of the witness, explain the insecurity of the forms of communication and interpretation. It is possible to escape from the challenge of interpreting, but one must tie, morally speaking, the act of

witnessing and the effort of remaining hermeneutically true. Freedom has the potential of moving indefinitely in its pursuit of
truth and limiting the impact of errors and mistakes. Without
falling into naive optimism, these remarks help us in understanding
that, if personal autonomy may be costly, it is worth pursuing.

15. It is profitable to read some thoughts of Kierkegaard
in our effort to give some identity to the act of witnessing. He
distinguishes the communication of knowledge, which is direct,
from the communication of power, which is indirect.

> When reflecting on communication one concentrates on
> the receiver. The reference is then to ethical communica-
> tion: a form of "maïeutique." The witness disappears,
> so to speak, to become a servant and help the other
> person.
>
> Ethical communication is that of a power with a certain
> obligation; communication itself does not aim at knowledge
> per se, but at power. When ethical communication offers
> an element of knowledge as its point of departure, we
> have an ethical-religious communication in its Christian
> form. This element of knowledge distinguishes religious
> communication from ethical communication in the exact
> sense of the word; the former, however, does not constitute
> a communication of knowledge, but a communication
> of power and more precisely a communication of power
> with obligation--"pouvoir devoir." The communication
> does not aim at knowledge, but at power. Knowledge
> is only a transitory moment in this communication. [6]

What is disturbing is the possibility of bringing together
those ideas with another from the same author (in his Post-Scriptum)
according to which we cannot escape from our solitude except
by the experience of suffering and dereliction. In those conditions,
the witness of Christ on the cross would be the only case allowing
us to reach back to God and man in the true act of communion.

16. There is nothing hopeless, however, in realizing
the instability of the human conscience witnessing to some truth,
of the conscience receiving the testimony, and of the latter as
well. It is good that those three factors which determine the
witnessing manifest also a certain life and that the witnessing
itself be evolutionist by nature. For we must, from the same
movement, extricate the potentialities of the object of our testimony and that of the person from whom we have received the
testimony and of the person to whom we communicate it. The
testimony has a transforming power for those who give it or receive
it. It also forces us to determine the different levels of our communication and to extract from them their implicit elements
as well as their promises. Understanding is the second stage of

knowledge which succeeds to an inner disruption before it heals the wound. One understands better what has been honestly communicated. To understand, however, is to interpret; and to interpret means that one is moving toward the assent and option necessary to recapture a lost intuition, no longer alive, and yet still a part of a promise since it can be rediscovered and universalized. The witness is not a mere spectator, he is a craftsman, he is a leader of the human destiny.

17. Should a witness lay down his life to be believed? To the complete commitment demanded by Pascal, Jean Rostand answered with a facetious remark: "I do not believe witnesses who are not willing to die!" [7] Fanaticism certainly obscures one's vision, while impartiality is the gift of a cold head, which may, indeed, be paired with a warm heart; but it is a matter of accepting death and respecting the authenticity of a fact. The commitment of the whole person, however, is not pure excitement of the sensibility. The thoughts of Pascal, if not always his language, have enough coherence to answer all objections.

18. There is, however, a far more serious dilemma. If the testimony is an unchangeable expression of the witness, it is a lie, for it is short of the total signification of the fact, and it does not take into account the normal development of both the witness and the recipient. An impersonal account, an objective communication which, detached from the act itself, is nothing but confusing empty shells. If, on the contrary, the testimony is mobile, what guarantee do we have of its authenticity, of its ability to resist the distortion of imagination? Life can deform such witnessing into some kind of uncontrolled creativity. In both cases, the testimony loses its certitude: in the first case, because it denies the facts of history; in the second case, because it becomes a story.

This final difficulty, however, is not insoluble in principle. On the one hand, a partial expression remains eternally true and valid if it is recognized as such. On the other hand, the transformation of a person continues to be meaningful; it can remain coherent if it conforms itself to a self-dependent conscience. The interconscious development, too, can be a faithful expression of the witnessing which continues to be at the center of the rapport. Communication and interpretation of the testimony are threatened in many ways. We are not left, however, without criteria to identify those dangers and avoid them. [8]

19. How far can the action of the Word go, which is at the source of the verification and proclamation? We cannot answer that a priori; nor can we decide ahead of time if a series of testimonies, i.e., a tradition, is indefectible in its final expression and infallibly oriented in its course. The analysis, however, of

what Hegel would have called "l'esprit objectif" in the language, institutions and the vast patrimony of culture incites us to raise again, and more directly, the following questions: does not a series of testimonies constitute a witnessing which the witness bears to himself? Is it not true that his attestations, even as they become anonymous and diffused in the minds of many, reveal an original idea developing according to a certain logic?

We must answer these questions affirmatively. Anonymity is but another name of a universalizing relation which expresses man's ability to communicate in this world; and the Word allows us to participate to its inner-self through this process.

The objectivity of a witnessing has its limits, however, because it is never free from an element of subjectivity. Anonymity is not impersonal. First of all, it does not free itself from a transcendental subject, i.e., the Word which controls some unforseeable determinations. Furthermore, we human beings are inevitable vehicles of ideas, influencing their course; and we retain the power either to consent to the inner force of the testimony, or to distort it, or cover it and smother it. This symbiosis is such that a series of interpretations and the accumulation of meanings in the course of time can distort the intention of the original witness and turn objectivity into a spiritual mockery.

20. We are back to our initial thesis: at first (see paragraph 2) the witnessing appeared to us as a personal activity, even when it originates in things and is strengthened by them. Now we can add that it does not benefit from the structures to which it has submitted; it does not find in them a protection from the human reality where it is born and grows. It is in the normal course of the personal and interpersonal development that the witnessing ultimately finds its meaning, verification and redemption. Its highest norm imposes upon us a tension which even our freedom cannot dispel.

Salvation, which in principle, is always offered, implies, however, that its application proceeds tentatively. To put things in the best possible way, the passage of time, which we do not perfect either qualitatively or quantitatively, makes of us imperfect witnesses. It leaves anxiety about the repercussions of any affirmation even in the case of the best and most certain witnessing. There is no fidelity to the past, no guarantee for the future, except that which comes from the admission of transcendence.

NOTES

1. See **Le Témoignage**, Paris–Rome, 1972, preface.

2. This expression is the title of a beautiful book by the late Gilbert Maire. It is also found in an inaugual lecture by Sir Kenneth Clark, **Moments of Vision,** Oxford, 1954, where esthetical criticism opens many doors to the philosopher.
The brilliant preface by Ronald Barthes to **La Vie de Rance** of Chateaubriand, Paris, 1965, was interesting to me for another reason: it demonstrates, unwittingly perhaps, that a selection of best texts by the critics does not necessarily correspond to the selection by the author, or at least differs in many ways; this means that the general interpretation of a work can be negatively affected by the choice.

3. Sir K. Clark, op. cit., p. 6.

4. Ch. Le Chevalier, **La Confidence et la Personne Humaine,** Paris, 1960, has described with great art the psychological processes of tenderness.

5. E. Castelli, op. cit.

6. Quoted by H. Vergote: "Dialectique de la Communication," in Revue de Métaphysique et Morale," 6, (1971), p. 76.

7. J. Rostand, "Carnets d'un Biologiste," p. 21 (quoted by P. Foulquie and R. St. Jean, **Dictionnaire de la Langue Philosophique,** Paris, 1962, p. 215).

8. For a longer exposé on that subject, refer to my article: "Les Deux Passé et le Problème de l'histoire," in **Explorations Personnalistes,** Paris, 1970, pp. 11–123; and in Chapter 24 to "Histoire et Dogme de Blondel ou L'Exigence de Tradition Active."

Chapter VI

CULTURE AND PERSON

1. Self-consciousness is always aware of its oneness, which is subject, however, to a multiplicity of contrasts. The "I" asserts itself by confronting not only other persons but also the outer reality.

Considered in its spatial individuality, self-consciousness is cast in a strange environment. How many powers of influence are completely ignored by the individual! We are touched by only a fragment of the reality of the world.

But how do we separate space from time? At the very moment I begin to think of a remote person, of whom I know very little, I am already left behind. What I know is already part of his past because of a necessary time-lag between knowledge and its object. We stagger away from reality in time and space. We constantly shift from space to time and the passing of time as if drifting aimlessly. In our present experience we are aware of such phenomenon and try to reverse it in an attempt to achieve a better control of our world.

2. In its temporal context, self-consciousness develops the invincible feeling of being inserted in a much larger reality. Although I cannot recall the first moment of my psychological birth--"mon éveil psychologique"--and am unable, therefore, to free myself from a dimension of universal continuity, I must not escape, however, the necessity of interrupting the same continuity for the sake of affirming the oneness and individuality of my conscience, vis-a-vis the reality which precedes it. My irreducible originality is more than a feeling of metaphysical awareness; it is confirmed by the certainty that there was a time preceding my very existence. I cannot understand myself without looking into the past from which I am necessarily detached if I want to face my future. The past, however, offers an inexhaustible wealth of experience on which I depend even when I realize that I must free myself from it. By my birth I interrupted the line

of continuity, and by my personal growth I somewhat neutralize its impact. The past is the greater self preceding self-consciousness, a potential "ego" which challenges my individuality. Because of its universality I try to enter into communion with the world of the past to affirm myself and reexamine whatever sources of influence may have conditioned me more profoundly than I would be ready to confess. I am a product of the world; a fact I can neither deny or change. I would like, however, to re-trace my path and assume freely the rise of my consciousness.

3. The relationship of culture to person arises in the context of that experience. Indeed, what is culture if not the rescued presence of the past, sometimes a remote past effected by a personal awareness of its reality? There is no culture without the conscious attempt to recapture the finiteness of the past. And the first stage of that recovery of the past, through personal experience, is the acquisition of a language. By doing so the child rises to an intellectual level the bio-social currents which preceded and conditioned him. Language is more than a gift, it is a process of active self-affirmation. If there were no potential intellectual activity in the soul of a child, the baby would never learn to talk, he would never master any sound beyond the primitive cries of the animal. This common truth is often neglected today; or one refuses to assess its importance.

It is true that the child receives and respects the morphological and semantic structure of a given language; hence the tendency to magnify the importance of the language at the expense of thought, the latter depending too narrowly on the former and assuming that the human being has received at birth some innate linguistic patterns. The discussion of such hypothesis is beyond the scope of this study. Let it suffice to say, however, that data show definitely the simultaneity of the comprehension and the rise of its object, or what is understandable. This applies also to the knowledge of matter which could not be understood if it were not understandable. The language of a learning child is even more intelligible than nature, for it is made of cultural symbols and not simply of pure reality. The experience of a great number of human beings is anonymously expressed in those symbols and by using them the child acquires the first elements of his culture.

4. To some extent the diversity of linguistic families does not create new problems. We always face a certain personal assimilation or transposition of symbols in the cultural achievements of artists, moralists and scientists. The language is always a matter of great importance. The way they use it affects morphology, syntax and semantics; in other words the complete mastery of the language.

Culture, in the real meaning of the word, adds to the fundamental understanding of the language a growing reluctance to be conditioned by anonymity. This is obvious in the arts (particularly in literature) and in the study of ethics (here the reference should be vague enough to include religion); a cultivated man can relate by symbols to other men, living or dead, in identifying and judging them. The situation of scientific culture (not excluding philosophy) is not different. A scientist does not want only to understand his field; he seeks entrance in the thought of Newton and Einstein, in the work of his colleagues still living, in the same way as the man of letters relates to Homer or Racine as well as to the popular contemporary novelist. In that case, it is not the anecdotal character which is important but the individual mind which creates a work and is immersed in it.

There is a culture, therefore, able to focus our attention on the thoughts and feelings of man. It goes beyond the usage of familiar language which affects us without relating us openly to the past. This culture, capable of relating the meaning of symbols to the thoughts of men, can be subdivided; it is one thing to enter into a semi-dialogue with the dead, through a meditation of Plato or Descartes for example; and another thing to dialogue with the participants of a conference on Philosophy.

5. In any case, no person becomes truly cultivated by passively repeating the past. We try to re-examine and understand it even better than we know ourselves. It is, indeed, a very ambitious task and somewhat elusive. The possibility of failure, however, is compensated by the opportunity of reviving the past in our own person, whatever the deficiencies of the latter. As we think of the past we give it a new coloration, a new destiny. Even the worst misunderstanding can bear fruits. They are like the good side of the disaster. This truth is illustrated in the field of "intertextualité": translations, free imitations of ancient themes show many examples of renewal of thought emerging in spite of disguises and deviations. A fortiori there is a new intellectual life when minds which assimilate thoughts are sensitive to their motions and nourish them without destroying their originality. In **Andromaque**, Racine is unfaithful, perhaps, to Virgil and Euripides but he remains true to the orientation of classic tragedy.

6. The posthumous career of a work is achieved by a series of processes: selection, clarification, metamorphosis, neo-synthesis or structures, combination of unrelated elements . . . etc. Sometimes a work of the past leads only to an occasional reading, which is however a quasi-pure creation, as Roland Barthes would say, or a new writing. The contingency of the exercise is inevitable. It will take different forms in the history of philosophy and in the history of arts; but it can be traced everywhere.

Should we conclude here that there is complete arbitrariness or absolute relativism? Should we infer that the original work is inaccessible as if the human eye could see it only through a distorting prism? Certainly not! It is not fatal that we come against the past as if it were an insurmountable obstacle, nor is it destructive that the assimilation of the past be at the expense of a certain truth. Those who have patiently immersed themselves in the study of Plato, Bach or Newton may have their own perspective and yet they are normally bound to reach a certain agreement as to the objectivity of the content of their study. Objectivity in diversity leads to certitude. A certain bias of the "pre-comprehension" periods does not prevent unity and exactness of comprehension. In the same manner the positions of several people in a room in relation to chairs and tables does not affect the substance of those objects although they may see them differently. Clarity and accuracy do not arise simply from an intelligent decision of the subject but also from the impact of the object. This is no less true when we deal no longer with chairs and tables but with a dynamic reality such as an artistic work with well structured ideas capable of development. A work passing from one mind to another certainly remains subjected to their influence, on the other hand, it exercises its own impact on them in harmony with its objectivity and unique potential. This was well demonstrated in the famous "Essay" by Newman.

7. The "en soi" of a work can be discovered; but it is open to changes, like its author himself. The greater a work or a person the more inexhaustible is their identity. It cannot be understood by a simple process of reduction to a form of fixed structure, or to a thing without future. It is important, therefore, to dissociate exactness of interpretation (something possible) from any finality of the same (something impossible). The truth of a work, like that of a person, is found in its constant re-orientation; for this reason the essence of a work includes its radiance. Any conflict of interpretation, whenever it occurs, expresses either a crisis in comprehension or the incoherence of the object; it may also indicate a lack of vision or understanding on the part of one or more interpreters. Nothing, however, allows us to deny the existence of an orthodox series of interpretations, unless we give orthodoxy a rigid meaning or dismiss the validity of coincidence or harmony of interpretation on the part of the most serious specialists.

Is it true that the culture fed on writings, hence on a dead past, deprives us of the possibility of a living dialogue? Plato was critical of writings for often their authors were no longer there to defend themselves. Nevertheless, pondering on a printed text leads to a silent exchange with the author, even when he has been dead for centuries. A difficult hermeneutic asks questions of texts and listens to its answers. It is a type of verification. [1]

There is room for discovery in the pluralism of interpretations for all true knowledge is open, not centripetal but altruistic.

8. Any person seeking culture runs the dangerous risk of being dominated by his culture. It is often said that the actor, assuming and playing many different roles to the best of his ability, destroys his own personality, lending it to other individualities, denying its very substance in a gift of self to his art. The same remark could be made about a certain group of scholars, whose availability undermines their inner self. They are consumed by the people they study.

At the other end of the spectrum the reader who uses an author to bring to life and exploit his most capricious phantasms suppresses the relation of culture to person. His assumption that all texts have more than one meaning and that there is nothing to gain in several readings when time should be spent in re-writing, leads to a complete separation of culture and person. Furthermore such an attitude when uncontrolled creates the risk of plunging the personality of the interpreter into a kind of childish anarchy under the guise of fostering creativity and "différance."

The poor scholar uses authors as substitutes, exempting him from the responsibility of facing himself. The dreamer, on the other hand, uses writings as if they were material without any intrinsic value. In the former we find a form of spiritual suicide, in the latter a kind of homicide; in both a contempt for the person.

9. In fact the relation of culture to person should be that of mutual growth. As we revive the past for its own sake our person discovers his own identity. It affirms its unique autonomy by contributing to the unfolding of an idea of the past. There is a mutual "causalité" and the growth of one helps rather than handicaps the other. In the reanimation of the past a common future becomes possible. The process, however, implies a willingness to die, so to speak, for the sake of an extension and deepening of the subject. Hermeneutics and interpretation are integrated in a form of "intersubjectivity" without which the future of the person would be undermined.

This further refers to tensions and risks. The concept presupposes a rational commitment to the possibility of knowing and understanding another person and his work for the sake of reaching a cultural "we" a "nous culturel"--the "nous linguistique." Of course, this implies a judgment of the persons and their works. Would the objectivity of the outcome be different from any other form of objectivity? The same elements of freedom and probability exist everywhere whatever the restrictions of logic or mathematics. There is no reason for retaining a kind of criteriology of culture on pretense that the "Logos" is not demanding enough or because the correctness of judgment is not recognized by some kind of a plebiscite.

10. We can answer now, at least partly, the question we raised. If we understand culture, as it is usually done, as a presence of a past and distant human experience in the individual awareness of a person, it must be recognized that such a presence is not immediate but communicated through a "semiologique" system. Language, learned by the child, is one of the most elementary forms of that system. The personality of the child finds in the use of language an opportunity to unfold and acquire the heritage of a past which precedes his spatial-temporal existence. It further develops through the discovery and mastery of a system of symbols. In the process the child becomes conscious of the universal dimension of human experience. At that elementary level interpretations remain anonymous and only dependence upon parents and teachers, who act as vehicles of language, is recognized.

11. At a higher and more specific level culture demands that its sources and subjects be identified and individualized by the recipient. This is necessary to foster an encounter of persons in the transmission of works, because a masterpiece carries the imprint of its creator. In this encounter we discover a reciprocity at the osmatic or genetic level of consciousness. It happens, of course, in different ways; for it is obvious that one does not participate in the same manner in the genious of another when listening to a sonata by Schumann or reading the thought of Kant. In both instances, however, one finds a mixture of feelings and concepts, but in different dosage.

Furthermore, the dialogue may take place at various levels of intensity, depending on whether the work is that of a contemporary or emerges from a distant past and is enhanced by a certain, unfamiliar "aura vitale." For that reason it is possible, independently of a variety of specific objects, to speak of cultures in the plural and not in the singular. There are many paradoxes in this situation for the zones of penetration of the "aura vitale" are not evenly distributed. For example, we may have some experience in sheep breeding or in metallurgy and understand perfectly well some details of the **Georgiques** or **Iliad** whereas the feelings of the "Prix Goncourt" recipient may remain inscrutable.

12. It is preferable for many reasons that the designation of sources and subjects be returned to the anonymity of the past in order to facilitate creativity. As it is often said, culture is what is left once almost everything has been forgotten. It is often less an explicit knowledge than a form of know-how, a method, an <u>hexis</u> of the mind; hence a certain dualism in the meaning of the word culture.

At times a compromise is reached, which is very well illustrated in the work of Bergson. He began by separating knowledge from know-how in his two-fold study of philosophy and history of philosophy. The Données immediates are the product of personal reflection whereas his short thesis, Quid Aristoteles de loco senserit is a scholarly monograph. But if we pass from there to **L'évolution créatrice** what do we find? At the end of the book the author has drawn a vast fresco of a retrospective development of western philosophy.

It is unbelievably superficial if not wrong. Under the cover of that fresco he has unfolded his own thought, which is far more interesting and very profound. The evolution of his thought, however, would have been impossible without his knowledge of many metaphysicians of the past--particularly Plotinus--who molded his mind and brought a forgotten past to his consciousness. His work is at the same time auto-cultural and hetero-cultural, divided into serious information and mediocre historical review.

One would be tempted to conclude that a good philosopher is often a poor historian of his own discipline and vice versa. Non omnia possumus omnes. And yet the imprint of the past is necessary to the elaboration of an original philosophy; so is a certain ability--"aptitude architectonique"--to understand and re-invent historical developments. Is is only a dream to believe in a more complete triumph of intersubjectivity? Or would dependence on the past handicap the soaring of a new genius and vice versa? One must reconcile two specific needs: to avoid confusion of literary genres--which must be respected--and engage in the kind of cultural transmission necessary to a mutual stimulation of persons.

NOTES

1. E. D. Hersch preferred to call it "validation" giving it a different method from that of the natural sciences. His objective is to justify the correct interpretation of what the author wanted to say. See his book **Validity in Interpretation,** New Haven and London, 1971.

METAPHYSICS

Chapter VII

BEING AND PRIMORDIAL RELATION

Being and its Primordial Relation to Other Beings

1. It is possible that the verb "to be"--"être"--in its primary meaning be proper only to Indo-European languages; specialists, however, refuse to infer that these languages have only one term to express the idea of being. [1] It is advisable, therefore, not to reserve ontological reflection to one part only of the linguistic world. Even with the Indo-European group, languages are not offering the philosopher the same resources. To refer to one example only, Greeks can designate the substantive being by using several words: ho ôn, to ôn, to eînai. On the other hand, Latin, German and French have one word only: esse, sein, être. Philosophers have to coin a second word, more or less artificial: ens, seiende, l'étant. Italian is more fortunate and has two terms: essere, ente. English is limited to one: being. Hence its limitations. The word opens doors to many confusions. In all languages, indeed, one may use approximations which soon become technical terminology, either to designate existence (huparxis, exsistentia, etc.) or essence (ousia, essentia, etc.).

Semantic evidence emerges from that variety. Let us take another example, the verb, "to be"--"être." It is clear that that verb has two functions: one, it joins two things together and creates an equation; two, it refers to existence and becomes an absolute affirmation. What does include the latter meaning? It is somewhat obscure; and the philosopher has the responsibility of clarifying the connotation he gives to the word.

We shall use two words when referring to ontological substantives: "be"--"l'être", and "being"--"l'étant," with the following signification. By "being" we shall designate the concrete individuality which is best expressed in the person but includes a certain dimension of universality. Furthermore, "being" will refer to individuals deprived of personal inner consciousness--"intériorité." By the use of "be" we shall designate the primordial relation of a being with itself and other beings. That relation is not purely intellectual, but existential without being separate like being itself--"l'étant."

2. Our first task is to explain our definition of "be"--"l'être." Is it a real definition or a simple description, or just a convention? It is true that in a sense nobody can define such ideas as fundamental as that of being and relation. At best one can reach a certain consensus on the conventional interpretation of their content. Through that convention, however, one must describe a certain experience and attempt to analyze it in depth.

In our study, "be"--"être"--is subordinated to "being"--"étant." In the metaphysical order the former comes after the latter even when they go together in the existential order. This subordination does not prevent "be"--"être"--from facilitating the relation between "being's"--"étants"--as we know it. It creates community and communication. Its universality gives us the feeling of being overwhelmed and somewhat lost in it. Its constitution, however, is homogenous. We immediately understand the relation which is both opposition and synthesis, as Hamelin said. It is in us and around us; but we grasp its meaning and universality. Ontic determines the ontological relation more deeply than it is conditioned by the same.

3. It is a fact that "be"--"être"--creates divisions in the "being"--"étant"--and between beings. Reality is pluralistic. There is a creation of beings in the true sense of that word. Bradley remarks with some hesitation that differences "have broken out." This original diffluence, or fluidity, brings into focus alarming forms of dispersion in the "being"--"étant." The subject--"moi"--is not only incomplete vis-à-vis itself it is also divided in its interiorite. It is also incapable of assuming its own relativism without transcendent help. It is separated from all other beings and the world which share in its weakness. There is an enlightening paradox here as we discover the community of mortal beings. We are creatures subjected to a Creator; beings have their origin in a Being free from our limitations.

Should we infer that "be"--"être"--is a tragic entity? We do not believe so. It is instrumental only, and has identity only in the being it supports. It shares in the tragedy of the being and overcomes it. It lies at the origin of a fluidity which is not the stigma of any being but the external mark of its finitude. [2] In other words the fluidity it refers to emphasizes the external character of being. It proves that we are mortal beings. It does not show a trauma. The tragic element is found in "being"--"étant"; it does not emerge from "be"--"être."

4. One must distinguish between the primordial and

primitive aspects of the relation which constitutes the reality of "be" and "being." By primordial we refer to something metaphysical. Without it the relation itself would disappear. This primordial relation embraces the complete temporal evolution of a being. The word primordial signifies an ontological notion; the words primitive and derived indicate chronological notions; hence the ambiguity of the word "arché" and the affinity of the two meanings of that word. The first phase of the temporal moment is more emphasized than the succeeding ones. It is what interests the historian; and yet its importance should not be exaggerated since the primordial remains part of the continuing motion to the end. The primitive being in relation to the primordial, is absorbed by the latter. There is a derived "be"--"être"--"étant." The former is necessarily received by the latter. They are attached as the shadow of a walking man.

This historical aspect of "be"--"être"--is recognized in those judgments which assume a series of data. If we say, for example, that Louis XIV is the greatest of all French kings, we assume that the proposition to be true must rest on the examination of the complete line of French kings. In non-comparative judgments, however, there is still a historical implication because there is always a relation. To resolve that Socrates was a wise person, requires that we affirm that Socrates existed at one time in history, that he was first a child, then a young man, an adult, that he thought and acted in history, sharing his wisdom with disciples who transmitted to us their experience. Past, present and future with their limitations and possibilities express primitive or derived modes of action of beings in their inter-relations. The primordial relation of a being to itself, however, will precede them logically, and dominate them metaphysically.

5. It seems in those conditions that "beings"--"les étants"-- emerge at the end or term of a relation, a primordial relation. There is a continuing debate on the interiority-exteriority of relation. Do we subscribe to the concept of exteriority? Do we identify "l'être"--"be" with a form of relation and the latter with the exteriority of the "étants"--"beings"? Finally, do we not recognize that the terms of a relation precede the relation itself? How far can we go in substantiating those affirmations? Are they not absurd if we give them absolute value? If relations are separable from their terms, they cannot fully embrace them without being destructive or, to say the least, they lead to an experience of agnosticism when the mind refuses to further examine the hypothesis. All this is strange when one realizes that thinking is the act of the thinker, that is the act of a being which is irreducible even in the identification of the two.

Often the difficulties we encounter show that the problem has not been clearly formulated. Although beings may show a great fluidity in relation to themselves and other beings they keep, however, their individuality and ability to communicate. This may not always be clear since it is not part of the exteriority dimension of beings. And yet it is in their exteriority that we observe beings and their primordial relations. A relation is primordial between two beings; but it is never pure. It is subordinated to its terms.

Intellectually, it is possible to conceive "being" apart from "be" although the distinction is impossible in concrete reality. One cannot conceive "be," however, apart from "being." What is true, in fact, is that "be" and "being" go together; their existence is simultaneous. They are one in their diversity, in their relation and in the exteriority in which we know them. The communion of self with its own consciousness and with the other self is intuitive. Communicativeness and its act can be analyzed and they alone make possible the relation between "be" and "being."

The exteriority of relations is twofold: it shows that there is a distance between the two terms and it signifies that there is a common foundation of these terms as well as real communication between beings. If beings cannot be comprehended at the level of concepts, they can be identified in their relationships, the latter functioning as media. External relations can be misleading, however, when one overlooks their relativism or emphasizes their rationality at the expense of their foundation in reality. When "being" is given priority over "be," it becomes normal that the interiority of the former find expression in the latter and that the relation remain constant.

6. With that kind of precaution, it is possible to assume that "be"--"l'être"--is a relation at least at the level of abstraction if not by nature. Most primordial relations, primitive or derived, can be seen as "principium quo" not as "principium quod." Ontological forms are discovered as a static world. Hamelin suggests that they could be assimilated to the roads followed by all beings and designated by the term "relations relatées." "L'être"--"be"--as a system or an order has a dimension of eternity. It is a structural, historical form which is petrified as it is realized in a series of "beings"--"étants."

Since the crystallization of "be"--"l'être"--goes on indefinitely as "beings"--"étants"--appear on the scene, the framework of this process can never be perfect. It can be defective as well as perfectible. The destiny of "l'être"--"be"--remains fragile for there is contingency in ontology. We must conclude that the static character of "l'être" is only superficial. Furthermore, although "l'étant"--"being--is in projection of "l'être--"be"--it can modify it. One does not repeat the other. Where there is repetition we find re-utilization and renewal; in other words, continuing creation.

7. This leads us to recognize the dynamism of "l'être"--"be." It comes not only from the influence "l'être" exercises on "l'étant" but also from the impulse the ability to communicate gives to "l'étant." We have observed a distance between "étant" and "être", the latter being at the origin of the former. This creation by dehiscence underlies a certain neutrality of "l'être." This is neither tragic or anti-tragic, but it is ambiguous. (§3) This ambiguity underlines two other elements: contingency and fragility. (§6) All those things are inherent to the temporal evolution of "l'être." (§4) They show its authentic dynamism, that of a creature--"l'être:" "be"--serving other creatures--"étants:" "beings"; all submitted to the supreme Being which creates them. There is a phenomenon of growth for "l'être" in "les étants and through them. Everything they do or submit to affects "l'être" and is affected by it.

Boethius thought that if A is on the right or left of B, B is not modified. He felt that the spatial relation has no influence on beings. However, even in remaining within the context of the same kind of relations, is it not possible to raise the philosophical question about the validity of re-examining the problem? What is, for example, the relation of any point of the circumference to the center, or that of an angle to the triangle? We would like to criticize the assumption that living beings are indifferent to spatial relations. That Peter may stand on the right or left of Paul constitutes a modifying reality for the latter, even if he is not conscious of it. In the primordial relation of "l'étant" to itself or other beings there is an increase of l'être." We are grateful to Hamelin and MacTaggart for having dissociated themselves from the tradition of Boethius and proclaimed the dynamism of the primordial relation.

8. Although the thesis of Hamelin differs from ours in this essay, we owe him for having suggested that the ontological relation is a correlation. The correlation is a complex reality. All relations preceding a system are not changed by the translation of the system. There is, however, a correlation between the system and its components. There is another one between the evolution of the system and the stability of its components. This helps us to understand the more general fact that all correlations--even primordial ones--are unequal. Correlatives have different rhythms and are often "déphasés." There are degrees of reciprocity.

"L'être" is not uniform. There are degrees of intensity and intimacy of detachment and separation. We must recognize differences in those forms of correlation which unite body and soul, physical realities, men among themselves, man and animal, earth and cosmos. Ontological correlations create a wide variety whatever their common elements, one of the most important being an element of duality; there is no passive state without action, no active state without passion. The spectrum of those correlations goes from incompatibility to cooperation, from violent exclusion to juxtaposition which is tolerant coexistence, from convergence to quasi-identity. Phenomenology and logic could examine each phase in detail to show that incompatibility has degrees, so has opposition which is more superficial than contradiction.

9. We are not asking ourselves what are the place and role of any negation in the ontological relation. Philosophers often introduce relations of identity and contradiction as follows:

$$A = A$$

$$A = \text{non } B \text{ (everything that is not A)}$$

They neglect the possibility that $A = B$, on the ground that B could then be reduced to A. They would rather introduce the consideration that B be part of the equation $A = A$. In that case the second A is slightly different from the first and assumes the existence of B; an assumption which denies the possibility of a perfect equation. Finally, the symbol $=$ signifies equivalence not identity. Negation is an absence of equivalence, a sign of imparity.

The use of an equation does not represent the total function of a connecting verb. If we could free ourselves from the narrow framework of the logic of substitution we would discover that the copula has a mystery of identification or non-identification which finds its source in the mystery of existence. What is the meaning of the obstacle for a person who suffers negation or the hurt of contradiction? Should we see it as an outcome of language or as belonging to the reality of things?

The radical negation of "l'être," which no longer distinguishes between contrariety and contradiction, is the most radical denial of being--it is in fact nothingness. The metaphysical dimension of nothingness is the antithesis of words which allows us to see the character of a creature and its being. This is the first truth we learn from the radical negation of "l'être." It reveals its contingency. It takes farther than we had anticipated the subordination of "l'être" to the supreme Being. Nothingness is gnoseologic and reveals the weaknesses of the ontic dimension.

A similar truth is expressed in the assumption that the radical negation of "l'être" is in fact the negation of its independence. Any effort to make of "l'être" an absolute at the expense of "l'étant" gives to the former the appearance of a Sphinx. It becomes an enigma, creating doubt and a possible denial of its reality. It is equally unrealistic to deny its presence or exaggerate it to the point of making a god of it.

The relativism found in "l'être" signifies that it cannot be perfected in or through its own unfolding. This has been well demonstrated by French neo-criticism. It is explained in the "synthèse totale" of Renouvier and in the "relation indéterminable" of Hamelin. We referred to it in section three of this chapter when dealing with the cause of infinity.

10. Nothing else could be said of the contradiction of "l'être," whatever Hegel may suggest. "L'être" can stimulate "l'-étant." The radical negation of "l'être" has only a heuristic value and brings into light the nature and limitations of "l'être" by appealing to the hypothesis of its non-existence; as if "there were not anything rather than nothing," to use the phrase of Heidegger.

One must distinguish the contrariety of "l'être" from its contradition. The former is not a pure negation for there are degrees in being; there can be more or less "être." The "plus-être" and the "sous-être" are fluctuations of a certain dynamism. To deny that is to yield to the influence of Parmenides, some Scholastics and those who subscribe to the concept of a "cadre formel" (§5 and §6), protected by many paradoxes. We find, in fact, destiny and adventure in the phenomenon of "l'être." This is one of the very few points where my thesis is in agreement with Heidegger's. After all, the "mé on" of Plato is not that far from our position. It rests on the conviction that the "non-être" is not nothingness. "L'être," as we said, has degrees and even a history.

It would be false to say that "l'être" is the opposite of "l'étant." They are interrelated; but they should not be identified, for "l'étant" does not change for the sake of another "étant." Does that mean that there is neither contrariety nor contradiction in it? No negation? No, but the negation of "l'étant" is originally quite different from that of "l'être"; although there again, we find a relationship between the two. La Senne used to make a distinction between what he called a "contradiction de chute," or negative and a "contradiction de conquêt," positive. The distinction applies more to "l'étant" than to "l'être" but it helps to see in both some ontic characteristics.

Even the strongest contradiction, that of nothingness, has a meaning for "l'étant" indicating its contingency. There was a time when it was not in the world; and the time of its disappearance will come. There is also awareness of the birth and death of other beings. The coming of death is a fact regardless of its universality and yet it does not convey the idea of nothingness because it refers to the reality of being. The consciousness of death rests on the ability to speak about it. The death of one or more beings forces us to take seriously the negative element in its most radical form of the experience of being.

11. The reader who has followed this analysis might be tempted to raise an objection. Have we not made the concept of primordial relation so comprehensive as to include all kinds of relations, creating confusion? Have we not fallen into the error of many ontologies and made of "l'être" a "deus ex machina" allowing all sorts of cheating?

We shall answer that in our thesis "l'être" is a transcendental relation. Let us try to be more specific. We do not give the word transcendental the connotation one finds in Kant (a condition a priori to knowledge); nor do we give it the connotation found in Husserl (a phenomenological reduction, or what is left of it); we give the word its ancient meaning (a common property above all categories). But this is not enough. "L'être" does not differ from an absolute simply at the level of rationality; it could be true of "l'étant" not "l'être." In so far as language is concerned, a coincidence in terminology enables us to use the traditional axiom: "ens et bonum--convertuntur" not "esse et bonum--convertuntur." We refuse to reduce "l'être" to one of its structures (§8), for example in the area of causes (matter, form, essence and existence). "L'être" is a transcendental relation in the meaning proposed by the medieval philosophers of the school of Bonaventura: it is potential communication for the achievement of communion. It is a constant invitation to being, a relation of the transcendent to exteriority. We can verify that in the intimacy of our person which is removed from its ideal and suffers because of its inadequacy. The completeness and limitation of our person, however, prove its contingency, which is the mark of "l'être" and "l'étant."

Transcendental relation and the relation of predication (prédicament) are not the same; the former originates the latter, allowing also the further distinction between primitive and derived beings. (§4) This is why we were able to open the scope of the primordial relation without abusing the need for logic. The presence of a variety of relations is justified when it helps to trace the analysis back to a transcendental principle.

The vocabulary we are using comes from the School, but the context is different. When we say that "l'être" is a transcendental relation, we simply mean that the relation is constitutive of "l'être"; as such it is primordial and affects all beings. By relation of predication (prédicament) we designate specific relations which proceed from the transcendental relation. It is difficult to know to what extent this definition is different from that of Aristotle, whose thought on that subject is not clear. It went through several stages and is absent from certain lists of his categories, although it might be present in all of them. [3]

12. In the last analysis "l'être" is the intelligible "chōra"

which makes possible and supports the "étants." It stimulates and limits them. It gives them future, but also the possibility of failing. In the created universe it underlines our total dependence, reminding us that all beings are composite and relative. It is not the relation per se which exists but the scope of its function. "L'être" is integrated to "l'étant" as an expressive norm of the latter. "L'être," therefore, has no being of its own; it exists only in us. It is, perhaps, what Aristotle wanted to say, as his text of the **Categories** suggests: the "stasis" is a "pros ti," but "to hestanai" is not. [4]

13. The primordial relation is a prefiguration of the "nous" - "us." It first creates a tie between the empirical and the ideal self of each being, which is never independent. Even its originality points back to its transcendental source. Between the two there is a humano-divine "nous" which is found at the most intimate level of our interiority. There the relation of a being to itself reflects our self-consciousness.

The relation of one being to others in the world is also a prefiguration of the perfect "nous," offering itself to all beings without being absorbed by them.

What form of being do we find beyond the "nous?" It cannot be the primitive being--"être primitif"--since it is the first chronological form of primordial or transcendental being, but rather a derived being which is the result of a free act. It is integrated to "l'étant"; it bears its mark, it has the structures and qualities essential to the development of the person. It is still an aspect of the "nous" at two levels: in the historical development of the humano-divine relationship in the inner self, and in the community of other beings.

A transfiguration of "l'être," is taking place but not to the point of its disappearance in "l'étant." This implies that the full development of "l'être" is esthetic. Discovering the unfolding of man's work in the world reveals his glory. One must say more than "plus entium, ergo plus entis"; what one sees is the elevation of "l'être" to the "nous" level where it can participate in all interpersonal relations in the realms of science, art and love. "L'être" cannot be eliminated from an order of creation but its exteriority can decrease, its limitations diminish as it enters more deeply in the glorious alliances of a creature with its Creator.

14. The reality of "l'être" cannot be reduced to a conceptual idea, although some philosophers try to do so. Great thinkers do not confine "l'être" to a supreme gender; but the Western tradition has attempted to objectify it in a form of logic. The formal frame (§6) should also be conceived as larger than the

conceptual frame which is only a restriction of the total intelligibil-
ity of knowledge. Such intellectual experiences cannot be confined
within the limitations of speech.

Contemporary philosophy emphasizes the affinity of
"l'être" and language. They are parallel, they say; language precedes
and expresses "l'etant." This assumption could be dangerous. It
could substitute a concept of "l'être" for its reality, and to the
idea of "l'être" a way of formulating it. It is not impossible to
suggest, however, that language can indeed express the reality
of "l'être." This is achieved in poetry, in the difficult terms of
science, in the interpretation of symbols, in the exchange of con-
fidences, in the meaningful silence following a conversation, in
the mutual understanding between speaker and listener. We express
the ontological power of language when we recognize its musicality,
for no autonomous form of expression is more complete or more
flexible than music. Music gives language its highest level of
reality and performance, a kind of personality as well as being.
Through language the objectivity of "l'être" and the subjectivity
of "l'étant" are brought together without depriving the being of
the artist of his individuality. Harmony is achieved.

15. On several occasions we have referred indirectly
to the whole question of values. They include the qualities of
both "l'être" and "l'étant," the ultimate values of Truth, Goodness
and Beauty condition primarily the personal being--"l'étant person-
nel," although they do not have being in themselves. They are
part of the ultimate source of being and yet they affect the individual beings they touch. In their function they remain diffusive
even at the final stage of the integration of "l'être" and "l'étant"
(§§13-14). "L'être" is certainly affected by those transcendent
values, and the use of the connecting verb--"l'être copule"--or
copula--shows and conceals at the same time the absolute of
that transcendence which can never be reached.

"L'être," however, is always ambiguous, revealing contra-
dicting values; its relations and structures in the interpretation
of symbols, are open to many options for "l'étant." Although spiritual, those values are not always moral in the assimilation of
"l'être" in "l'étant." In fact, they can be demonic. In other words,
"l'être" shows, even in a state of disgrace, its transcendental
vocation. The evolution of "l'être" verifies its divine destiny as
well as the ebb and flow of the cosmos. We cannot pretend, therefore, that there is only a superficial difference between the rational
"esse" and the "verum" or "bonum" (§11) even if they have the
same origin, the same field of influence and the possibility of
joining together. "L'être" carries within itself both a promise
and a threat.

The freedom of "l'étant" is the cause of that ambiguity.

The course of ontic freedom would be different from what it is in this world. If there were no form of ontological exteriority, it would then be a creative power without darkness and possibility, without a "meonic" alternative. It would rise to perfection. Our freedom in this world is conditioned by a dimension of "non-être" (§10); for this reason the unveiling of ultimate values remains partial.

16. We have established the principle that the primordial relation is at the same time universal and a correlation. As a result "l'être" is univocal. We do not imply that it is a gender but that the primordial relation is identical in all beings, allowing mutual communicability among them. A being, however, is irreducible, though it may enter into communion with other beings at the level of consciousness through knowledge and love. Nothing is more confusing in the history of philosophy than the debate on univocity and analogy. We shall not spend much time on that question which often can be brought down to a difference in terminology.

For us, the correlation of "l'être" cannot exclude the diversity and inequality of "les étants," but they are part of the same universe. The profound unity of all beings can be explained first by the mysterious causality of divine creation and second by the co-operation of persons in their effort to reach perfection. This kind of unity presupposes the role of mediator of "l'être correlatif."

In that context of correlation we should as a final question. Does not the divine source of being need the world as much as the latter needs God? Is the univocity of "l'être" undermining the theistic thesis? The answer is no if God is willing to enter into a relationship with man and offers him the intimate communion of the Logos. "L'être becomes then the Word which is the sign or expression of the Supreme Being, the Creator. The sign itself is not God, but given by God; it is a call which we can either accept or reject without distorting it because its transcendence cannot be touched.

God becomes in us relation to Himself by virtue of the distance between creature and Creator. He shows the weakness of our condition and is the remedy. "L'être" which separates us from God becomes the way to bring us back to him freely.

NOTES

1. A. C. Graham, Being in Classical Chinese, in J. W. M. Verhaar, Editor, **The Verb "Be" and its Synonyms,** Vol. I, Dordrecht, 1967, p. 14.

2. A. Guzzo observes that the four causes of Aristotle cannot be applied to God and consequently to that philosophy. There is only a general ontology of the created world. **La Filosofia, Cancetto, Struttura, Caratteri,** Torino, 1961, p. 69ff. We would readily apply this remark to our study of "be" to distinguish it from the study of "being."

3. L. Elders, **Aristotle's Theory of the One,** A commentary on Book X of the Metaphysics, Assen, 1961, pp. 14, 34-36, 149-152, 194-196.

4. See W. D. Ross, **Aristotle,** London, 1956, p. 22, note 3.

Chapter VIII

"L'ÊTRE," ULTIMATE VALUE?

Is "L'être the Ultimate Value?

1. It is difficult to translate into French (or English)[*] what Aristotle calls "ousia" in certain texts of his **Metaphysics**. Translators hesitate between "essence" and "substance." The terminology of ontology has many ambiguities, more particularly when it deals with the "couple" which is constituted of "l'être" and "l'étant." It is, therefore, necessary to clarify the connotations we give to those words. We look upon "étant"--"being" as a concrete individual who exists and "l'être"--"be" as the primordial relation of each being with itself and other beings. "L'être," when understood in those terms, reveals the incompleteness and flaw of each created being and the "extériorité which singularize all beings. "L'être" is, therefore, a principle of relation and correlation which precedes each created being; it also follows "l'étant" in its development, enriching it with all kinds of further relations. We also make a distinction between antecedent and consequent "être" and between relating and related, relation or correlation. Finally let us observe that the tension between beings varies or fluctuates from simple juxtaposition of beings to their asymptotical function. It follows that "l'être" is never fully "être," whatever the tension index.

"L'être" is the mark of the Creator on his creature and, although it designates essentially the creature, the sign that God is in relation to his creatures as their Creator. God is also "related relation"--"relation relatée" which His divine action becomes part of human history. In the case of the "relating relation"--relation relatante" the tension index is infinite; in the case of the related relation it varies according to men's receptivity. We could also say that "l'être" is the univocal norm which rules the order of beings on behalf of the Supreme Being which reveals, but also hides, its transcendent creativity.

---

[*] Not in the original.

2. Now we begin to see why we would ask ourselves whether "l'être" is an ultimate or absolute value. There again we must agree on the meaning of words.

Is value a preference or an excellence? We could answer that value is an excellence which justifies a preference since it is observed in a process of evaluation. It is intrinsically tied both in its origin and destiny to personal beings.

As far as the adjective "ultimate" is concerned, it can designate the end of a line of evolution in the substantive it qualifies. Or in the context of limited perfection it may help in sorting out subsequent meanings of the substantive.

3. It is necessary to affirm that "l'être" is a value, a universal value since it is the norm of all beings--"étants." The Creator gives away such value, making of it the condition to and factor of cohesion in the universe. "L'être" is the means by which and through which we can realize our existence as individual beings. It further determines eternally the constancy which is verified in its temporal deployment. It is the relation and correlation at the origin of all evolution of being. It dominates all thesis and antithesis. It imposes a limit to the continuity in creativity. "L'être" is the normative law of all beings; in that sense it is identical to its function and is found in each being.

4. Can we infer that "l'être" is an ultimate value? Yes if we suggest that it is not determined by time, even when identified at a given moment with a particular being, or is part of the "nous" of individual consciences. But it is born again, so to speak, in all beings whose existence it monitors. It is part of a continuing creation and of the time which flows always new. There is no substitute for such value, for it is a constitutive element of ontic and ontology. It has the paradoxical status of an "in se" which is "in aliis" without being either accident or substance, but a mystery to all beings--"étants."

5. "L'être," however, is not an ultimate value in all aspects.

a. No philosophy of the person and no concept of God could subscribe to Heidegger's thesis of the subordination of "l'-étant" to "l'être." The worst danger for "l'étant" is not to limit "l'être" by defining it but to forget its own concreteness for the benefit of a purely formal being whose only function would be the multiplication of self in the series of existential moments. If we diffuse that relation we transform our transcendent "ego" in a simple a priori form of our becoming or development. We renounce our real vocation to keep of our being the concept only of a simple succession of changing conditions; our action becomes pure compulsion to realize a certain image of our self. In that case there is devaluation of the being, its future and past; devaluation of the image it has of self and of God. To make of "l'être" an ultimate value would amount to the destruction of the world of "étants" and reduce it to a shadow or an empty phenomenon.

b. If "l'être" were raised to the status of an ultimate value, it would be separated from other ontic values to become a pure receptacle of beings--"étants." That kind of process would, in fact, empty the universe and distort our concept of the nature of God. With Heidegger we must say that "l'être" is neither "l'étant" nor God. But our perspective is quite different from his. There is no rivalry but rather a conspiracy between "l'être" and "l'étant". If we give "l'être," however, an ultimate value, we inevitably demote "l'étant"; we cause tension between the exteriority and interiority of relations vis à vis their terms; we sacrifice the communion of "les étants" limiting it to a process of communication with "l'être."

c. It seems unthinkable to assume that "l'être" is the ultimate value, unlimited perfection, the substratum of all values. It could not be done without dismissing all the objections we have raised. There is no worse mistake than opposing ontology and metaphysics and claiming that the former could maintain its axiological value, when in fact it would be divested of its authenticity.

6. Are the "transcendentaux" inherited from Neoplatonism and enunciated in the trinity of Truth, Goodness, and Beauty, without connection with "l'être" as we analyzed it? No, we do not suggest that, since "l'être" is by definition the primordial and universal relation which can give birth and meaning to other relations.

In reality the three "transcendentaux" are a manifestation in "l'être" of the creative Being, whose imprint is in each of us. Through them he reveals himself naturally to man, in all humility on his part and inevitably for us. "L'être," however, conceals the divine message it intends to reveal, creating division between thought and language, introducing symbols which translate and distort. The symbol is an epistemological and ontological prism; it gives us some ontic freedom with creative imagination and elective discrimination.

Our ontic freedom allows us to insert exchange values-- "contre valeurs" in our existence, with the limitations imposed by "l'être." Whatever the impact of error, malice and ugliness (to name a few forms of evil), "l'être" will not let them destroy the radiance of real values. It will not allow itself to be affected in its own nature because the primordial relation cannot be touched by the relativism of derived relations.

7. To delete Truth, Goodness, and Beauty from the list of ultimate values can be misleading. In fact one would dissociate perfection from the perfection value. It is, perhaps, the privilege of perfection to perfectly integrate the presence of the Perfect; in other words to bridge the gap between ontology and ontique. The "transcendentaux," however, share in the weakness of "l'être," regardless of their intimate relation to the Source of all beings. The symbols we use in observing them in the development of other beings do not allow perfect vision. "L'être" reminds us of our relative condition, whereas there is something infinite in the vocation of "l'étant." Stimulated or restrained by "l'être," the person, which is "l'étant" by excellence, discovers that all ultimate values are in its inner self and that in spite of its createdness, its identity is absolute and the potential to fulfill itself is real.

Chapter Nine

THE FINITUDE OF THE CONSCIENCE

1. What is finitude of my conscience? It is perhaps the fact that it is determined at each moment; determination easily understood since my action as well as my being has a definite form, a certain quality and quantity, a positive mark which identifies me and is not replaceable since it is one with my thought, my immediate "cogito."

2. This first statement needs to be clarified. By finitude we mean limitation; it is not evident, however, that I am fundamentally limited in my own self since my individuality is open and its perspective universal. Furthermore a limitation implies a negative element. But there again, I have no proof that my person has any negative and yet essential element. The fact that I am determined is clear and is observable in the evolution of my person which is gradually individualized. My determination is also the sign and guarantee of my eternal right to claim my autonomy, which explains all my struggles and my doubts. How could I be alienated from or rejected by my real self--"mon chez-moi"?

3. In my determination, however, there is an element which I do not control; hence the necessity to constantly make new projects in order to fulfill myself and become what I want to be or accept what I am. In reality, I never succeed in consciously becoming what I am. There is always a hiatus between what I am essentially and the existential realization of the consciousness of what I am. This gap brings to light a negation, since I have not achieved my ipseity.

I am conscious of my finitude since I am a "being"--"étant"--in "l'être," or an existing being alienated by virtue of all relations and directions through which I am aware of my existence from the very moment of the rise of my consciousness. The self-awareness of the "je"--"I" is grasped in the realization of a difference which is no less evident than the discovery of one's identity. The "je," therefore, is known in the paradox of a continuity expressed in discontinuity, consequently, each act of a person is separated from all other acts, in spite of a common substratum which denies separability.

4. It is as if my limitation would be pushed back each time I am ready to overcome it. The finitude I experience is in a sense a dimension of my infinity; and this gives me, perhaps, the best understanding of my situation. This infinity rests on the positive, fundamental determination of the "person"--the "je."

5. Behind that infinitude, which remains and cannot be overcome, one finds another one, at the level of nature and beyond the control of the subject. I know by experience that I cannot overcome that limitation. I infer from what I know that I cannot comprehend my ipseity. It remains always inaccessible.

6. If my situation is paradoxical, it is not, however, a contradiction. On the one hand my identity is given me as an unlimited presence without inherent self-negation. It precedes me and goes with me in all my actions and situations. On the other hand I am acted upon as if my identity was detached from me. If my individuality is not limited, its manifestation, however, is; I am, therefore, divided in my inner self. This condition cannot be reversed; it is part of my experience, it is an insurmountable qualification of my existence.

7. We should distinguish, however, two kinds of limitations or negations. One is very close to my conscience and does not separate me from my true self. It is not an obstacle; if it were it would be as the result of a choice and it would not destroy me. It would rather incite me to action. It would not separate me radically from my "moi" but from my "non-moi" which is not my true self. The "non-moi" is the second kind of limitation. It is beyond my control and the sign of my estrangement and blindness.

Another point should be made here. Infinitude has two dimensions inside us. One thing is the limitation of which we are conscious, which enables us to pursue with a sense of security our self-development--we can see an analogy of that experience in a series of decimals, for example the progression of the type 1/3 (0.33). We are sure a priori and a posteriori of the course of our ipseity for there is a constant re-affirmation of our conscience which casts light upon its path. It is another thing, however, to face the unforseeable character of some of our acts and situations; we do not feel completely removed since our conscience embraces all new acts but an element of disparity is there to remind us of our separation--something we can see in the disconcerting formulae: $\sqrt{2}$ or pi.

8. Mobile and immobile finitudes are also found in my relationship to other people, with further complications since the other person is in a situation similar to mine and the encounter of our finitudes will be like the square--"puissance 2" - of one. Let us explain this point.

a. The openness of my individuality and yours means that we share a constant possibility of communion. Furthermore the availability of this openness is comprehensive of all communions which have marked the past of our consciences. The intersubjective conscience is free of finitude. It is observed already in the reflexive or pre-reflexive "cogito"; but it is more radical in the "nous" for two reasons: it is a primitive reality which cannot be erased by any solipsisms. This "nous," even when touched by oblivion, survives as a link capable of bringing together more subjects without being altered in its capacity by the multiplicity of dyads.

b. The meeting of finitudes, however, reveals only the potential of interpersonal life. It also brings to light the separations and negations affecting the consciences. The actuation of the "nous" is always difficult; it remains unequal to what it ought to be; it is fragmentary rather than universal although it might reach out to universalism. The fragmentation of the "nous" is above all a conflict of consciences or a separation less traumatic. The encounter of finitudes is always a surprise and often an obstacle before it becomes a game in some favorable circumstances. [1]

9. Those facts should protect us against the temptation of assuming that we are an omnipotent monad. All our efforts will never make it possible to draw from ourselves one single living, complete alteration, or give birth to a "pour soi" which would be an "en soi." The genial artist comes near to the goal by creating characters who are in fact phantoms wandering through the skies of his soul. The monad which assumes in vain the power to create "ex nihilo" another monad is led inevitably to the discovery that its own hypertrophy is not capable of adding any substantial change to the universe, but it is capable, on the other hand, of empoverishing and diluting its own substance and alienating itself rather than acquiring the miraculous power to create another being. In easier terms let us say that my finitude is in a negative sense my inability to bring to life the presence of another being and in positive terms it is my surprise before the real presence of that being. The latter is not deductive; it is always new in each of its individualizations, even when covered under a coat of banality either self-imposed or forced upon him by me.

10. Mobile and immobile finitudes take on a new dimension in our relationship to God, whose immanence and transcendence are absolute.

The created person enjoys, in a sense, a very close relationship to the absolute Principle of his being. The person touches God by an intuitive act, or more consciously every time he realizes his dependence on God, whose power sustains his existence. It is quite possible that the person is unable to identify God by name but the vital relationship is real and the person is conscious of the impact of a presence.

It is true, that a person touches God only for an instant, soon aware of the overwhelming power of the Being who gives him being. We find Him because He has found us. That distance from God, however, does not remain, at least not consciously; it is constantly denied by the person. The immanence of the divine presence is true. The second stage of consciousness is that of a wall higher and more insurmountable than any other obstacle: from a maximum degree of immanence one passes to a maximum transcendence. If we experience only the former and know God in the intimacy of our being we would transform Him into an object; but God transcends our experience and leaves us in the confines of our worldliness. We must rediscover Him in our obedience or rebellion, as we know the tension of being alternatively drawn by Him or rejected when we abandon his presence.

In our finitude we are the victims of a certain ambiguity: nothing is more present to us or more absent from us than the divine presence. When we think that we have overcome our limitations, they are still there and such awareness is an ever greater separation.

11. All these feelings of our inter-personal and human-divine relations underline the necessity of practicing the kind of dialogue which will reflect our finitude.

Dialectics as a method implies a negative dimension since one of the interacting elements can be denied. It recognizes the existence of a limit which is then moved or removed. We call that the movable limit--"la limite mobile," by contrast with the immovable limit.

The dialogue rests on an element of novelty; this is why it can be so difficult and rare. It presupposes a gift; it represents our only hope to overcome some immovable limits because it is, in fact, divine grace. Any dialogue with self is the irruption of an element of singularity from our empirical ego; through it the transcendental "je" - "I" integrates its own image in the series of our actions to enrich and change them altogether. The dialogue with another person is possible when the encounter of two finitudes gives to each individual what he could not discover by himself. A fortiori in the dialogue with God, or prayer, a widening and perhaps suppression of our finitude takes place. This is possible whatever the infinite distance between God and man, when we perceive only the echo of His voice.

12. All created conscience is ambiguous. It touches both the infinite and the finite. Whenever it tries to free itself and claims infinitude, it contradicts itself. We may find an example of that kind of contradiction in the logico-mathematical paradoxes and more particularly in the mathematical infinite.

Galileo remarked that most natural numbers and square numbers are bi-univocal--"bi-univoques." To each number of one series corresponds a number of the second series and vice versa. Although the first series may seem larger than the second, it has, however, a bi-univocal relation with it; that is, with one of its components. Hence Euclid's axiom "Totum parte magus" does not apply.

Similar paradoxes have become evident, though not all in the same way. For example, Cantor asks himself if cardinal numbers, finite or infinite, are all necessarily cardinal. The answer is yes, if all quantity has a cardinal number and if that number is the highest one. On the other hand, as Cantor demonstrates, any quantity has an "n" element, and the totality of sub-numbers is 2n. Hence, sub-numbers have a cardinal number higher than the one we had first discovered. Here we are confused. [2]

More recently, Gödel has demonstrated the non-contradiction of Mathematics. He reaches the conclusion that:

> all systems capable of expressing arithmetic are necessarily incomplete and one of the undecided propositions of the system is precisely its affirmation that it is not contradictory.

This result, confirmed by parallel investigations in other areas of arithmetic, leads to the general conclusion that "formalization cannot be final." [3] No convention is self-determined. One is, therefore, obliged to move from one "métalangue" to another in some kind of indefinite process in order to avoid begging the question of contradiction.

Let us say to conclude that the paradoxes of the infinite lead to a direct contradiction and the "undecided"--"l'indécidable" of Gödel--to a danger of contradiction. One way or the other the infinite is being questioned either by a conflict of propositions in relation to the infinite or by an indefinite repression of axiomatic systems. Hence, what should we think of our intellectual effort to break down the barrier of our finitude? And what should we think of the presence of the infinite in reality?

13. Specialists do not answer this question satisfactorily. They are divided into several schools which illustrate the antimony we referred to. There are obstinate "finitistes" and no less convinced "infinitistes"; and there is a third party: those who consider the problem as void of meaning.

The "finitistes" are in the tradition of Aristotle and Kant. The nineteenth century proponent of this thesis was Renouvier, who thought that the infinite can be only virtual not actual, both in abstraction and in reality. An indefinite collection cannot constitute a totality. In the dialogue that L. Couturat conceives between himself and a "finitiste" of Renouvier's school, the latter says:

> Je vous accorderais encore que la grandeur infinie et continue est concevable, parce qu'il ne s'agit là que d'un infini ideal et potentiel qui n'existe que dans l'esprit. Mais "ce" que je ne puis admettre, c'est qu'une telle grandeur existe dans la réalité, car ce serait alors un infini actuel qui me parait contradictoire. [4]

Mathematicians of the "instuitionniste" school (Brouwer) follow the same line of thought. They accept from pure intuition the only element which can be built upon; but it is possible to count indefinitely not infinitely; the antinomies of the infinite cannot be resolved because one cannot be free from the limitations of knowledge without reducing an infinite which, in fact, cannot be comprehended. Brouwer believes that a calculation of infinite quantities implies the rejection of the principle of the "tiers-exclu." [4a]

From the point of view of logic the aristotelician Professor A. Dumitriu, erases those antinomies by remarking that they result from sensorial confusion. He quotes the famous example given by Peter of Spain who later became Pope John XXII,

> Omnes apostoli Dei sunt duodecim
> Petrus et Jacobus sunt apostoli
> Ergo Petrus et Jacobus sunt duodecim.

> L'erreur consiste dans le fait de confondre le sens "collectif" avec le sens "distributif"; par sa signification collective, dans la première permisse, "omnes" forme la classe de douze apôtres; mais comme il n'est pas distributif, il n'attribue pas le prédicat "sunt duodecim" à chaque membre de la classe ou à deux apôtres.

The error found in the paradoxes of the infinite is of the same kind.

Dans la proposition considérons la serie de "tous" les
nombres ordinaux possibles, inclusivement "Ω", le plusgrand,
le mot "tous" n'a plus le sens collectif ou catégorématique;
. . . La proposition ne peut avoir qu'un sens distributif
ou syncatégorématique, c'est à dire: considérons chacun
de "tous les nombres ordinaux possibles . . . [5] On
ne forme pas une série nouvelle.

14. "<u>Infinistes</u>" as we may imagine, disagree. They follow
Leibniz:

Je suis tellement pour l'infini actuel qu'au lieu d'admettre
que la nature l'abhorre comme l'on dit vulgairement,
je tiens qu'elle l'affecte partout, pour mieux marquer
les perfections de son auteur. [6]

In modern times, this position is held by L. Couturat
who is a convinced Cantorian. He resolves the paradox as follows:

Sans doute l'ensemble des nombres qu'un opérateur peut
énumérer verbalement ou figurer par l'écriture est toujours
fini et comme on peut toujours l'augmenter, il sera bien
qualifié d'indéfini; mais l'ensemble des idées-nombres
qui préexiste à toute énumération et qui seul la rend
possible est essentiellement infini. [7]

It is the distinction, therefore, between image and idea,
or between enumeration and normative idea which is being used
here. Couturat believes in the actual infinite rather than in the
objective idea of the empirical operation.

The strong point of the "<u>infinitistes'</u>" position is that
mathematicians move with great freedom in the calculation of
both infinite and finite members. Certainly, some reject the actual
infinite at the level of abstraction and concreteness as well (Poin-
carré, for example). [8] The layman, however, who opens a book
of mathematics, may have a different impression.

15. There are, finally, the "indifferents," all those who
try to avoid the issue on the ground that it is void of all meaning
and interest. It is possible to number among them B. Russell and
his "Theory of Types." The class to which an individual belongs,
he says, represents a type immediately superior to that entity.

The antinomy suggested by the concept of class is avoided,
since such concept is no longer thinkable . . . What is
true of a class is true of all predicates, for a class is
nothing but the extension of a notion, i.e. a predicate. [9]

The hierarchy of types is the same as that of predicates.

Russell, however, recognizes the pragmatic reality of his solution. Pure formalists too practice the same polities; it is that of the ostrich.

> What is the meaning of the laws of numbers? How do we know they are true? Do numbers exist? All these questions have no substance. What is left is only a game with the appearance of reality. . . . Those systems have no factual content (statements); they are only signs (marks). **[10]** . . . One system is not more true than the other even if it fits a certain operation better (and even that is very mysterious).

16. Certain "finitistes," "infinitistes" and "formalistes pur" leave us unsatisfied. One has the impression that the first are too rigid and the third group superficial.

Would it not be better to think that the "infinitude" of the human mind is the condition of the creature? It is both rooted in the infinite and condemned to be finite; so much so that it is necessarily unlimited or indefinite because of that twofold character. **[10a]**

It is profitable to keep in mind the principle of Bernard Balzano: the real calculation of the infinite is not that of an infinite multitude, but rather the determination of the relation between two infinites. **[11]** We understand and work with that relation only.

This is an elementary truth; not as common as it would seem, because it implies the generalization of the notions of division and limits. It applies to infinitesimal calculations; and is it not, a fortiori applicable to reflections on the "transfini?" Balzano himself did not accept a hierarchy of actual infinities in the concrete world. **[12]** His principle, however, remains valid, at least for the philosophy of mathematics.

17. There are several categories of paradoxes: those of the series of infinities; those of the adjective "imprédicable" which might or might not be a predicate; those of a type "I lie," etc. . .

It is certainly possible to apply to the language which expresses those paradoxes the same distinctions as those suggested and yet criticized for their sophism by Dimitriu.

We must, nevertheless, examine the epistemological and metaphysical problems, whatever the logic of our position. Paradoxes take us back, in many different ways to the realization of our finitude or better our "indéfinitude."

The first lesson to draw from our difficulty in the area of logic and mathematics, is that the concept of absolute "<u>objectivation</u>" of the subject is unthinkable. The act of conscience cannot be entirely projected or objectified. The "<u>je</u>" - "I" always precedes and goes beyond the "me" or the best representation we may have of it. In the case of the liar this unevenness is clear. One could suggest also that the two acts of understanding and inventing can never be completely formalized.

The second lesson shows that the "objective" paradoxes of the representation of the subject are different from those of the subject itself and they manifest an internal limitation of the formalization process. The reason for that rests on the kind of relation existing between the objective representation of the subject and its nature. It has been said that:

> La proposition indécidable de Gödel est bâtie sur le modèle du paradoxe du menteur. [13]

Ladrière concludes that, generally speaking, the fundamental limitation of formalism is,

> de ne pouvoir parler adéquatement de la transcendence dans le langage, de l'effectuable c'est à dire du fini. [14]

Although that conclusion could not be reached for many centuries, the perspective under which it has been formulated was known in the past. Albert of Saxony wrote:

> nulla res creata potest distincte repraesentare seipsam formaliter.

Venetus applied this thesis to propositions on the "<u>insolubilia</u>"; [15] and Proclus said that:

> the limited cannot ignore the unlimited nor can the latter ignore the former from which it receives its form. These relations, however, are transcended by the Ineffable One. The fundamental position of the soul could be that of the difficult equilibrium between spoken reason and abysmal silence . . . [16]

18. One could wonder why we considered the infinite in the preceding paragraphs with no reference to the concept of perfection. One could object also that our study has been limited to the extensive and quantitative infinite, reflecting the intensive and qualitative infinite, which is more important.

Let us remind ourselves that our incursion in the area of mathematical symbols was only a means to focus our attention on a more fundamental problem: that of the condition of creatures. We remained within the confines of the conscience and its language without asking ourselves how those symbols would apply to the physical world. Furthermore, logic paradoxes, that of the Liar, for example, let us beyond the field of other paradoxes such as the paradoxes of classes or of predicates, and certainly beyond the field of cosmological reflection.

The analysis of finitude and infinitude, the vague perception of the infinite within our own conscience corresponds to what one discovers in the realms of the mind. Precisely because we chose the perspective of the ontic of the created conscience, we can move from reflecting on the extensive infinite to a reflection on the intensive infinite; and we can do that while remaining in the same universe. What happens in the intellectual order is simply an aspect and a symbol of what is taking place in the conscience as a whole.

When we speak of perfection, absolute Perfection, we often refer to moral goodness. How can we forget that it rests on an ontological good as soon as the conscience becomes aware of the perfection of its act? The answer could be found in the fact that the words--infinite and finite--have been used historically sometimes in a logico-mathematical study and at other times in an ethical-metaphysical reflection. The problem of analyzing the concept of finitude in the physical order, necessarily leads to the examination of the quality of an infinite existence, that of the "Being in plenitude" - "l'étant en plénitude." We cannot think of the latter without referring to the concept of moral goodness which is one of its constitutive elements.

The metaphysics of God, however, is not our subject; and yet it cannot be excluded from the study of the inherent "indéfinitude" of a created being--"la forme d'indéfinitude inherente à l'être"--in primordial relation to other beings.

19. We limited ourselves to the task of analyzing the characteristics of the created conscience in ontic singularity and in the act through which it is identified. We do not have to examine the human consience as subjected to a terrestrial "Dasein." In other words, everything we said could be applied to an angel as well as to a man.

The moment has come to sum up our findings on the phenomenology of the human conscience examined under the aspect mentioned above. What have we found?

We have discovered the inevitable presence of a certain solitude. "L'indéfinitude" creates a hiatus between "le pour-soi" and "le pour autrui" and the being of God (par. 5 to 8). The finite-infinite relation, where a created conscience is revealed, does not necessarily point to a network of personal relations; and it does not vindicate the assumption that the "je" - "I" is a doorless, windowless monad. It introduces us, however, to a dynamism made of a duality at the level of action and passion. Solitude is a dialectical moment which alternates with a dialogue. It is, in fact, a "semi-solitude" which may become a "mediation," while fragmentation becomes a symbol. It should not be confused with a form of isolation or dereliction, since it is the condition of the development of the mind in relation to other minds.

20. We are able to develop a concept of the universe precisely because we experience a fruitful solitude. Each person has a representation and not simply an image of the universe; a representation which can be progressively perceived and amended. Without the solitude of the person there would be no conscious awareness of the universe; nor would it be cooperation with it; for there would be confusion of object and reality.

Since each person has a universalizing and universalized perspective of his own, the universe becomes multiple (complex) and each concept reflects that multiplicity. The bridge between the person and the universe is the creative imagination of the mind where the dimension "autothétique et altruiste" of the person is realized.

21. The degree of solitude, a product of "indéfinitude," leads us to an asymptotic development which pushes into the infinite communion with self and others, and the universality of consciences. Should we, therefore, deny the possibility of communion and substitute some kind of indirect and superficial communication based on objective instrumentality?

We do not think so. Firstly, because our person is not fundamentally negative (§§ 2, 6, 8). Contrary to Spinoza's axiom, all determinations are not necessarily negations. A first affirmation is "infinitisante," not "infinitisée." It is touched by the infinite and yet independent. It cannot be free from the infinite unless it be touched by it. This is possible in the ontological alternation between infinitude and finitude. One finds in the person, therefore, a mysterious fugitive but real communion with self, others and the divine source of being in a continuing creation.

Then the "être" of the "étants" appeared to us as a form of exteriority which is the sign of a created universe. "L'être" is not an entirely finite relation; it has one foot in finitude and the other in infinitude. Its ambiguity comes from its transcendental character, i.e. "supra-catégorial," through which the Creator creates a universe of creatures, stimulates them, calls them to grow both in Him and in a universal correlation. "L'être" is univocal;

"les étants," however, are not. It is in the latter that the former exists, i.e. in the infinitude of the Creator and the finitude of the creature. It is the aspect of the "Logos" through which God becomes in us a relating relation--"relation relatante"--to teach us how to build up a polymorphous communion. There we realize our created reality in his pure actuality.

Finally, communion between consciences does not end with the experience, but remains, in spite of solitude, as a promise or a possibility, more than that, it is a constant reality as long as there is grace, for the dialogue is not conditioned by dialectics. (§ 9) Grace is synonymous with freedom; freedom is born of love. In God freedom is identical with His loving creativity which is the dynamism of all beings and of the universal correlation. To us it gives the free imagination of love--"la libre invention de l'amour"--which makes communion possible and goes beyond it. There is also a subtle relation in the very fabric of our action and passion between the infinitude of our condition and the finitude of our essence. This confirms us in the reality of our solitude, discovered now as the mark of our created dynamism; it is no longer isolation which is a temptation, a sign of evil.

22. Does the "indéfinitude" of the human conscience imply ignorance and powerlessness? There again, some distinctions must be made.

Ignorance and powerlessness are, in a sense at least, tied to the createdness of the creature. The simple fact that I want to increase and renew my knowledge shows that it is never perfect. I even deny that absolute unity be a perfect reality. The void, therefore, that we can see as a residue of past communions, becomes the hope of communions yet to be. (§ 7).

Even "l'être" reveals to created beings their future course. It consists of a "aiôn" and a "chôra" both intelligible because created. It is a time and space which do not belong to the world of mathematics. Although they can be divided, they are not material. Does that mean that the universal dimension of the conscience is compromised or abolished? Certainly not; the conscience, being inserted into an intelligible spatio-temporality, has the capacity to interrogate itself prospectively and retrospectively and increase the intersubjective "nous." The conscience is always able to overcome the limit forced upon it by "l'être." In spite of the latter, or because of it, it fills the vacuum around it. The conscience knows and can do all things, provided it is free, without becoming irrational, and autonomous in its independence. When there is ignorance, it is an educated form of ignorance--"docte ignorance"; when there is powerlessness it is seen as a permanent possibility of power.

23. The conscience of a created being does not necessarily experience failure and guilt. We have no reason to tie intrinsically suffering, death or sin to the very structure of human destiny. There are levels of creation which are not conditioned by our personal creaturely condition. An analysis of the deepest level of being shows that this is true; even though the same level of being cannot be separated from our personality since it adds to it some definite conditions of existence.

We are unfortunately conditioned by our "Dasein." The negative element in us is aggravated by a material spatio-temporality and by the opposition of the mind as well as its tendency to err. This is either forced upon us or the result of a choice. Finally we are burdened by an insurmountable culpability of many forms and various degrees. It is good to know, however, that those limitations are not per se related to the fact that we are created beings. At the same time, it would be ridiculous to overlook their tragic character which shows our human finitude and the real tie existing between our personal existence and the reality of evil. To study that tie would be the subject of a totally different study.

NOTES

1. Permit me to refer to this subject in my article, "Le heurt initial dans la rencontre des personnes," in the collected essays, **Begegnung**, Graz, Verlag Styria, 1972, pp. 23-30.

2. Cf. St. Barker, **Philosophy of Mathematics**, Englewood Cliffs, 1964, p. 83.

3. R. Blanché, **La Logique et Son Histoire**, Paris, 1970.

4. L. Couturat, **De L'Infini Mathématique**, Paris, 1896, p. 488.

4a "In practice, anyone who decides to accept only constructive proofs in mathematics may have to reject arguments which employ the principle of excluding middle in relation to infinite sets (i.e., if he cannot explain the unsatisfactoriness of all non-constructive arguments in the way suggested by Gödel." W. and M. Kneale, **The Development of Logic**, Oxford, 1962, p. 681.

5. A. Dumitriu, "Le Problème Des Paradoxes Logico-Mathématiques," in Scientia, July-August, 1968, pp. 4-5. The author agrees with Wittgenstein ("Tractatus," progos. 3323-3325).

100

In Scholastic Philosophy "catégorèmes" are words which have their own meanings (substantives and verbs); "syncatégorèmes" receive their meaning from the former. They combine: adjectives, adverbs, prepositions, etc. . .

Dumitriu subscribes also to the Aristotelian distinction between separate accidents (Virgil lived in Rome) from inseparable accidents (Virgil was born in Matoue). The semantic bifurcation of attributes is, in his own mind, the source of sophisms hidden in "insolubilia."

6. Quoted in epigraph by Bolzano, **Paradoxen des Unendlichen**, Leipzig, 1851.

7. L. Couturat, **De L'Infini Mathématique**, p. 469.

8. Cantor distinguished 1: The absolute or divine infinite, 2. The concrete "Transfini" in the created world, 3. The abstract "transfini" as mathematical measure (number). There are four possible interpretations for the last two:
   a. Rejection of the actual infinite, abstract and concrete.
   b. Acceptance of the actual concrete infinite, rejection of the actual abstract infinite.
   c. Acceptance of the actual abstract infinite, rejection of the concrete infinite.
   d. Acceptance of the actual infinite, abstract and concrete.
I borrow this list from S. Breton, **Philosophie et Mathématique chez Proclus**, Paris, 1969, pp. 100-101.

9. R. Blanché, op. cit., p. 327.

10. S. Barker, op. cit., pp. 98-99.

10a. To those who would object that in the order of phenomena "indéfinitisme" is the same as "le finitisme" one can say that "le finitisme," in the strict sense of the word, excludes all novelty in the course of time, which is not the case with "l'indéfinitisme" which opens the conscience and makes possible an even progress.

11. " . . . eine regelrecht vorgehende Rechnung des Unendlichen . . . nämlich nicht der Berechnung der unendlichen Vielheit sich, sondern nur eine Bestimmung des Verhältnisses zwischen dem einem und dem anderen Unendlichen," **Paradoxen**, par. 28, p. 43.

12. **Paradoxen**, par. 27.

13. J. Ladrière, "Les limites de la formalisation," in **Logique et connaissance scientifique**, published under the direction of J. Piaget, Paris, 1967, p. 317. The author adds that "elle (la propositon de Gödel) est cependent construite de telle façon qu'elle ne conduit à aucune contradiction." It is true since the "propositions undécidables" of Gödel are neither derived nor refutable. As derived, however, they could be false or even contradictory without giving any indication of that at the level of self evidence--"au niveau de système d'axiomes considéré."

14.   J. Ladrière, <u>art. cit.</u>, p. 332. He also says, "ce qui est auto-référentiel comporte une dualité irréductible entre l'acte d'expression et le contenu qui est visé dans cet acte," p. 330. I reached the same conclusion, although in less precise and less technical terms, in my book, **Personne humaine et nature**, Paris 1943, p. 38, (edit. 1963, p. 95).

15.   See A. Dumitriu, "Le problème des paradoxes au moyen âge," in <u>Revue roumaine des sciences sociales,</u> series on Philosophy and Logic, t. 9, n. 3, 1965, p. 136.

16.   St. Breton, <u>op. cit.</u>, p. 172.

Chapter Ten

IMPERSONAL APPEARANCE

How do we Explain the Impersonal Appearance of the Conscience?

I. Pros and Cons

1. One finds between human conscience and human personality the distance existing between a psychological experience
and a metaphysical conclusion. At the time that difference becomes
evident one must somehow overcome it because the human conscience contains at least potentially, the affirmation of its ontic
specificity; furthermore, the metaphysical conclusion is rooted
in experience and does not simply transcend it. In other words,
a human person is a universal entity--"singularité universelle"--and
it is in the paradoxical equation of those two terms that one
discovers its mystery.

The function or equation becomes self evident when
one reflects on the fact and meaning of the "cogito": phenomenology and philosophy find a common level free from all threat of
dissociation. When we deal, of course, with superficial feelings
or wandering images, it appears dreadfully wrong to give the
subjective experience such a scope that the description of those
emotional experiences is equated with the very essence of our
being or expresses the fundamental structures of all personal
beings. But it is a different case when we examine the very act
constitutive of the "je"-"I." We touch there all requirements
of both conscience and person. Their mutual relationship is illustrated in the act of reflection.

2. This thesis, however, is not evident to all thinkers.
In a sense, it is even outdated in the larger context of the crisis
affecting the study of metaphysics. A first attempt to deny the
personal character of the conscience can be attributed to Jean-Paul
Sartre in his early image on the transcendence of the "ego." He
recognized at the base of all human experience a non-reflective
conscience--"conscience irréfléchie" which is not fundamental

to the "soi" and is absorbed, so to speak, even in its "translucidité" by all objects it embraces. The transcendental conscience (i.e., the "conscience de"--which is per se "donatrice de sens") is an impersonal spontaneity--"une spontanéité impersonnelle"--a non-substantial absolute whose being is at the level of appearance only. Sartre does not see any profound difference between the "je" and the "moi," for they are two faces--one active and the other passive--of the same objectivity which moves from the "pour-soi" to constitute the "ego" of "le soi." Sartre can write, therefore, that "le cogito affirme trop" (the cogito says too much); or again: "My 'je' is not more certain for the conscience than the 'je' of other men. It is simply more intimate:" and finally: "The absolute conscience once purified of the 'je' has nothing left of a subject." [1]

In **L'Être et le Néant,** Sartre could not maintain his basic anti-personalism and he reintroduced the problem of the person in his description of the conscience and existence of the other--"autrui." At the beginning of his work, however, he had attempted to destroy the system; he used the conscience not only to undermine the theory of the personal substance but also to restrict and humiliate the person.

3. Since then many attacks have been more radical. It is not simply the person, but also the individual conscience which is being devaluated. New trends have emerged. Levi-Strauss substitutes an objective analysis of the unconscious to the so-called romantic exaltation of the conscience. "The ultimate goal of human sciences, 'he says,' is not to constitute man but dissolve him." [2] The outcome of his analysis is a system of structures which is transformed according to the norms of involution to give myths the possibility of being thought by man, but unconsciously. These myths can relate to each other in a vast network. Men are nothing but the silent performers of a symphony; and the conductor is an expressive thought of the unconscious.

Levi-Strauss builds up his theory on a certain concept of language, which can be traced to the positivism of Greimas: "All sign and statement to be intelligible must be translated into a more explicit sign or statement; and this ad infinitum. The closing of a discourse is achieved in the circularity of the inter-preters; the common image of that circularity is that of a dictionary. The meaning itself is nothing but the possibility for a sign to be reproduced by another sign: the semiotic function is the 'virtualité du transcodage.' ". [3]

4. We could go on listing examples of the same kind, which all aim at the elimination of the true person, and of the conscience in order to keep only a singular thought-speech current ("ça parle en moi, ça pense en moi"). The diversity of metaphysical

assumptions, which is found behind these denegations, has a rather simple cause, although it is not always identified; the socio-cultural change due to demographic growth of mankind. Four billion people on the earth lead us to a civilization of termites. We are erasing surnames and their pretention. Theoricians should be aware of that reality. Men of letters and science assume the responsibility of spreading it. Foucault raises a black flag to proclaim the death of man; Robbe-Grillet writes novels without characters. Roland Barthes reduces inspiration to an objective performance or a combination of forces . . .

Facing those new manifestations of a superstructure, classical Marxists suggest that everything can be explained in terms of economic conditions and industrial production. They touch here a secondary mechanism of a more profound tragedy. It is the explosion of human demography, made possible by technical progress but regulated by the mathematical law of geometrical progression which unleashes all the processes leading to an ideological warfare against person and conscience.

We cannot undertake, in the following pages, to analyze the problems and limits of the cultural evolution we witness; nor can we identify the symptoms of the reaction of a rebelling youth. Our intention, in the above preliminary remarks, was to define our subject. Since the crisis can be traced to a dissociation of the conscience from the person, it is the relation between the two that we must study in order to alleviate any possible irritation experienced in the failure to identify them thoroughly or separate them definitely.

II. The Infra-personal Conscience

5. There is in us a basic animal psyche. Some call it conscience, others unconscious. It is difficult, in any case, to refuse it a structure. It has been thoroughly explored by psychoanalysts. It is an element of continuity; and yet it would be erroneous to give it a form absolutely identical for all men. It has an individual or quasi-individual nature, whose components are combined in different ways and express themselves in pulsations or receptive dispositions.

This elementary conscience is incomplete like all biological individuality. It is even incoherent; and as such disappointing. Inner tensions are often contradictory. The infra-personal conscience in us, however, is directed toward the person, even when it foreshadows the latter rather unclearly. It is also overdetermined-- "surdéterminée"--by the rise of the "je"-"I"--which controls it in its rebellion or in its efforts of regression. It may appear personal when, in fact, it is pre-personal; due to the fact that the dignity of the person always reflects itself on it. When my conscience seems totally absorbed by its "sensori-motrice" condition, exploring the field of its impressions and vital reactions, it is not entirely controlled by the imperatives of its adaptation, as would be the case of an individual taking a meal or running after an autobus . . . My person is probing my conscience, inviting it, invading it. I discover the personal in the pure state, as soon as the ape has yielded to the man. The "surdétermination" of the inferior reason does not begin only with the age of reason; it is already present in the total potential of the human fetus which is oriented from its very beginning to full personal development, if nothing comes to stop its growth.

6. The pre-personal conscience is a reality, therefore, although indirectly; it is real by the knowledge we have of it and by its ontic status. Indirect does not mean ineffective; on the contrary, it often manifests itself with great power. A further indication of that is the phenomenal difference between people; a real separation seen in the temporal procreation and the break down of generations. A long series of human beings is like a breathing monster, a panting creature. The love of a couple causes a merciless rupture, even in intercourse. Without implying with the Cathari that physical love separates man and wife, as if it were the punishment of sex, it is evident that the child born of it will gain a growing independence. The child severing ties obeys a law of ingratitude. His person begins by ignoring all debts to parents and has no intention of acknowledging them. Whatever may attach him to his parents, he denies their deep "alterité"; he hardly accepts that they do not understand him; and he comes finally to the realization that they cannot, in fact, understand. Unconsciously, he takes revenge, shall we say, against them, for having been thrown into existence without choice. It is also true, however, that he acts out of love for his own life which he wants to protect jealously. Although there is mysterious continuity, the generation of men is a succession of injustices, i.e. of ignorance and cruelty.

We find the same law at the social level; thinkers of one generation forget the debt they owe to the preceding one, although they feed, so to speak, on their substance. Exceptions to that rule, due to the influence of education, prove that culture may correct nature to a certain point, without altering the fundamental law of ingratitude. Personal conscience, forgetful of its ascendancy, starts its career by a fall; it cannot "surdéterminer" the infra-personal nature without assuming its burden and then withdrawing in some invisible zone.

7. Such is the pre-personal aspect of the conscience. There is another aspect, however, which should be called post-

personal, because we constantly fall below our true self. We become feeble and we decay in the expression or image we give of ourselves. This law of fall is verified in the analysis which slows down our vision. Since we cannot reach the status of a divine person and we remain behind our ipseity, we are threatened by the evil of division in our "moi" as well as in our "je." The language which serves communication with self and others is the accomplice of the duality which handicaps our personalization; for example, the impoverishment of prose follows the ambiguity of poetry. We gain in our knowledge of things, we lose in our knowledge of self. Applied to the person, analysis causes a series of opacities. Analysis renders real services to material communication; but it cannot prevent our falling back into interpersonal conscience; good and bad are mixed in the way we express ourselves; self-expression may help us to move in the material world but it re-enforces our humility.

8. After the analysis one observes the "habitude," another way of being humiliated as well as helped. The paradox of the created person is found in its ambiguities. The "habitude," however, has more weight than the analysis. We are wrapped in it as in a sheet. Thanks to it, however, we have the illusion of not losing anything of our continuity when we forget our identity and are divided. We find in it the advantages and limitations of our animal temporality. The risk is that our determination may reverse itself and the lower part of our self may rule the higher level. Everything has been said now on this "servante-maîtresse," sometimes "hexis," sometimes "routine" and we do not have to add anything.

9. Pre-personal or post-personal, the conscience is infra-personal, indirectly however. This means that even in the foreground of our experience (through the phenomena it generates) it is subordinated to the future and past of our personal conscience and consequently of our person. At the beginning or the end of our experience it is virtual and cannot exist or be known otherwise. We cannot say that the "je" is other than itself; nor can we say that the infra-personal conscience is different from the "je"; but we must reserve for the "toi" the dignity of being different from the "moi." On the other hand, the infra-personal conscience is for the "moi" and the "nous" a relative "non-moi" or a relative "non-nous"; it is found in the motion of the personal life and yet separate from it.

III. The "Constructions Anonymes" of the Person

10. We can be mislead by a language which has no normative rule but its own. Philosophers pay much attention to the

autonomy of structures and their patterns of transformation. They cannot deny that an isthmus attaches them to their subjects and that they all affect the language. Indeed the language would be nothing without speech which expresses and controls it. Is not language constituted of personal pronouns, proper names and many other morphological elements which show the imprint of our need for clear expression? It would be naive to act as if speaker and listener did not count; or if the referee was nothing but a code, depriving the language of any ontological dimension. Theoricians are the first, in fact, to free themselves as soon as they open their mouths, of those restrictions they put on the use of language. They must renounce their formalism and believe in the reality of the person.

11. It is difficult to develop a personalistic conception of the language against linguistic positivism. The exercise, however, can be beneficial. We must recognize that the impersonal appearance of the conscience may arise from the patterns of language which express the person. We just alluded to personal pronouns; they are an excellent illustration of that. The term "je"-"I" can be emptied of its content at any time and refilled, so to speak. This is due to the universal use of the same pronoun; it does not belong exclusively to any of us, although it is used each time in the singular. It remains per se indifferent to its recipient, and yet it makes possible the reciprocal comprehension of all subjects. The exchangeable quality--"interchangeabilité"--of the "you" - and "he" and of all personal pronouns, is conditional to communication.

Reflection shows that this flexibility of language underlines the comprehensiveness of personal life. Nevertheless, that exchange, seen superficially, may depersonalize communication; one forgets the speaker and listener to concentrate on speech and its subjectivity. Hence the explanation of a false interpretation of the phrase: "ça parle en moi, ça pense en moi." In reality, anonymity is that of the person; the impersonal appearance is an illusion. The conscience is of a different nature, depending on whether it refers to impersonal things or to the infra-personal conscience.

12. We could make similar remarks about all forms of anonymity proceeding from the person. They lead to a false concept of human impersonalism--"impersonnalité humaine." The empty form of the transcendental "je" (Kant's interpretation: the "je" is the abstract condition of all possible objects) takes a concrete entity in the person. This concept of "réification"--giving a concrete form--can be traced back to Kant and his disciples and found also in Huser. Max Scheler comments: "If we omit the plurality of the individual 'je,' what is left is not a supra-individual 'je' as a universal reference of the 'monde'-world--but a complete void." [4]

The transcendental "je" is a fictitious form, analogous to the potential infinity of optic. It helps in defining the metaphysical problem of the development of gnoseological and axiological realities; it can also hide the solution. It is a temporary hypothesis, almost suspended in nothingness. It establishes only a negative truth, namely that the personal conscience proceeding from that transcendental "je" is not alone and is not divine. It does not suggest a splitting of the reflexive conscience into personal and impersonal forms. We could not suggest that one of these forms would be minor and derived while the other would be major and first. It is, in fact, the personal subject which is the creator of the transcendental "je" and gives it an appearance of reality. We should not be the victim of the image we have of ourselves whatever assistance it may give us in understanding our own actions and feelings.

13. Another error is to imagine a "no man's land" preceding and preparing the encounter of persons separate in time and space. We anticipate that encounter with a feeling of emptiness and expectation. The fact that our conscience is real (a posteriori) implies the reality of the other conscience (a priori), since we know that a person exists as a person only in the concert of other persons. The congenital solitude of the human being should not be understood as an absolute isolation. The complexity of our emotions comes from the certitude that other persons exist and the uncertainty about their true identity; hence a state of tension which can be resolved only through anticipation whose function is to act as if it were the lights of a car on a dark road. This acceptance of other beings becomes so important that it may substitute itself for the "je" and in doing so create again the illusion of an impersonal conscience.

14. As a matter of fact, this expectation not only prepares the encounter (harmoniously or not) of other personal subjects, but also the perception and conceptual elaboration of material "qualia." The end of that process is an objective picture of things and ideas. The anonymity of nature--or, better said, its impersonality--invades the scope of our vision and threatens our individuality. Although we need an intensive personal activity (particularly in the area of the intellect) in order to grasp the scientific nature of the world, we do not cease to look at ourselves to discover things through a structure of notions related to them and meant to draw our attention. We no longer see things in their relation to us; we resume that relation or at least we recognize a mutuality of relations; and this triumph of objectivity remains whatever our efforts to alter it, because we depend on scientific reality, i.e. on objectivity.

The impact of science and technology may lead to a denial of the person; this is all the more true when we subject ourselves to scientific analysis, submitting the exteriorization of our body and psyche. In these conditions, concern for self is nothing but a reaction of self-defense and an effort to stop the contagion of things in our mind--"la contagion des chores." In fact, the captivity of the person is now complete, at the expense, of course, of our objective vision. The anonymity of the latter-- "l'anonymat de l'objectivation"--corresponds to semi-lucidity destructive of the "self" unless we discern clearly the boundaries of the object in the context of our total experience.

15. As we suggested we can depersonalize ourselves to a certain point, and be a more integral part of nature--"nous naturaliser"--whenever we are ready to be assimilated by things and disintegrated by our own ideas. We find that danger even in our inner mind; indeed both personal and interpersonal lives can be easily and immoderately conceptualized. The "je," "tu," "nous" tend to change from personal to impersonal pronouns in the surroundings of external, objective nature.

It is not science alone nor technology which are behind that trend; a certain phenomenology of the subject which is identified with the object is also responsible. When we detach acts and functions from their sources, a network of often very subtle interactions is left (for example, the image of my ego, as seen by somebody else, and perceived by myself in a kind of feed-back). This quasi formal network is artificially separated from concrete, real persons; it leads to a divorce of psychology and metaphysics or, worse, to a deterioration of phenomenology wrongly applied to the metaphysical knowledge of the world of the person. The outcome of this can be seen in the contemporary works influenced by Nietzsche; they propose a bizarre cosmogony built upon a desire or will, or some other mental exercise identified as the desire or will of the person. The "je," affected by the phantoms created in his inner self, believes that he is nothing but an epiphenomenon; his self-criticism becomes a self-denial.

The real man moves in two directions. On the one hand, he allows "qualia," erected in ontological principles to float in the universal matrix; on the other hand he can take hold of himself only in the form of "hupokeimenon"--an undefined substance, completely deprived of all individual character.

16. Another way of yielding to impersonalism consists in the divinization of the personal "Logoi." Each one of us is unique or called to identify his uniqueness. The plurality of minds is no less certain than the possibility of their agreement. Neither one, however, should be exaggerated. If instead of taking refuge in an objectivity which would unite us mechanically, we opted for plurality in order to dissociate us, one from the other, radically, we would reach a form of polytheism of souls--"polytheisme des

âmes"--and intellects destructive of the ideal "moi." The latter would be turned into some kind of vampire which would destroy our concrete existence or abandon it to its sad fate as if it were a negligible entity. The soul, if exalted, no longer flows in the psyche it is assumed to control; it goes beyond it with other souls, with the freedom of a star among other stars.

Let us suppose now that we bring it down from its "empyrée" and allow it to take possession of our self. Will our situation be better? This new process is, in fact, the sign of a malady of the personality, fanaticism. The "je" is motivated by a force which crushes his liberty instead of strengthening it; the "je" is confused about his identity, taking the image of self for reality; it also compromises his moral development.

17. All constructions which are the work of the person are confusing. The person erects an interhuman or theandric image of the "nous" where the "je" and the "tu" disappear in some kind of ecstatic confusion. False mysticism falls into the same error; it translates to a higher level the same limitations which prevent the animal from reaching perfect individuality inside the group. Pseudo-mysticism eliminates the conflicts of the "Mitsein," which is a noble effort. It does not, however, achieve a "Fureinandersein"; it rather distorts and degrades the "nous" of the interpersonal communion--something quite different from the oneness of a blind mob. The feeling of fusion substitutes an homogenous identity for the heterogenous identity of consciences. It is not sensitive to the need of a reciprocal genesis which is the foundation of personal dynamism. The failure of the "étants" is caused by their yielding to a mirage.

18. This confusion is often traced to a desire for a deep sleep without nightmares. The personal conscience, however, protests against this defection and prefers tragedy to serenity. One of the extreme manifestations of this reaction is found in the feeling of distress which affects some experiences when we are unable to integrate them to the "je" or the "nous." The "Sehnsucht" of the German romantics took that form. When one hears a children's choir, for example, one realizes that the young singers are unable to express the meaning of what they sing, or, indeed of what they are. They stay at a certain distance from an inner paradise which remains, therefore, close to us; we cannot enter with them or through them. The function is impossible and yet something in us demands it. That kind of feeling so deeply felt is one element of the artistic experience.

It is also the counterpart of the confusion we speak about-- "confusionnisme." It implies the desperate will to break the barrier which rejects all ipseities. We can see in it, however, the esthetic expression of man's destiny which is to raise the psyche to the level of personality and with it the spontaneity of nature.

When conditioned by the eschatological need to fulfill itself, the person witnesses to its inalienable essence; it renounces not so much the building of anonymous mediations so useful in delivering it of its inferior egocentricity and animal servitude, but the feeling that those mediations point to an impersonal fatality, the ultimate outcome of its operation.

IV. The Presence of the Logos

19. We do not imply here that the impersonal appearance of the conscience has no other origin than the anonymity of our constructions and their mistakes; nor do we suggest that the contamination of our minds by matter as discovered through science, is also the culprit. We would not deceive ourselves if we were not free to deny ourselves in a certain measure. But this lack of true freedom--"contre-liberté"--obeys a norm beyond us which controls the freedom we have. This norm of subtle, invincible wisdom is the "Logos" which originates our "Logoi." It precedes, accompanies and follows all our actions. We escape determinism, but we are inserted in a dialectic.

The first act of the Logos in the "étants" is "l'être." The latter is the primordial relation of each "étant" with himself and other "étants." "L'être" is not the Logos, the divine Logos himself, but his manifestation "ad extra." It is the form of exteriority, the sign of the condition of being created; it is a divine condescension in the realm of creation.

The person is an "'étant' par excellence"; and the conscience of "l'être" is a call to order it constantly addressed to "l'étant." The mediation of "l'être" is not entirely and directly ours. Its impersonal appearance expresses the fact that the created person is limited and must go to the neutralization of death to fulfill itself. We encounter in the norm of "être" an invigorating obstacle, a pedagogical or ascetic negation which conditions our development. The unlimited meaning of objective convergences is unveiled in this presence which invades all our faculties. It rules our thoughts; it instills the play of our actions and interactions.

20. The work of the Logos is not limited to the giving of the initial being to all personal "étants." It consists also in the sustaining of all our structures, giving them correction and possible extension. All the systems we build are duplicates of a universal system which creates and supports the development of derived beings--"être conséquent." A long series of variations occurs which are our imitations of the Logos and its emanations.

The work of the Logos is divesified and graded. The myths studied by Levi-Strauss, for example, reveal a norm of transformation which is an aspect of the collective thought affecting all individuals contributing to it. There is no doubt that Levi-Strauss' systematizations belong to the infra-personal or extra personal realm, this due to a certain contempt for "le pauvre trésor de l'identité personnelle." They are fragmentary and often too ingenious if not pretentious. Notwithstanding these reservations, however, they make possible in a logical way the hypothesis of a hierarchy of ontological circuits which appear and develop in the destiny of the "étants." One can say that the emanation of "l'être" is not only a descent in relation to the Logos, but also an ascent, dramatic and awkward, toward the same.

21. Beyond "l'être" which introduces the Logos to "l'étant," there is a presence of the Logos itself in "l'étant," as if it were the soul of our soul. Is it not the "sur-consciente" source which gives us our uniqueness, our vocation, and our liberty? This mysterious source of the "je" may seem impersonal, like a voice suppressed by its echo. We try a song whose origin is enigmatic and confusing.

Nevertheless, intuition and reflection could lead us to an opposite conclusion. As the Logos could be found behind the activity of "l'être," it is not possible to suggest that in the same manner a supreme Person can be found behind the superficial impersonality of the Logos? The Logos, indeed, creates and comprehends our persons; consequently we can hold it to be more personalized than we are since it gives us personality. The mediation of "l'être" is the mask of the mediator. The anonymity of the latter is the appearance that its universality gives to the personal order. Since it creates and comprehends "l'étant" in "l'être" and vice versa, it is the direct author of both. Its plenitude, which transcends us, is so far beyond our reach that we conclude that it is impossible even to apprehend it; hence we are reduced to a monologue about it. The Logos is a difficult "god" but alive. In reality, it is the transcendent "Thou" of which the transcendental "je" is only a substitute, lifeless and inconsistent. At the peak of our personal and inter-human experience there is One who must have a supra-personal character; in other words eminently personal.

22. Thanks to that Being we can push back what we called "biological ingratitude." Now we must obey this God-Logos by becoming receptive to his active presence; what the mystics call theopathic passivity. The use of that term is debatable for it signifies a state as perfect as the perfection of our activity. Whatever the meaning of the word, however, the conclusion is clear: the life of the mind is the efflorescence of the life of the person. Unity between them is intimate. The former is in the latter and for its sake.

One could ask if the impersonal appearance of the conscience is not absorbed in the inter-human and theandric "<u>nous</u>"
when one reaches that final phase where the created "<u>etant</u>"
assumes its "<u>ipseity</u>" when discovering that of the Logos. As soon
as reason operates we receive the promise of it; as Claudel once
wrote: "<u>des qu'il y a proportion, il y a entretien</u>," - "as soon
as there is relation, there is communication."

NOTES

1. J. P. Sartre, "La Transcendence de L'ego," Paris, 1972 (a new addition
of the article published in <u>Recherches Philosophiques</u>, 1936), pp. 25, 37, 55, 79,
85, 87. I agree that the "je" and the "moi" cannot be separated. In a different
context I shall use both terms with approximately the same meaning.

2. Cl. Levi-Strauss, **La Pensée Sauvage**, Paris, 1962, p. 326.

3. Quoted by M. Constantini in the journal, <u>Résurrection</u>, n. 36, pp.
85-86.

4. M. Scheler, **Le Formalisme en Éthique**, p. 384.

Chapter Eleven

COMMUNICABILITY AND COMMUNICATION

Communicability and Communication Between Consciences

1. All personal conscience is endowed with the irrepressible ability to communicate in an interpersonal milieu. Even the misanthrope cannot avoid that necessity. To find refuge in the wilderness is another way of declaring one's humanness. This constant truth is expressed whenever we say that the human person is submitted by nature to an order of communication. We can see there the pre-reflexive then reflexive expression of the act through which the person affirms himself as a person, or at least an indication of that act. Communicability is understood as an inevitable disposition of all persons, not as the act itself of communicating between persons. This is why communication, even in its subjective foundation goes with the person but does not constitute it an "étant."

2. Seen under a different light, communicability manifests the presence of "l'être," of which it is the corollary, in each "étant" and between all "étants." "L'être," indeed, is the primordial relation that each personal "étant" has with itself and other "étants." If we consider communicability in infra-personal and extra-personal "étants," the primordial relation of "l'étant" has less interiority than the person. There is something added to the real tie between a stone or even an animal and their own existence, for neither the stone nor the animal are conscious of their primordial relation to themselves or to others. They do not have to ratify their being; they receive it in the universal interaction. The only dimension of inferiority in that case is seen in the network of relations. Hence the definition of "l'être" we gave at the beginning of this paragraph applies first of all to the personal conscience; then, secondarily to other infra or extra-personal beings. In assuming that communicability manifests the presence of "l'être" in "étant," we establish the principle which has a universal outreach.

3. The primordial relation of "l'être" is a correlation.

As primitive in "l'étant," this relation insures communicability between all aspects of "etant" between themselves and with "l'etant" itself. It also guarantees communicability of all "etants" between themselves without giving priority to any of them in relating that communicability to the rest of the universe. This equal submission to the primitive relation erases all "sens uniques" and unilateral privileges in general ontology. It makes this relation recognized everywhere and in all directions in the fundamental ontic and inter-ontic of all created beings. The radical relation is thus a radical correlation.

4. "L'être," however, apart from the "étants" has no meaning and no communicability. It is secondary to them, although essential to their existence. This is evident in the case of the derived "être" which is real in the effective operation of the "etant"; it is also true, however, in the case of the radical or primitive "être"; it can be verified even in the fundamental ontic and inter-ontic basis of the communicability we have studied.

4a. We have just made a distinction between derived and primitive beings--"êtres." It is another way of recognizing that "l'être" has a history. On the one hand it is given to created or worldly beings: "étants mondain"; it is its primitive aspect. On the other hand it takes part in the development of those beings; it is its derived aspect.

Is there a very serious difficulty? We have defined "l'être" as a primordial relation of "l'étant" to itself and other "étants." That definition applies to the primitive "être," but not to the derived one. How should we define the latter? What is the element of continuity between the two? If it is true that multiplication of beings occurs ("plus entium") as well as an increase in being ("plus entis"), should we not conclude that ontology is divided into two irreconcilable parts?

The difficulty could be caused by the ambiguity of the term "primitive." There is a chronological primitiveness and in that sense the derived "être" is not the primitive one. There is a metaphysical primitiveness, better called "primordialité": in this secondary sense the derived "être" is not free from the radical one, for the increase in being "plus entis" - whatever its element of novelty - does not modify the fundamental condition of the primordial relation of "l'être" with "l'étant." The new being, derived from the activity of other beings, is always a gift for all other created beings--"une grâce pour l'étant mondain." That being is not created without being received at the same time; it always remains a primordial metaphysical relation or correlation to all beings in their development. The transcendental character of "l'être" (in the classical ontological meaning of the term) is not diminished but rather verified and strengthened by the constant enlargement of its network.

5. The beings we are cannot be confused with the relation or correlation which brings us into existence. Because of this we are led to postulate the existence of God, i.e. of a Supreme Being which is not like other beings but is the source of their communicability. God subjects himself, so to speak, to the rule of ontological equality of the being He gives us; and yet because of his Uniqueness, He is free from that rule, whose function we explained earlier. (§ 3)

It is not the place here to justify the affirmation of God's existence; it will suffice to show its seemliness by the analogy of "l'être." Why not object, however, that it would be simpler to assume that "l'être" could, indeed, be identified with all created beings? Would it not be enough to think of an "ordo ordinans" immanent to all beings without being conceived in divine terms?

Let us say at least two things. First of all, if we take seriously the personal conscience, it is impossible to equate it with "l'être" or "l'étant." One could do that only by raising the primitive being to the level of the "nous" it anticipates; but even in the "nous" one would find again the problem of the relationship of the human "toi" with the divine "toi" - "Thou."

Furthermore, communicability implies that personal beings be individualized. This state of separation is strange, in a sense contradictory to each person who cannot subsist without the constitutive ties of the "je" with the "toi." The separation cannot be primitive for it would be destructive of the personal spirit. In these conditions communicability seems to be like a divine instrument which heals a wound of which we are conscious without being able to remedy it. Hence, communicability makes the act of God probable at least. The "être" is a demiurgic instrument which reaches all beings and holds them as in a net. It allows the active co-existence of all beings in one universe. Without it there would be not even a multi-universe--"multivers"--but either an acosmic paradise of consciences, all perfectly reciprocal, or a centrifugal flux of evanescent and non-intelligible phenomena. In fact, the world is neither one; the "étants" are there in constant but rectifiable diffluence; this twofold condition points to a creator and ordinator of the world, who orders the "être" like an intra and extra-ontic relation and provides universal solidarity and cooperation among all "étants."

6. Communicability is neither conceivable nor real without communication which is its true entity. To be real communicability must rest on a fact, namely the separation of the "étants." That separation is threefold: first it divides like a sword the inner self of the "étant"; then it scatters the "étants" like galaxies, projecting them far away from their creative source which remains transcendent. Furthermore, communicability which is neither

conceivable nor real without a "pluriversalisante" creation, can reverse the movement of separation and make possible a concrete communication bringing all beings in a form of transcendent communion.

7. Before we go into the analysis of communicability, we should underline one more thing about separation: its point of departure.

We easily conceive of the distance existing between consciences; we have an image of it in the relation between stars and night. This concrete image is not purely arbitrary, for it is true that human consciences have a perceptible space as their field of operation. The latter cannot be reduced to a network of abstract relations translated in mathematical terms. It also expresses an organic "Sitz im Leben," unfolding a motion of material contact or withdrawal for each of us. The separation of consciences, however, is first of all a spiritual distance: ignorance of the deep self, ignorance of the other person, ignorance of God. If it were not for that spiritual distance, would there be divergence of judgments and behaviors? Would the world, as we know it, be in a state of conflict? Would a free person turn against another?

There is no doubt as to the answer to those questions. It would be false, however, to regard that distance, and a fortiori, the distance of perceptible space as essential to the reality of personal beings endowed with creative freedom. Growth is conceivable without the dislocation of duration. We can understand freedom as faithful to the pure norm of autoposition without aggressiveness. In other words, personal autonomy is conceivable as different from biological or juridic autonomy and realized in our earthly experience. Kant's morality points to our harmony of liberties which gives autonomy its highest statute without undermining the collegiality of all subjects but rather liberating them from a milieu which partially denies them.

8. Once again, we must prevent all abusive simplification and recognize that we are amphibious; there is in us a relation above all relations, a communion in free reciprocity; and there is the adjustment of the person to a certain development, affected by the limitations of communication. Communicability is the revelation of the "être"; communion is that of the "étant." The latter goes beyond the former. It is not always possible to deduct the existence of communicability from an instance of communion, although one may indicate the other's direction.

The human person, therefore, moves within the zones of its primordial ends and contingent means. The "étants" are analogous, for each one is the original partner of a reciprocal communion. The "être" which is the principle of communicability in a world of separated beings, is univocal, for it is the foundation of all language; and language itself is the best example of univocity. This complex structure of the personal order respects the diversity of human experience and the possible unification of its components.

9. From communicability, which manifests the nature of "l'être," we pass now to communication which is a derived form of the "être" in the "étants." The act of the "étant" modifies the initial ontological relation leading to the emergence of an operating "nous" open to somewhat undetermined participants.

The French language condenses in one word the meaning of three Latin words: "communicans," "communicatio," and "communicatum." The ambiguous differences in meaning would have to be clarified for the sake of a more precise phenomenology. Let us limit ourselves to one important point. As soon as there is intention to communicate something to someone, a series of dehiscences occur between transmitter and receiver. It is, in fact, the beginning of the message. The person represents himself, uses symbols, becomes concrete; in other words expresses himself in a language. It enters the anonymity of objectivity. That operation is mysterious; it is a kind of self denial and death, but not completely. The voice that has made the sound remains in it, even when it is not identified. The hand which writes leaves its imprint on the paper then disappears but the meaning of the message remains. Nothing is more striking than the example of the recording. The intention of the messenger is protected. He is no longer there and yet the auditor is aware of him. The transmitter has engraved his word on wax and by doing so projected himself into the future; and the receiver listening to the record is meeting a voice of the past. These two opposite motions are complementary precisely because the message is not tied to the transmitter; it is embedded in the wax to establish a lasting present common to both transmitter and receiver. The relative stability of the matter brings nearer consciences otherwise separated. Sign of a real absence, matter becomes the instrument of co-presence.

10. The message is separated from the messenger but it has no entity outside the consciences it brings together. It is complex by nature, as a vehicle it is material, as a meaningful exchange it is spiritual. It is renewed every time it is understood; active and passive it has an hermeneutic "aura" which requires a certain community of language and concepts. Matter is the vehicle of a message only when it is receptive to a multitude of inter-conscious acts which are understandable and understood when they all participate in the same Word.

This means, of course, that all electronic and mechanical transmissions, so complex today due to technical progress, are real only when they originate in and return to the mind. What

Berkeley said about the material world, whose reality depends on its ability to be perceived, applies to communication. When we say to another person, "I have received a message for you," the telephone call or the telegram are the products of a machine associated with the action or reaction of consciences. The product, however, has two services to offer: it is a servant without which consciences would not be touched; and a servant able to keep the content of a message always valid even after the departure of the sender and before the arrival of the receiver. The transmission-machine breaks down a wall but the interlocutors it liberates join only partially and indirectly. There is, therefore, in the message considered as a vehicle a little more and a little less than the nudity of two consciences.

11. It is possible, therefore, to include in the message something other than the messenger; and this by the decision of the latter. The best example, of course, is the resistance of a messenger to the communication of truth--a false message. The personal "étant" certainly cannot attack the radical communicability of "l'être," without which the person would have no reality. In the same manner the "étant" cannot prevent completely the meaning of a communication since a false message can be submitted to a critical inspection, more refined perhaps than the lie itself. Language, however, can be used, equally well, to tell the truth and to lie. The intentional alteration of truth, even when limited, is one of the most grievous threats to the conscience. Willful falsehood widens the separation of consciences precisely when communicability was a means of union. It is a failure which affects not "l'être" itself, but its outreach. It complicates communication. It is a deception leading to "la guerre des communiqués."

12. Another source of break-down in communication is the involuntary error of either transmitter or receiver. As in the case of lying, error can occur at either end of the line but it affects the message only in the acts of giving and receiving it. In the conscience of the transmitter there is a problem of auto hermeneutic in which the message is interpreted as if it were already received. This hermeneutic determines the choice of words; it is very important in giving the message its final meaning. It has not, however, been systematically studied by philosophers. It seems that they give their whole attention to the hermeneutic of the receiving conscience.

There is a physical zone between emission and reception where an accident may happen without engaging the responsibility of the person. A study of communication shows with greater clarity the phases and anomalies of what takes place in the natural transmission of sounds and graphic signs. It is possible to build machines to prevent accidents. Other machines, however, request transmission of information in code which has to be deciphered; in the course of the operation the possibility of mechanical failure cannot be ruled out. It is true that the engineer has normally built a machine capable of controlling its operation and eliminating its inexactitudes, all things which are not possible in the case of natural transmission.

The transmission of information, restricted in its scope, neutral as to the nature of its content raises many questions in the mind of the philosopher. Those questions, however, are secondary when we deal with analytical technological or even logical information. Such information calculates trustworthy factors for the memory, transmission and correction of data; it does not know, however, or understand the content of the processes. On the contrary, it takes a simple lie in one conscience only or even an involuntary effort to underline the complexity of the operation, beyond the limitations of the machine.

13. Falsehood and accident are, in the last analysis, the two important factors which determine the pathology of communication. A third factor, however, may find its way between the other two and aggravate them; it is the number of intermediaries, conscious or material. A message passing from one person to another is inevitably affected by several distortions even more so when it is transmitted through space by mechanical devices. Statistics of sociologists are clear on that point; and the study of mass media leads to the serious question: what is left of the conversation with a politician, for example, or of the official account of a given event when those reach the average person? Manipulated by journalists and commentators they are affected by the receptive conscience which is in turn affected by prejudices and opinions. Error is often like a snow-ball and the reliability of the process is often minimal. It would be beneficial if quantitative studies could determine certain laws of the patterns of distortion as reliable, as the law of gravitation or the principle of degradation of energy.

Outside the sector of electronics, however, which is limited, any further attempt would probably be delusive because of the great inequality of messages, and the diversity of the psychic milieux. There are certainly many degrees of exactitude: meteorological information is transmitted more accurately than political motivations. Health bulletins about the condition of an illustrious person are more elusive and contradictory than the news of his death, etc. . . In one case you have a tower of Babel, in the other you reach a sudden consensus without error.

14. What is the conclusion of our study? If there is one it is that the surest communication should combine the following elements:

a. It occurs in the restricted circle of persons;

b. It is transmitted from one person to the other, avoiding irresponsible anonymity.

c. It facilitates the discernment of truth, relations between members of a family or professions, etc. . .

On the contrary if communication takes place in a large, heterogeneous circle, it produces confusion particularly when strong emotional reactions are involved. It then blows up like a bomb, leaving only scattered fragments. Only communication dealing with technological data have a chance of being received in the human community without repercussion because it is factual and inconveniences no one. As far as science, strictly speaking, is concerned one must remark that communication reaches experts only and is soon distorted when handed to the masses.

15. We have not yet considered, however, a possible form of resistance to lies and errors; a slowing down that any communicated idea might oppose to forms of communication. This "braking" effort can be the result of discrepancies between communication and the personal source of information. The same effort can also initiate the autonomous course of a thought which will unfold according to its own nature. The initial idea does that as it is propagated; it enters in "symbiose" or in conflict with its communicators; it is at the same time influenced and influencing, it contains some of the pretentions of the transmitters; it has a power to rebound; it manifests an inner logic capable of overcoming all obstacles, as we may observe in the history of many institutions. Sometimes what has been communicated over a period of time has a power of auto-cleansing, thus verifying the saying that, "truth is the daughter of time." The process has been difficult; a single aspect has at times overshadowed the whole thought; then a new emphasis has emerged. At the end of the exercise, however, a certain equilibrium has been achieved. Nature also has its own feedback and the process of communication ends in the wisdom of an information both matured and verified.

16. Such an objective is possible but not necessary. In some instances it is only a dream and we cannot escape a certain pessimism as we look at the history of communication. The latter is different from the communion between persons because it does not unite consciences in perfect mutuality; it gives them something external to accomplish but it does not bring them together in the oneness of a common act. There is, therefore, a certain alienation of the self in all communication but it should be overcome and the separation of consciences should be healed. Does that in fact happen? Is communication equal to such a task? How do we explain a certain sluggishness, a number of deviations especially encountered in collectivities? Is it not clear that the whole operation can be distorted?

17. One could search for philosophical or theological answers to those questions. We should remark, however, that the above "exposé" is centered on the intellectual component of communication. Hence it is not an accident that we met the process of information in our reflection. Between communication of data and communion of persons there must be an interpersonal tie of another kind to consider: the one provided by our living past by the heritage of someone else; this in contrast to the dead past studied by historians. There is in each one of us the mark of various traditions; it affects our present, giving it a certain reality. It is that chain of influences integrated to the life of the individual which gives him an individuality reflecting past years and past experiences, race, nation and religion. All that emerges from times long gone while giving meaning to the present. That heritage in each of us is an intermediary between uncertain communication and the plenitude of communion; it allows us to erase or change as we wish; it is part of us; it is us. It is tradition in the best connotation of the word: it is both remembrance of the past and power of rejuvenation.

18. Ultimately, what do we do with communication? We acquire it and assimilate it to our being. As "étants" we also integrate it to the inter-personal network which is beyond the fundamental communication of the pre-reflexive being. If "l'être," innate or acquired, is a correlation of "l'étant" with itself and all other "étants," as we showed earlier, it gives autonomy to the "étants" in the universe without giving them that kind of independence which is a form of arbitrary isolation or a monadic sufficiency.

No personal "étant" can be produced by others; this is what gives it originality and autonomy. The opposite is also true: no personal "étant" can produce other "étants" and this, of course, is the source of interdependence of "étants" in communication. The "étants" are called to give themselves in this world as "asymptotic preparation" or an echo of their transcendental communion which help them to promote their reciprocity through knowledge and creative love.

ADDITIONAL NOTE

Philosophy of communication goes beyond the problems of information we have just referred to in paragraphs 11 and 13 of this chapter. We should underline, nevertheless, the great interest of a research which resulted in breaking down some barriers between logic and phenomenology, for example the work of P. Watzlawick, J. H. Beavin and D. D. Jackson, **Pragmatics of Human Communication**, New York, 1967.

In their effort to identify a few fundamental axioms of communication, Paul Watzlawick and his collaborators depend on the **Tractatus Logico-philosophicus** of Wittgenstein when they suggest that communication does not convey a message of reality but of a practical translation of data affected by our senses; all the rest is silence. It is quite possible not to share that insight of their mystical existentialism and to give more ontological content to language. Their position, however, has naturally inclined them to emphasize those paradoxes related to the boundaries of thought and expression. They divide them in logico-mathematical paradoxes (of the type: "La classe de toutes les classes ne font pas partie d'elles-mêmes"), semantic paradoxes (of the type: "I lie"), or pragmatic paradoxes. The last are so called because they deal with behavior and are different from simple contradictions since they cannot be resolved by a simple choice of "yes" or "no." They are injunctions of the type: "be spontaneous!" or again propositions which under scrutiny express two irreconcilable predictions.

In order to illustrate their thought the authors expand curiously on the theory of Gödel on unresolvable propositions. Since it is necessary in that case to leave the system to be able to decide, they introduce the concept of "méta-communication" and then a "métalangage" or "métaconnaissance." They show that the paradoxes of communication can have a therapeutic value as well as a pathogenic one. Indeed, those paradoxes can be a source of creativity by game, humor, symbolism, etc. One has to agree with that insight and find it very helpful for the study of language, grammar and semantics and more generally for the studies of human relationships.

On the other hand, Watzlawick and his friends think that our knowledge can hardly go beyond the level of complexity of the type: "I know that you know what I am thinking of you." As far as higher complexities are concerned--"I know that you know that I know that you know what I am thinking of you," etc. . . one should rely, according to them on mathematical symbols and computers.

General remarks are in order: (1) as the sentence becomes more complicated it fails to add to the experience; it reminds us of the sound of the needle of a turn-table on a scratched record. Nothing new is added to the original affirmation; (2) if too much complexity does not stop communication it becomes repetitious of a series of data (I know that you know . . .) and changes into an historical relation; (3) if I substitute for the formula: "I know that you know that I think of you," the following: "I know that you know what I think of you," I do not change the "je-tu" relation but I give it a new content. This requires a new complexity of the language, although the fundamental requirements of communication do not change, namely communication is not a communuion but necessarily includes an objective reality.

Chapter Twelve

INTERSUBJECTIVE CAUSALITY

1. We can examine now the relation to others in two different and yet interrelated contexts: the first is that of "I'-étant," the second that of the "étants." The first is in us and we begin with a communion or reciprocity of consciences already established. The enigma then is to understand why and how the consciences can go their separate ways. In the second context, that of separated consciences, the link between them, the network which holds them and organizes them in the same universe, is "l'être" itself whose instumentality facilitates their relation. Their communion, however, is to be observed beyond simple communication and this is also an enigma.

In both perspectives relation, which is dynamic and in process, calls one's attention to the problem of causality. But one of our most puzzling experiences in the study of philosophy is precisely our failure to unravel the mystery of intersubjective causality. The fundamental fact is clear: we recognize our created-ness and the impact of mutual influence. However, the why and how of those facts remains hidden. I can try to describe the rise of consciousness and its exchanges with others but the essence of such reality escapes me as well as the analysis of the causality of the "moi" on "moi" - the "I" on "me." I have only a glimpse of a movement which eludes me. The "transitivity" of the relation seems, therefore, undeniable and yet inexplicable.

It is surprising and somewhat scandalous that so many philosophers have remained indifferent to that kind of antinomy. They have re-examined and criticized the mechanical causality and the biological causality, identifying the specific nature of each; but they seem to ignore the metaphysics of the genesis of the conscience and of its influence on other consciences.

2. One thing is certain: analytical thought here does not correspond to reality which is misrepresented, distorted, impov-erished. Bergson has perhaps separated too much the intellect

from life; but he is fundamentally right. One must maintain that the analytical intellect is never free from its subject; the presence of the latter remains in the separation movement. As we drift from a subject we can still reconstruct it through comparisons and corrections. External knowledge is never final per se.

It is not final either in the case of the perception of material objects, nor in the relation to other people, whatever its special conditions. It is certainly easier to twist reality in the analysis of a person than a thing. The real person can be bypassed, his thoughts and feelings ignored. Conversely the "méconnaissance" of a person is easier than that of the material objects we constantly see. Furthermore, we do not doubt the presence of a person beside us even if we ignore him or her; on the other hand we have access to the psychic interiority of a few people whereas material objects have none beside the relation of their molecules. Finally, we have access to the person through analysis whenever intuitive sympathy reveals and purifies.

3. We find here, at least partially, the meaning of the analysis of the movement of the consciences, namely that this type of knowledge is unique and incomparable. It is strictly personal or interpersonal but it cannot be repeated and it does not embrace the external reality. Any interpersonal relation is a unique event as communication between individuals but it is not a perfect intellectual analysis. St. Augustine said, "you can see the face of a person but you listen to your conscience not his." There is, of course, a partial discovery of the person in the look of his face. It is a beginning which will unfold and be strengthened through love when our eyes admire what others could not see.

Bergson distinguishes two types of knowledge: comprehension and intuition; between them exist channels: the "schéma dynamique" and the "jeu des métaphores." Furthermore the "transmutation symbolique" is the ideal instrument to express a loving relation to the other. That relation experiences ups and downs; it has strength and weakness but it finds its authenticity in the recognition of the singularity of the other person. Individuality is not a limitation; it is, in fact, perfected by a universal horizon in theoretical and practical knowledge. Relations between people will manifest such potential through the use of symbolic language which allows the association of general concepts and sensorial images and gives them an irreplaceable meaning.

4. Has our initial difficulty disappeared? Not at all. It is not enough to discover the uniqueness of one experience to dissipate the mystery. Although a relationship can be experienced, it cannot be explained. It cannot be fully understood. Our experience is not clear even to itself; we can give something of ourselves without fully understanding what we are doing. In that context,

Leibniz and Malebranche are more convincing than Hume. They did not deny causality--how could that be possible in the order of subjectivity?--but they traced its source to a divine center. We cannot truly take hold of ourselves and others because we cannot understand the Creator and substitute ourselves for Him. We can only receive his Word. To receive Him is to accept the second place of the creature; it is to reverse the manipulative movement of the intellect and accept values which reveal and yet hide the very nature of our reality. There is, therefore, a mystery of "l'être" and "l'étant." Relationships always have an unexplored area. This is experienced in human encounters and more fundamentally in our encounter with God. We cannot fully understand human influences because we cannot exhaust the meaning of our tie with the Creator, although God gives himself to us in our "étant" and in the unicity of our "être."

Everything happens in the "Dasein" to make us conscious of our nothingness whenever we deny that relationship to God which gives us our identity and supports our relationship to others. The insignificance of man in the universe and in the history of mankind, his humiliation before the power of the individual and collective unconscious are certainly compensated by the scope of self-understanding. The intellectual tragedy, however, and the stress of our mortal existence have no outcome but despair or transcendence. This is why reflecting on subjectivity and intersubjectivity necessarily leads to a religious choice.

5. It is possible to go further in the description of the intersubjective causality; the following five points merit our attention: 1. the active intention of the "moi," 2. the expression of such intention, 3. its perception by another person, 4. the modification of the mind of that person in response to the activity of the "moi," 5. the perception of the "moi" of this response.

This scheme is helpful in revealing the influence of the "co-effectuation." It must be used, however, with caution since it exposes us to the danger of agreeing to a concept of perception of the other by analogy; it also leads us to a dissociation of body and psyche, giving to the former the most important causality. With that caveat in mind one can see a diversity of cases where such schema is relevant. The active intention, therefore, can either be affected by a desire to influence another person or refrain from the same; expressive behavior can be more or less spontaneous or voluntary, etc.

In fact, the distinction between "l'étant" and "l'être" must be used here to unravel the complexity of data examined by the phenomenologist. We consider, therefore, intersubjective causality under two forms: that of the "étant" and of the "être."

6. The causality of "l'étant" is tied to intuition whenever there is direct influence; the "moi" grasps the alterity of its partner in its originality and uniqueness; it renews the "nous" which exists between them by its active influence. The body of the other person becomes then transparent to its own spirit. It is obvious, of course, that we experience such intuition and engage in that action in an inceptive fashion only; they develop sporadically, during chosen periods but with great effort as if they were groping in the dark. Those privileged moments must find in the ensuing time a confirmation or verification allowing the elimination of pseudo-intuition and a de-mystification of pseudo influences.

7. More often than not, the mediation of "l'être" is present in the causality of "l'étant." The theory, therefore, which sees the knowledge of the other person as resulting from reasoning by analogy, should not be rejected but properly understood. Furthermore, we cannot reject the concept that we affect others by our bodies, but we must limit the scope of that assumption. The body is not identified with the mind; it is detached from it, although we do not fully understand how.

It is obvious that in our daily life we "guess" another person better than we discover ourselves in him or her. The separation of our consciences overwhelms our relationship; such separation, however, is never final or complete but rests, in fact, on an inceptive or remaining unity. The body of the other person becomes then neutral. We see that body and interpret its gestures as if it were a mirror of ourselves, the echo of our voice, the touch of our hands on our own body. We internalize that experience--free our "cénesthésie"--behind the physical appearance of an unknown other--"autrui"--rebuilt in our own image and resemblance.

Consequently, our influence on another person is normally the result not of a real intuition but of a simple and rather limited perception. We use bodily appearances as instruments to act on a person as if he were a thing. Whenever the person escapes that fate, the corruption of the mechanical causality, and is restored to the influence of an interpersonal causality it is through a kind of groping induction tying together analogical knowledge and action to promote a loving relation of the consciences. The subordination of "l'être" to "l'étant" and their integration have an important place in the destiny of people.

8. It is important to underline the axioms ruling the intersubjective causality, to show its effectiveness and metaphysical originality.

1) There is a synchronic element in the "diachronie" of that causality: the conscience-mother and the conscience-daughter generate one another. [1]

2) The effect is not separated from its cause; this is why it would be preferable to speak of an influence of persons not of a causality. Even when human contacts cease and physical or moral distance affects the relationship, there is a reality of separation which is not the same as the distance between two balls on a pool table because the contact between persons is internalized; all separation in the infra-human world would be only metaphoric.

3) Consciences are not similar to the trays of a scale or to the pipes connecting containers in a laboratory. The activity of one conscience does not necessarily invade the passivity of the other; the plenitude of one is the emptiness of the other. The merit of Leibniz was to understand that all perception is active and that there is a causality "idéale," a relation of perceptions besides physical causality and spatial impulsion. He thinks, however, that: "une monade agit lorsqu'elle accroît la clarité de sa perception et elle est dite agir sur les autres parce que cet accroissement doit être compensé par une dimminution proportionnelle chez les autres." [2] This last affirmation cannot be verified in the interpersonal relation nor in the mutuality of consciences.

4) The ontological superiority of the cause vis à vis its effect is debatable in the intersubjective order. A personalist philosphy cannot accept the following proposition of Proclus: "Tout être qui en produit un autre est d'ordre supérieur à son produit." [3] Proclus does not demonstrate convincingly that cause and effect are equal. He bases his reasoning on the implicit assumption that the complete absence of hierarchy is unthinkable. He suggests the argument, anankē stēnai, that if the effect is sterile it is inferior to its cause and if it is fruitful "tous les êtres seraient egaux," what he considers to be absurd. How does he not consider the possibility of reciprocal causes? Is it really absurd to deny the primacy of a person? [4]

Proclus is right, on the other hand, to maintain that a cause cannot be inferior to its effect: "Si un être pouvait rendre un autre plus parfait que lui, il se confererait à lui-même cette perfection avant de la donner à son derivé." Language, stripped of its sacredness, has still power to convey the truth that the perfection we give to a person, though made, is real and can be acquired.

Materialism can be defined as the possibility of seeing the plus emerging from the minus. According to Bergson, however, the conscience which is the opposite of matter is the emergence of the plus from a relative evolutionary minus only. The fact that the dynamic reality of life dominates the succession of its forms is what differentiates the "evolution créatrice" of Bergson

130

from materialism. The source of life, therefore, cannot be inferior to the stream of life even if a new form is better than the old one from which it proceeds.

9. The charter of causalities could be shown as follows:

1) There is first the creative causality of God forming the personal consciences. They are "étants" inferior to God and yet they are already called to know him by grace in a sense to beget Him relatively and according to his design.

The inalienable superiority of God does not rest on an axiom of universal causality but on the intuition of a "surplus" which conditions our coming into existence and the unfolding of our intellectual activity. [5]

2) There is then the intersubjective causality at the level of mutual influence between created persons. It aims at reciprocity, definite and yet diversified; in principal it is permanent.

3) Finally there is the emanation of matter, its dispersion. Here the effect leaves its cause; there is less contact; there is no strong causality but a spatio-temporal fragmentation. The transitory reality disappears; determining conditions only remain. Vis à vis its antecedent, the event can unfold with independence and novelty--what some people see as a combination of freedom and necessity. There is connection not implication, legality not interiority. The "conditionné" can surpass its "conditionnant." It is no longer, however, a relation of cause to effect comparable to what we see in a relation between persons.

Two movements, apparently similar, are opposed to each other in our experience: one is a "diffluence" which individualizes things by separating them, the other distinguishes among persons while uniting them. The reciprocity of consciences and the love emanating from them can save from the "diffluence" which incites and pervades us. We can transform, in fact, at least up to a point, the "qualia" of our nature into qualities expressing our person. The relation to a person reaches its climax when it is the intermingling of two expressive qualities in the same "nous." The communion of the "étants" overflows its interiority and expresses itself in its materiality which becomes a gift to each other.

10. Transformation, however, is not necessarily transfiguration. . . It is inevitable that we transform certain "qualia" of our nature into expressive qualities of our person. This alchemy is inherent in the scope of our creative imagination and our liberty; but we do not necessarily take decisive steps toward ourselves in all our daily actions. The value of our vocation to "ipseity" cannot be ignored; this would lead to the obturation of the con-

sciousness of a transcendental presence which is its source. Certainly the rise of our freedom confirms our origin and its necessity. The same freedom, however, can turn us against ourselves. There is a derived freedom standing against our original freedom. Our self transformation then is no longer the transfiguration of the qualia but the disfiguring of the essence of our person.

Something similar happens in the relation of consciences: creative imagination can produce either a destructive hostility or a humiliating complicity. This is the multiform activity of moral evil. In its most subtle form it is collective escapism of the "soi." It is also a mutual influence, vocal or silent, but verifiable on the scene of the world.

The bad causality, however, has its limits. The metaphysical suicide of the "étants"--"suicide métaphysique"--is impossible, and prevented by their "être" or the primitive relation which both separates and unites them. Their unhappy differences neither destroy that relation or the initial reality which constitutes them as "étants."

What does one do in the effort to reverse the fundamental values or the characteristics of the "étants"? One denies one's unique vocation or helps someone else to do the same; one attempts to create a different "nous." It is a decision at the same time attractive and senseless.

The worst result of the kind of aggressivity trying to destroy the other person is in fact the least dangerous. By definition the "je" of the other person cannot be touched, only its periphery. The soul withdraws and escapes from whatever or whoever kills the body. In fact, the failure of aggressivity is proportional to the horror of the crime. In the case of degrading complicity or of reciprocal permanent hatred the failure is less visible because the soul of the other person is truly influenced. Their causality, however, is not fully intersubjective; they do not reach the core of the soul; they do not establish an absolute negative communion.

First of all, the negative element signifies that the selfish servant of the "moi" and the "toi" never reaches a static goal for an absolute goal cannot be static. The consciousness of the "not yet"--"pas encore"--points to the infinitude which is of the essence of the life of the subject. Furthermore negation can play an opposite role, by allowing the flight of the "étants" or a rebellion against themselves. Such negativism, however, is limited and it shows that in spite of the moral atrocity of human history, the dyadic transformation remains possible. It is the cause and the end of all empirical transformations of all qualities of expression. At the very center of decadence there is a remaining spark; it is indestructible, an act of judgment and hope.

132

11. The form of exteriority which "l'être" imposes on the "étants" and the materiality which burdens the persons before it is eased by their eventual interactions is an invitation to consider negation under a last aspect. We have already discerned in it a limitation of each being in relation to its Creator. Then we saw in it a sign of the indefinite dynamism of these beings, creatures. The same negation is also the factor which allows them to run from each other, fight each other according to the nature of their freedom, making their individual choices, taking their risks. Negation appears now to us as a mediation at the very center of intersubjective causality. The divine creation in us and a fortiori the inter-human influence have a moment of emptiness and annihilation. Of course, nothingness is always in relation to the "étants." The action of the "étant," however, on another "étant" either to bring it into being or to modify it, represents a discreet withdrawal of the cause, which is humbled by its effect. This allows the rise of the other as an antitype of the cause or as a completely new reality. The transitory character of the other, either as a negation or a novelty adds to the problem. This applies to all cases of intersubjective causality whatever the variations of the metaphysical and moral order.

12. The action of an "étant" presupposes also a zero phase--"un passage par le zéro." In that context the analogy of mathematics is relevant. As the zero has no sense in itself although it is present in the arithmetic of numbers, in the same way in the intersubjective tie one finds a kind of void indispensable to the totality of the relation. It is a mark creation puts on the creatures to facilitate their interaction and prevent the confusion of the "étants." It helps the "étants" to surpass communication and it gives nothingness a dignity which is perhaps eternal. The person overcomes the limitations of his nature by the unfolding of the expressive qualities of the "moi" and "toi" and by the growing community of the "nous." Thus, the person finds the way to a communion which brings to maturity the relation to other persons.

Everything is found in the experience of personal causality. It is tragic, since it bears the bitter fruits of a negation. Whoever intervenes brings about a separation of persons, a death in transitory action, a response which might be a rebellion of the effect against the cause. More deeply, however, causality is tied to the survival of the "étants" for it depends on a transcendental communion. It brings potentiality to consciousness, freedom of intervention to the limited range of choices; it gives a glimpse of the indefinitely perfectible synergy of persons through the mutuality of love.

NOTES

1. I expanded on that subject in my book, **Explorations Personnalistes,** Paris, 1970, pp. 85-90. See also **Vers Une Philosophic de L'Amour et de la Personne,** Paris, 1957, pp. 135-145, and **Personne Humaine et Nature,** Paris, 1963, pp. 145-161.

2. Y. Belaval, **Leibniz Critique de Descartes,** Paris, 1960, p. 434.

3. **Eléments de Théologie,** edited by J. Trouillard, Paris, 1965, p. 65.

4. It is not necessary to underline the revolutionary effect of the Christian doctrine of the Trinity on Neoplatonism. For Proclus, causality aims at what is superior and better. It is different from the "causalité cathartique" which frees from the less good (prop. 158); those two causalities are also different--at least logically--from the productive causality, or are only one aspect of the same. Furthermore, for Proclus, it is only the act of the mind which is productive. (prop. 174).

5. We concur here with the ontological argument of Gabriel Marcel and H. de Lubac.

RELIGIOUS PHILOSOPHY

Chapter Thirteen

THE SACRED AND ITS PROFANATION

1. The sense of the sacred arises when the ultimate mystery of our being or that of another person is unveiled to our consciousness. This feeling is like an intuition. There must be a mystery, i.e. a transcendence over phenomena; such transcendence must affect our experience, although it cannot be fully grasped conceptually or explored. The sense of the sacred demands a minimal distance and a paradoxal coincidence; it is like an asymptotic approach when the infinite is on the edge of the finite. The awareness of such a situation, however, occurs like a painful irruption. Something happens to interrupt the monotonous routine of our life. Love, joy, suffering, fear suddenly reveal a new dimension both final and unreachable of what we really are at the deepest level of our experience. The sense of the sacred, psychologically different from ordinary psychism, destroys our tranquility and gives us a perspective which embraces both retrospectively and prospectively our whole psychism. It is like an initiation to a new level of reality which surprises us; we cannot control it, whatever its obvious presence and immediacy. There are many paradoxical elements: innerness and distance, transcendence and immanence, growing approximation and flight toward the infinite, a spark and an inferno, a symbol and a bare reality.

2. The sense of the sacred has this paradoxical trait of being at the same time essentially cognitive and radically non-conceptual.

One might debate that it be intellectual. It is true that a priori it seems to overshadow the mind; indeed, it does at least for all things which are not essential. The confusion it creates, however, by disrupting all superficial normality is the price to pay in order to reach some knowledge of the principle, of "ipseité" (one's selfness). This knowledge seems to be fundamental. It can be compared to the knowledge of a substance deprived of its accidents. The impression of void, however, can be misleading. Accidents are, in fact, examined, since feelings have emerged in connection with some specific event. Accidents are experienced, organized, integrated in a reality which transcends them and at the same time uses them to allow its own presence to be discovered, giving a greater meaning to all fragmentary and common elements.

Maintaining that "ipseité" cannot be verified because it is inexhaustible and structureless; is in fact to suggest that knowledge is nothing but a collection of general concepts without ordering or unity. Is it possible to deny to a study of "ipseité" the category of knowledge, simply because it is not a concept, although it stimulates and organizes related concepts? The knowledge of the individual has something ineffable because the subject cannot be limited, not that its nature is not well defined, on the contrary, its potentiality cannot be contained; the sense of the sacred is the meeting of a being at the deepest level; it immediately leads to a physical and mental behavior which would be inexplicable if it were deprived of cognitive power. The imagination soars to reach the enigma and absorb it in its silence.

3. One of the first results coming from the experience of the sacred is the emergence of many emotions with a dominant connotation of respect. The word itself is incapable of perfectly expressing the meaning intended. It is a respect which combines veneration and enthusiasm; it also expresses surprise and fear of a possible familiarity as if we were facing again a primitive state of being, a synthesis capable of finally reabsorbing the fictitious universe where the "Dasein" had placed us.

Rudolf Otto has sorted out those emotions in the famous formula: "mysterium, tremendum, et fascinosum." It defines less a cause than an effect; less the sacred than a sense of the same, more particularly its irrational aspect which corresponds to a non-cognitive, a priori form. This form should be added to the other a priori forms enumerated by Kant and attached to a "normal rationnel" that it may produce some "idéogrammes." There are, however, some restrictions and a risk of imbalance in Otto's description, which the author himself has recognized. [1]

4. For Otto and Durkheim the notion of sacredness is closely associated to the experience of profanation. However, before we deal with this deterioration of feelings, complicated by a sense of malediction, looked for or endured, we must define a concept of transgression which is more primitve and general than the experience of rebellion. I refer to the transgression of the order or things--"l'ordre phénoménal." The sense of the sacred fascinates and terrifies by what it reveals. It goes beyond the normality of daily life and reaches into an unknown sphere of reality. It is not simply a form of escapism into the invisible; it is a transfiguration of the visible; what is beyond the phenomenon speaks through it without interfering with its course. There is

a transgression of a special kind: a presence of the ultimate in the context of what is relative, a confrontation of the absolute with those conditions which resist it while making its presence possible. Hence, the fascination and fear of a conscience which uses ideas and images to comprehend what is ineffable, transposing in the former what springs from the latter.

5. Two cases, however, should be distinguished, depending on the object of our relationship: our own self or another person. When the conscience suddenly has to face itself not in some kind of projected narcissist image but in its unmasked subjectivity, an intense sense of the sacred arises. There is something almost unbearable in this inner revelation of the divine which transcends our moral and psychological distortions. What dominates this return to this original integrity, however, is not fear but attraction. Whenever this return is perfect--a practical impossibility--the will moves to its center where all psychic states share a common nature, like all waters do when rushing down the same slope.

On the other hand, when the sense of the sacred arises from an encounter with another person or with some infra-personal reality, the revelation is a shock and feelings are often dominated by fear. This fear is before the "mystère ontique" ready to unveil itself. It is like a pure state of the soul; it is metaphysical, not physical. There is no fear of being abused, but fear of discovering what is at the bottom of one's existence and of being swept by the will of the gods. It is not an epidermic suffering, but a kind of intimidation before the fundamental and irreducible strangeness of certain forms of the universe. If curiosity arises, and even subsists, it is never ordinary; it demands heroic efforts. Such feelings can be pathetic when their signification emerges from confrontation with death or some kind of natural catastrophe. The metaphysical experience has then a physical repercussion either of pity or panic. It can also happen that even the perception of the other person be submerged by the threat. The approach of a fast-driven truck, the attack of a wild beast afford very little opportunity for deep introspection, but they immediately release a biological fear: a mortal danger is menacing.

A metaphysical awareness may then develop but it will center around the victim, not the aggression; although it is not always easy to assess the contribution of each to the total experience. Psychological causes can be very complex, depending on the individuals, objects and situations. The revelation of the sacred will vary also with the different areas of concentration.

6. We have spoken, so far, of the sense of the sacred; but what is the nature of the sacred itself, behind that experience?

In a sense the sacred and the "l'en-soi" are one. The

former seems to dwell in the latter, as if it were its very being. This can be explained by the fact that the sense of the sacred is realistic and develops at the priority of its proximity with the noumenal world.

In another sense, however, the sacred is not the person but a challenge to "l'en soi" which never reveals itself perfectly. There is no sacred without a frightening distance although it cannot be truly experienced, as indeed, the distance from a point on an infinite curve to a zero cannot be measured. The sacred is a movement towards "l'en-soi" of the person, it is not "l'en-soi" as such. It is, in fact, a movement or, better, a dual-movement because the approach presupposes a distance.

There would be no sacred, however, if it were not for "l'en-soi" which sparks the intuition whose light can reach out indefinitely. It is the "ipseité"--one's selfness--which reveals to the person his distance from his true self or from those who relate to him. And it is the "ipseité" which tries to bridge that distance. The experience of the sacred enables the individual to transcend himself or to help others in the discovery of their own transcendence. The connotation of the word transcendence here is difficult. It does not refer to an indefinite phenomenal outreach but to the "cause ontique" which makes possible the eternal status of being.

7. Our unique "ipseité" creates our own sacredness; and the sacred expresses to the conscience the perception of its infrangible, original freedom. I cannot escape from the need to be myself, the auto-determination by which I am obliged to create myself freely, is my own destiny. The interrelation between destiny and liberty, whatever the constructive or destructive use of them, remains as long as I exist. The root of my sacredness is to be found in my being conditioned by it. Condemned to be free, we are fascinated by our freedom. We can rest now on nothing but our subjectivity which depends, however, on a power which transcends us, opens to us a mysterious world and carries us away in its orbit, swept by the tide.

Such is our experience of the sacred that when we encounter it in another person the intensity of our perception is renewed and amplified. A positive confrontation then occurs, the two apprehensions of the sacred supporting each other even when at first one experiences distrust. The sacred character of the "we" can be transformed if the encounter of two persons develops along the line of reciprocity and not simply of pure co-existence. A common destiny raises to a higher level the freedom of communication; liberties are two in one.

The development of dyades can manifest, therefore,

a full scale of sacred forms, all very complex as they serve many ends: privacy, conscious coexistence, effective cooperation or love.

8. There is also a sacredness of things quite different from the inner consciousness and free determination which characterize human beings. The "en-soi" of things, however, is sacred by virtue of the purpose which justifies their existence and supports our own sacredness although it remains insensitive to it.

Things are not so much sacred in themselves as by their power to arouse in us the sense of sacredness and free us from the burden of matter.

Although their inner sacredness is minimal it adds to the beauty of things by underlining the way people relate to them. Religion--like poetry--has sacred objects, places, dates, rites, and rhythms which enable adherents to synthesize their creeds and unify their attitudes. In common worship, however, opportunities exist for private interpretations, for the individual mind discovers itself in corporate action. It pulls from its intimate self what is hidden and projects it in symbolic forms. Hence the development of a large collection of evoking pictures, [2] which, at times, can be disturbing when individual intimate forms are dislocated and exaggerated in their external representations. And yet the destiny of a person could not express itself if it were not for the symptomatic and representative character of material things. The network of realities created by space and time brings together in some form of unstructured community those who can communicate and express themselves even if only obliquely.

Finally, the sacredness of material things and that of human beings are more closely related in the infra-human living world as life takes on more and more complex forms. Symbols are more intelligible to us in the animal realm than in the science of geology for we can experience in our humanity part of the animality since man is a superior vertebrate. If the uniqueness of the animal is not entirely intelligible to man it remains, however, an essential part of our being. We disturb it by interferring, we enrich it by transcending it.

9. To understand the "en-soi" of man and what is human leads to a discovery of the sacred in its divine context even before the transcendent God is apprehended. If we recognize, however, that our ultimate destiny depends on the inevitable exercise of our freedom, we concede also that the latter is given to the human creature whose end is in the Creator. Our human condition is both necessary and contingent. We must be contingent and this for two reasons: first, we are not creator but created and, second, we are unfinished, so to speak, undetermined. Within the framework

of our own destiny, our freedom is that of a creature called to re-create itself; therefore, it gives us a limited but real capacity to deny our "self" and in doing so challenge God himself. Hence there appears a form of transgression which is not simply disturbing the realm of phenomena (cf. par. 4) but undermining the original thrust of the noumenal realm.

At that point the sacred becomes an event, a call to metanoia [3] with the risk of option and through the difficulties of a rebellion always possible. In other words the ultimate is finally determined in the drama of a Creator - Creature confrontation. The sacred is then further defined as we relate in our "self" either to God or to Satan. There is a new element of "fascinosum et tremendum" depending on whether we are searching for the ultimate of a demonic relationship or the ultimate of sainthood. The "other" at that point is not simply a created partner, man or thing of a daily experience, it is the frightening face of a transcendent demon or, on the contrary, one image of God which is being imprinted with authenticity upon our personal history.

One of the profound errors of philosophical reasoning on such matters as the "mana" has been to reduce the sacred to some kind of primitive force expressing also the social dimension of the phenomenon. The truth is that the sacred is a gender with many specific differences. We have already distinguished three important ones along the following lines: the call to the ultimate expresses itself as a divine reality which completes the person, or as a demoniac force which is the counterfeit of divine grace, or again as a Saint whose God is Creator and source of grace. In that light, the sacred leads one to adoration, a prayer more intellectual in its form than demonstrative or explanatory.

10. It remains true that sacredness does not exist separately; it depends on the being of a thing or person. Should we say then, as we have tried to show in earlier analysis, that being and sacredness are inseparable because of an essential relationship between the two? There is an "ontique" sacred. Is there an ontological one?

To this question we must answer no--at least a general no. Being per se is not sacred but neutral; as such it is even destructive of sacredness. It is the source of externalization, originality, and univocity before the rise of all other specifications--"Le 'nous' d'avant le 'nous'." All those formulas, which we have coined in the writings we have consecrated to the notion of being, demonstrate that although it has a history being is not by nature independent of other beings. Its instrumentality does not enable it to help us in reaching the absolute. In fact it does the opposite. We would be even tempted to consider it as the source of its own disintegration. To say that, however, could be an exaggeration;

but, on the other hand, one can easily understand the antipathy any emphasis on the power of being may cause in the mind of many religious people. In the God of philosohers they suspect the presence of an ontological God which they oppose to the God of the Revelation.

Heidegger who exalts the concept of Being and subordinates everything to it, is very careful not to identify too quickly being and sacredness or being and deity and whatever our differences I must agree with him on that point.

11. There is, however, an isthmus through which being and sacredness are joined together; this possibility is due to the fact that the being expresses a dimension of infinite which is inalienable. We are subjected to a relation of externalization which we try in vain to overcome. Precisely because of its insurmountability this dimension belongs to the "ipseité" which is constitutive of sacredness. It is not, of course, a positive component of our "ipseité" but the sign of a natural deficiency which is always present and rules out any identification of the created with the uncreated God.

12. Does that mean that all "interontique" relations between persons are conditioned by the being itself and cannot escape from its mediation? No, we do not believe in such assumption. There are privileged moments when the communion of two persons is absolute. There are instants of grace when sensitivity to the sacred is more intense and really fulfilled. They do not free us, however, from our ontological condition; and this for two reasons: first, because they represent a point of arrival possible by overcoming an initial separation, they are not a point of departure; second, separation is overcome only temporarily before communion is brought down again to the simple level of communication.

A similar observation could be made of the "ontique" relation of the "I" to itself; for there is also communion and communication in our inner personal life; they constitute an "interontique" relation which brings us into contact with our Creator. Intimacy is never isolated, but rather inhabited, so to speak,-- "peuplée"--and in relation to its transcendent principle. Communion of man with God, like relationships within the human community, falls back, even more than the latter, into a form of communication. And yet our communion with God, which is essential to our consciousness, benefits each time from the light which causes those privileged moments of communion with divine grace.

13. Nevertheless, it remains true that being reborn in and through the self is a necessary condition. It reminds human beings of their createdness. It marks the time of creation. It

determines the continuing condition of being created; it is the witness and even the herald of our dependency on God. This dependency is natural; it is radical and complete, although not final. We receive from God the possibility of personal autonomy and interpersonal communion without the ability to identify autonomy and independence or intermittent communion with the "<u>circumincession</u>" of the divine Persons. Thus, the being remains the primary relation between created persons. It conditions them while remaining their inferior; it prepares the levelling of "<u>ontique</u>" and "<u>interontique</u>" relations which give it its ultimate meaning.

The person, therefore, lives on two levels: the level of being, which is the most intimate and final, and the level of becoming which occurs at the time of our metaphysical beginning and of our chronological renewals.

14. The series of relations which constitutes the history of beings is not limited to an immanent activity. The external relation multiplies and reaches out in outer contacts which are in harmony with the inner experience of the individual. We pass from an essential presence to an existential representation, to an idea of the being which cannot be identified with its action but is rather a product or emanation of its presence.

We should not be surprised, therefore, to see our faculty of comprehension extending the notions of being, coordinating them and at the same time evading systematically the conditions of existence. By doing so, the ontological understanding of the notion of being does not serve the sacred but rather profanes it. Neglect here is a form of profanation. The success of a profane representation of the world is both undeniable and superficial. Sophisticated minds are not satisfied by the exercise of incorporating the experience of man into a larger organization of things, depriving its original "<u>phénoménalité</u>" of the "<u>noumenal</u>" dimension and reducing it to a simple flux of existence without ultimate meaning. The objectivity of scientific and philosophical knowledge would be too limited; a perspective which can be accepted only by superficial minds. It would become what Pascal calls a "<u>divertissement</u>"; or "<u>fascinatio nugacitatis</u>" which covers all the ground from superficiality to illusions and perversity.

15. Language itself is an example of that form of escapism. The simple fact of referring by name to the sacred is a form of desecration; in the same manner, profanation may initiate a long development of what we call profane. As we identify a mystery we circumscribe it, reducing it to those external aspects we can verify, using concepts and terms of reference easily classified and exploited.

A concept, indeed, can be open to modifications by new

experiences; for it remains flexible. One could not deny, of course, the value of a general knowledge which helps in defining things; the common traits of things are as important as their singularity. When a concept, however, is intended to define living persons it betrays them, transforming them more or less into things or by-products of their ideal essence. Consequently to speak of a concept of sacredness is like alienating oneself from the sacred, at least when the sacred is a call to "ipseité" and when the sense of the former is an answer to the latter. By mentioning the sacred by name I vulgarize it; I manipulate it; which cannot be done without depriving it of its "specificité."

We have already assimilated the sacred to a gender with specifications (§ 9). It must be understood, however, that we have here a word which has been affected by a common usage. In reality the sacred is not per se a type of being like the physical components of a human being; it is rather a universal disposition (although not general) which is found in each being in a unique fashion.

16. The profane is not purely receptive; it does not precede reflection and free decision. The example of the child is clear. The child receives his language either from his bio-social nature (assuming the existence of innate linguistic patterns) or from his environment (which creates in the child the properly conditioned reflexes which partly constitute and determine most of the spoken language forms).

There is, therefore, an innocent earthliness--"profanité innocente--which has nothing to do with a determination to avoid a vision of the absolute. The need for renewal of our being (§ 12) is neither an actual sin nor an original sin, but it demands to be objectified. Language is the best instrument of this process. It plays the role of a spring-board; it is propaedeutic with a peda-gogical value in the development of the personality. [4]

Even if we are not responsible for its profanity and do not exercise the role of desecrator, profanity, however, is submitted to our reflexive consciousness which examines the nature and outcome of its spontaneity. Our ability to reflect--at the level of theory and practicality alike--cannot address itself to the problem of profanity without examining the corollary problem of desecration. Reflection itself changes as its exercise unfolds, looking into the sacredness of its object without relating it to the source of its own object, without relating it to the source of its own activity. The process can be frightening. The first innocent injury gradually becomes aware of a distance and obstruction which already consti-tutes a form of profanation. The philosophy of language and thought is now, willingly or not, a religious philosophy.

17. Everything we have said so far leads us to recognize

the axiomatic ambiguity of being, understanding and speech. All tend to desecrate, which allows one to manipulate them without rejection; in other words to use them for the "re-sacralization" of personal life"--"resacraliser la vie personnelle"--and integrate them to a motion they first ignore or oppose. In this context Heraclitus' words are verified: whatever fights against itself can also reach harmony, like the "harmonie palintrope" of the arc or lyre without the free thrust which affects understanding and language; for in them, finally, the dialectic of sacredness and profanity unfolds.

18. What we have described as profane is only part of our understanding. Dealing with language it would be convenient to classify profanity and prose together, and sacredness with poetry. But this would be an oversimplification and a certain misconception of literary forms. What we call prose can lead to the discovery of the sacred particularly in the realm of things; science may end in a form of ecstasy, for there is sacredness in truth and its conceptual expression. And as far as poetry is concerned it may be better fitted to convey sacredness because of its focus on the ultimate. It runs the risk, however, of worshipping only the echo of one's own voice, creating by so doing the worst form of desecration, the kind which hides under the cult of words and superficial emotion by taking the chaff of words for the grain of reality.

In fact, there are two possible directions for conceptual thought and language--the latter often initiating as well as expressing the former; but it is not necessary to label them prose and poetry. Whatever the name we give them let us say that one contributes to an objective organization of phenomenon and the other leads to the recognition by imperfect symbols of the call to sacredness identifiable in the various phenomena.

19. Let us underline a specific point related to the role of language. We have assumed that language desecrates the sacred by naming it. (§ 15) It does that very thing, however, only in part; and there is a counterpart. The naming of the sacred is heuristic and spell-like; it helps to receive the action of the inner power which is at the center of all reality and express our reaction to it. This function, which acts in the unfolding of sentences, is admirable provided that it becomes humble before the Logos and gropingly makes an effort to join and speak in our own "logoi."

This perspicacious fidelity, however, is not always guaranteed. Our response is pretentious and magic when it tries to penetrate the absolute by virtue of a simple formula. At that moment the concept is paralyzed and the language becomes the desecrator; the sense of the sacred is hypertrophied and sickly when we attempt to subject the sacred to the phenomenality of the object in order to satisfy the selfish interest of the subject. A process which is unthinkable.

The "sacralization" process is then affected in two different ways. On the one hand it distorts the "Logos" degrading it to the level of "muthos." On the other hand it gives to language the dimension of an absolute which makes of it an idol. The magician with his tricks is a convincing example of that transformation. The writer, the poet, the philosopher and their free creations are no less exposed to such linguistic profanation as they idolize their thought and meditation. "Homo loquax, homo mendax." A constant difficulty is to trace the boundaries between the awareness of ontic sacredness and all verbal expression of an illusion of the same.

In the absence of "l'étant," therefore, as in its presence, the human adventure never enjoys final security; this is, of course, the price of freedom and personal temporality. There are no exceptions to that rule, not even for the man of action. The "causes sacrées" are in the lives of individuals and groups, a mixture of authentic revelations experienced in the "en-soi" and of inconsistent fictions or even dangerous constructions of our own making.

20. Sacredness has a real value and is discovered in different ways and forms in the three ultimate realities: beauty, truth and goodness. The concept of ultimate value, however, could be self contradictory if what is ultimate is not the value examined but "l'étant" itself. Would not such a contradiction be the worst of all profanations and illusions? Its danger would be to simplify or prevent the identification of authentic values, to give an absolute character to what is only partial in goodness and reality.

All those objections are not equally valid. Sacredness is the first and highest in the hierarchy of all values. Its ultimate value, however, should not be understood as that of the "étant" but a call to the latter to assume its imminence in the consciousness of the individual.

One should maintain, furthermore, the concept of the ultimate value of sacredness and other participating values that facilitate the act through which we seek other "étants" and relate to them. Nothing else goes deeper to the heart of reality.

Finally, at the apex of our experience of human sacredness, once we have overcome the false sacredness of the demonic, we encounter that sacredness which comes from God. The fact that the experience of sacredness might appear as a disintegration of the faith in the Person of God does not prevent, in fact, our spiritual ascent to Him. There is no final symbol of eternal life but sacredness shows the presence of the absolute at the center

148

of our freedom if there is a Creator of our liberties and a community of persons.

NOTES

1. See Otto's conversation with J. Hesson, **Religionsphilosophie,** Munich, 1955, vol. I, p. 228. He is far more in the tradition of St. Augustine than of the school of Kant.

2. Cf. A. Farrer, **The Glass of Vision,** London, 1958, and M. Eliade, **Le Sacré et le Profane,** Paris, 1965. Imagination is the individual way of expressing and anticipating human experience. It has three constituting elements: the individual, the conservation of experience (material and intellectual) and the imaginative content. Its function is to create images which preserve an experience. These images can become more universal and circulate from individual to individual giving them the possibility of interrelating more creatively.

3. See E. Castelli, **Langage Théologique et Langage Sacral,** introduction to the Colloque romain sur le sacré, 1974.

4. Another form of "profanité innocente" may come from reserve or modesty which is the respect for privacy where the sacred resides. To avoid profanation, modesty often invents alibis for a "profanité par ,diversion," such as humor and other means to keep the sacred object at a respectable distance. In that case profanity itself can be an homage to the sacred, protecting its rights and constitution, the only noble form of secularization. In social contracts it is a sign of charity, respecting the sacredness of the other person and protecting him from contempt. It would deserve a special psychological and historical study for it is quite different from both the "divertissement," condemned by Pascal and the "néo-barbare secularism."

Chapter Fourteen

INSPIRATION AND TRANSCENDENCE

Artistic Inspiration
As A Path Toward Transcendence

1. Whether in literature, music, or the plastic arts, inspiration has been considered as a visitation of a divinity or of a superior power. This is almost a constant of history. Religions have viewed it as a phenomenon of possession: the enthusiast is, according to etymology, one who has a god within. Philosophers since Plato have more than once identified this possession with divine or demonic delirium. In Greco-Roman antiquity, the muses were charged with giving and even with dictating to the inspired the substance of his work.

To all these external testimonies is added--and this is more important--the conviction of the great artists themselves. It would be easy to collect texts to show that they have generally attributed the better part of their work to a source quite other than their own efforts. They have been conscious of having received a gift in privileged moments. Baudelaire aptly describes what he felt at such times and what pulled him out of himself, so to speak, while contributing an unusual efflorescence to or transforming his personality. Speaking of inspiration, he declares: " . . . I prefer to consider this abnormal condition of the spirit as a true grace . . . a sort of angelic exaltation, a call to transformation . . . This marvelous state has no precursory symptoms." It is "an intermittent obsession . . . from which we should draw . . . the certitude of a better existence." [1]

This description is sufficiently valid for the different species of "possessed," among whom certain authors include the "prophets," "the obsessed," the "automatics" (referring in the last case to the surrealists). [2]

2. The "possessed" are not, of course, the only type of artist. There are also workers or artisans who labor patiently

149

and without sudden or repeated illumination. [3] But we might ask if these two types do not really reveal certain predominant characteristics which never exist in complete isolation. In every real artist, there exists a spark and an anvil: sometimes the spark leaps at once; at other times, vigorous pounding of the anvil makes it leap forth. The role of work is enormous in the conception, organization, execution, and communication of the work, but the declaration of Paul Valéry expresses the proportions: the gods give us the first verse and it is we who make the second. Or rather, in the phases enumerated above, there is an instant when the two factors appear to combine--the acceptance of the gift and its active expression. Often enough, the whole expressive effort even appears to consist in trying to recapture the initial or superior gift, so that the greatest expenditure of energy, far from diminishing the gift, only makes more evident the necessity of its stimulation.

3. This perceived duality is mysterious. Thus, we should not be surprised if certain minds are impelled to reject it. They attempt to reduce inspiration to what it is not. This can be done in several different ways: biologists have proposed chromosomes, sociologists, collective influence. Both thus attempt a deeper exploration of the notion of the unconscious proposed by psychologists. Structuralists, of course, rely on a philosophy of language, in their effort at definitive liquidation of the subject and its guardian angels, in order to give formal explanation of the genesis of a work.

4. All of this has become commonplace; a few examples will be enough. Roland Barthes, anxious to establish a positivist position delivered from the celestial visitations dear to the classics and the transcendent self dear to the romantics, would like to view inspiration as mere performance. The artist represents the dramatic interplay of several harmonious forces: his inspiration is nothing more than the success of this interplay and his work is the ultimately-accidental prowess of a well-situated performer provided with good feed-back.

Unfortunately, Barthes' structural analyses leave him defenseless before the question of ultimate meaning or even the relationship of various meanings. When the linguistic schemas of Barthes, the theoretician, give way to the spontaneity of the literary critic, his judgments impress us as picturesque, but arbitrary; his soundings are penetrating, but miss the mark.

But there is a more serious and fundamental objection. This manner of conceiving inspiration explains nothing. In proposing the idea of performance, one rules out recourse to all non-quantitative criteria. All complexity is successful, in so far as the harmony of empiric forces henceforth has the right to be labeled a work of art. This view leads to a disastrous equating of the sublime and the mediocre.

Certainly, consonantia is one of Saint Thomas' signs of the beautiful; and "maximum unity in the maximum truth," has rallied many votes since neoplatonism. But we lose interest in the quantitative wrappings of such formulas, once we prescind from the judgment of taste which supports them. We appreciate the fact that a clever pedagogue might be able to dissect a classical tragedy and aid us to understand its coherent multiplicity. But if his notion of coherence or of harmony is devoid of lived experience and lacks a consequent scale of values, what is to make the **Britannicus** of Racine superior to Feydeau's **Fil à la patte**? Who knows whether or not Feydeau's vaudeville has not a more unified complexity than Racine's play? Unitas multiplex is aesthetically valuable only if evaluation of the quantitative depends upon evaluation of the qualitative. André Malraux rightly insists that art begins with quality.

5. Analogous remarks could be made about other attempts at reductionism. The Marxists willing to reflect on this question become more and more aware of the chasm between the infrastructure of society and the creative power of the artist; they should abandon the attempt to specify, whether in theory or practice, the link between the inspired individual and the collectivity. For example, in associating the tragic vision of Pascal with vexation of the nobility of the long robe in the seventeenth century, they are thwarted by the fact that the same nobility of the long robe was represented among the Jesuits, among the freethinkers, and indeed among the Jansenists. But there is only one Pascal.

Freud himself admits the limits of his explanation in terms of the unconscious when he writes: "The artist is originally a man who turns from reality because he cannot come to terms with the demand for renunciation of instinctual satisfaction . . . But he finds a way of returning from this world of phantasies back to reality; with his special gift, he molds his phantasies into a new kind of reality . . . " [4] This gift is thus "special." The adjective inserted in the phrase in passing attests to the fact that reductive analyses, no matter how ingenious or plausible, leave something unexplained and that this residual element may well be the principle element of the phenomenon to be observed.

Let us return to this double evidence: on the one hand, all that is large and new is explainable only by itself and does not yield adequate understanding through analysis; on the other hand, inspired authors do not have the impression that they owe their success to a sub-conscious, but to a sort of extra-conscious or supra-conscious. They are right! To appeal to subconscious maturity is to concur in an explanation which is too convenient not to be suspect; it confuses the introduction with the synthetic conclusion. Properly speaking, the work is conceived in the light, even if it is executed in shadow.

6. Charles du Bos was interested in this unexplained residual element and it set him on the road to an ontological transcendence. Poetry cannot be reduced to a poem: the mystery of inspiration cannot be denied on the pretext that it is the mechanism of expression. The failure of reductionists lies not only in the fact that there is a oneness of work and author, a residual originality proposed to our value judgment. An additional fact: the residue is fecund, the source of an indefinitely creative surge. Du Bos estimates that it is impossible to explain the more by the less and he grasps in this more the presence of still something more.

Where does this something more come from? It all happens as if the artist and his work have been swept by a breeze; he knows neither whence it cometh nor whither it goeth. It clearly does not depend on laborious means or on exterior influences which are the condition of aesthetic victory, not its cause, and which supply the matter, not a form.

The need to recognize the influx of a force superior to empirical individuality or collectivity is particularly striking in the category which du Bos calls "spiritual" and distinguishes from the "sublime." The spiritual is commencement; it is less a state than a gift; we find it, for example, in a Shelley or a Wordsworth. The sublime is a state or a climate; it results from a concentration or an elevation by which the artist poises himself at the summit of himself, so to speak, and in which we are led to this height. Milton is sublime rather than spiritual. "In my view," writes du Bos, "spirituality is situated at the beginning, at the point of origin: we certainly do not move toward it, we flow from it; current or source, we surrender it passage." [5]

Some receive the spiritual element at birth; others, the more usual case, are in this respect twice-born or, as Wordsworth, acquiesce to it by the counter-shock of nature on their spirit. But whatever the mode of approach, a grace has come; it is fundamentally the effort itself, if there is effort; and it is distinguished from the grace of the sublime, because the artist is at the disposition of, and his work open to, something infinite.

7. From the problem of inspiration, we are led to the problem of genius. Du Bos was haunted by this problem. The greater the discrepancy between the work and the man, the more enigmatic the presence of genius. A genius is often one in spite of himself, which is even more astonishing. Another consideration: the more original his genius, the more aware we are of the man's inadequacies

by comparison. "The completely original being always elicits in us the idea of someone greater than himself, because he does not exhaust his ideas, his archetype, in the Platonic sense of the term." [6] His maximal value demands maximal transcendence. Charles du Bos is so convinced of the validity of this position that he sees behind the mystery of genius nothing short of the mystery of God. The spectacle of genius seems to him so richly instructive that he assigns it a more important role in his religious conversion than he gives to moral meditation. In the exceptional gifts of the spirit, he perceives the visitation of the divine Spirit.

It matters little to him that great men are sometimes self-proclaimed atheists. The great atheist offers almost a greater occasion for the theistic argument than the mediocre believer. The presence of genius is indeed less static than active, and if we eliminate God, we deprive ourselves of "the first element of a satisfactory explanation," for inspiration. [7]

Once aware of this line of thought, du Bos does not hesitate to affirm that genius turns, objectively and without assistance, toward God. Later he would nuance his induction: he would adapt it, he would complete it, but the argument would remain. Keats serves as an example: "Keats the genius, was always slightly dominated by Keats the man: the latter was in a position of transcendence with respect to the former." [8] Had he not died young, what contribution might the flowering of his genius have made to the flowering of his humanity? Would he have given back his very genius to God? Du Bos believes so. But, whatever the value of this conjecture, we still glimpse a sort of parting of the ways in the path toward God, then the possibility of a juncture of the two paths; the logic of free existence competes with the logic imposed by the call of genius, and both surge forward together toward personal destiny.

8. Thus there is a religious end to a journey which began for our author with worship of the soul, with worship of a deus of the self, superior to the disparate selves. Unlike the restriction of the latter, this deus is an energy which constantly rejuvenates us without inhibiting us. But what is its nature? "Is it truly God or someone or something other?" [9] To clear up this uncertainty, let us recall that du Bos was helped by his reflection on genial inspiration. He gave art the exalted mission of expanding the consciousness of life and his reflection on art led him to discover the divine source of this consciousness. The divinity he encountered was truly a transcendent God.

9. He reached this peak, of course, by several lines of research. The one we have just examined with him may appear too rapid and too ambitious to demanding philosophers. Therefore, it may be useful to repeat the process in an effort to control the stages of his progress from beginning to end.

Charles du Bos' initial astonishment derives from the fact that the generative emotion of the work of art can be translated into an adequate form. We notice this, for example, in the paintings of a Giorgione. Another point of departure which is less interior, but still comparable to the one above, is offered by Malraux: he makes art not the copy of natural forms or existing models, but the transformation of such forms and models into a style. Of Romanesque architecture, he says: "it is defined by what it contributes, not by what it copies." This remark is valuable for all creation: art is "that by which forms become style"; it is essentially stylization and is irreducible to the real world; it is "fascination with the ungraspable." [10]

Thus the artist has the power to transform by structuring or to structure by transforming; and we should not forget that this involves some sort of figurative change; the transformation is not unimportant; it occurs at the interior of a specific world, the world of aesthetic values. The question now is to discover the origin of this creative power and the beauty which is its object or result.

10. Camus would reply that the man of genius is a revolutionary who creates his own standards. And the Italian philosopher, Luigi Pareyson, would explain his remarkable theory of "formation," by which he understands that art is a "making" which in the making, "invents at the same time the manner of making." More than the other formative activities of man, art supposes both the invention of the thing it produces and its compatible laws. [11]

But such descriptions, pertinent though they may be in their own order, do nothing to advance our quest. Whence comes creative power? The question arises again. And once again let us listen to André Malraux on the subject. He discerns a metaphysical question behind the aesthetic one which suddenly enlarges the perspective: "The greatest mystery is not that we have been tossed by chance in between the profusion of matter and myriad stars, but that, in this prison, we pull out of ourselves images powerful enough to deny our nothingness." [12]

The phenomena of the sensible or intellectual world are the curtain over a more profound reality. But do the meanings which the artist discerns in or imposes on the phenomena raise the curtain? Or rather do such meanings depend on a negative ontology," are they all sorts of incantations uttered as one circles around an insurmountable obstacle? Many questions at once arise about the truth-function of art, about the compatibility or incompatibility of art to concepts, and even the inert or active character of the being which art reveals! If we consult contemporary philosophers, we rapidly discover that they fall into opposing schools, even if they do agree to admit that there is something beyond appearances.

11. If they will go beyond apophaticism, some will see in the creative surge--which is always supported by something material--a participation in the vital dynamism of active nature (natura naturans). This was the attitude of Schiller, the German poet. He extolled the "naiveté" of genius and said that genial "inspirations are the inspirations of a God (all that constitutes sound nature is divine), its sentiments are laws for all time and for all sorts of men." The expressions of genius, characterized by the perfect disappearance of the sign in what it signifies, are "divine oracles in the mouth of a child." [13]

Gratuitousness and transcendence are affirmed, and the universal scope of art is clearly seen as the result of its superior origin. The plurality of styles and the hermeneutic distance not withstanding, the genius of Homer lies in the fact that he has survived the packing and unpacking of cultural baggage throughout space and time. But if the divine elevation of Schiller is not the absolute transcendence of a non-cosmic God; nevertheless, it allows the genius to experience a personal awareness of a mystery.

The poetry which he calls "sentimental" or modern is a retreat toward original naiveté. Whatever Heidegger may perhaps think, Schiller is indeed not very far from Holderlin and from Heidegger himself for whom the "care" of the poet "remains near the lack of god, without fearing the appearance of the absence of god, until from the region of the missing god, the inaugural word, which designates the Lofty One, may be granted." [14]

12. Continuing our rapid inspection of certain characteristic positions, we may now turn toward a more convinced partisan of divine transcendence: Etienne Souriau.

He first asks us to distinguish two aspects of inspiration which are inaccurately confused in the same word. On the one hand, there is "the orientation or active setting up of the dynamic alignment toward the given realities of another mode of existence"; on the other hand, there is "the strengthening or dynamogenic surge that prolongs the efficacy of the initiating process." [15]

In simpler terms, let us say that there is, on one side, the call of the work, which rouses and guides the operative contribution of the artist; on the other, there is the contribution itself.

Souriau conceives of the work as an autonomous being which tends toward existence and orients the soul. It is a call to us from the gods. The operative contribution itself comes from an interior influx; it is not transcendent, it has its origin in what the author nicely calls an "anaphora" or a "sudden and oblationary elevation of our powers to put us at the service of what calls us." [16]

Some artists experience the unity of self: they are the "demonics," in Goethe's sense; they are exposed to a dangerous enthusiasm which makes them accept their initial reaction to the call as valid, as if an exterior agent superseded them. At the opposite extreme, the hard-working individuals sense their disunity and do not feel their anaphora. But these differences are only psychological and do not affect the fundamental problem of inspiration, which is one of access to a supra-existence.

For Etienne Souriau, there is an "angel of the work" and "the worst has his angel as well as the best." We have plenty of souls--and plenty of work--which are virtual. However, it is in the direction of "the angel" (I was about to say "good angel") that we must look for a "shadow of God," if not God himself. The orientation is not properly speaking a direct revelation of God: the sublimity of the supra-experience which awakens our soul, through the work, remains, in many respects, an enigma. But it is a quasi-intuition of a divine will. The call which orients us is an echo of a transcendent world which offers a presentiment of God. Above all, God is in the harmony of the call and of the anaphora; and we ourselves can be the shadow of God when we help in the initiation of others.

What God is thus presented to us? He certainly differs entirely from the god of Romantic vitalism, he is the Other who questions us. "God questions--God is the question--and man makes himself the answer. Man is according to his response." [17]

Sublimity is the criterion of the orientation. "But did not one man write the **Vita nova**, another paint the Man in a Helmet, another jot down the notes of the String Quintet in E Flat? Even lacking other proof, these facts are so obvious that they already show that the sublime life is possible." [18]

The paths to transcendence, and finally to God, are many and inspiration furnishes one without excluding others--on these points Souriau and du Bos express agreement. Their destination is almost the same: a transcendent God who is a veiled God. The meditation of Charles du Bos on art, or more precisely his reflection on the origin of genius, leads him to a theism which is perhaps clearer than Souriau's. But we must not forget that he found in this theism only a temporary haven and that he perceived that a pure theism, one dissociated from its historical tenets and props, would have been somewhat fragile or artificial. [19] He was finally converted to Catholicism by the supernatural revelation of God in the Christ.

13. Artistic inspiration is not the Transcendent, it is only a path toward Him. Why then is the end of the voyage shrouded in mist? Why does God remain veiled? This is Bremond's problem

in **Prayer and Poetry.** Limiting himself to poetry and referring to the experience of the mystics as a term of comparison, Bremond resolves the question in many ways.

He believes that poetry is a grace and that it tends by its essence toward prayer. But the poet wishes to communicate his experience and has the gift to do it; unfortunately, this is not true of the mystic. The poet speaks; the mystic is silent. The poet is even impelled to speak, he needs an audience. Haste and vanity, which he more or less admits, keep him on the surface of his experience. "However, to pass through the living and hidden God is to enter into the mystical order, to accept detachment, the night of the sense and of the understanding, the gratuitous initiative of the heavenly Father, the docile response to the grace of charity, the actual union of our will to the divine will." Lacking this, the poet can even block mystical experience and use his gifts to hold God in check. The poet, if he is not a St. John of the Cross, is a living paradox: his prayer does not pray, but it stimulates prayer.

While writing a penetrating article on this subject dedicated to Bremond, Gabriel Germain also interviewed Raïssa Maritain, for whom poetry has a nature and laws of its own. The knowledge which poetry yields is imparted in the joy of creating new forms and touches the world rather than God himself; the mystic, on the contrary, touches the uncreated Abyss and rests in supernatural attachment to God. [20]

Finally, we should emphasize the calculus of operations which poetic expression demands. The artist has a technique, he ought to be skilled at construction and his construction risks erecting a screen between himself and God. This idea is already in Bremond. Nevertheless, I do not believe that expression of itself degrades intuition: such occurs only in the degree to which we yield to the temptation to adore the work of our hands. This is the most common and most irreligious form of the secularizing movement.

14. After this panoramic view, it is time to draw some conclusions.

The transcendence of inspiration involves the human subject, that is to say, first the creator, then the spectator, and then the critic of the work.

It also involves the object of artistic intentionality, that is to say, above all the work to be accomplished or the accomplished work: poem, symphony, picture, etc. . . and, indirectly, previous works which were provocative or served the artist as models.

Finally, it involves the world of aesthetic values, that is to say, especially beauty and her cortege of gracious and sublime values, then counter-values (ugliness, for example), and then annexed values, whether incorporated or associated (for example, the true, the good, the sacred which, in a certain sense, penetrate and dominate all values).

What do these transcendencies signify? What binds them together? In what order do they make their appearance and adjust to the new situation?

15. It all begins in the _aura_ of aesthetic values. They precede us and accompany us like a cloud exuded by the sacred. This mist has many elements and various densities, as already suggested. A Viennese waltz, a popular song, an oratorio of Handel do not have us breathe the same air. The sacred itself is a genus which unveils for us something beyond appearances and its extreme species go either to God or to the devil. But it is still God who attracts and dominates the full range. Let us define our thesis without further delay: without a supreme incorporation of beauty in the divine sacred, there would be neither creation nor aesthetic contemplation, and inspiration would remain entirely inexplicable. Not only would it be inexplicable, because it would not imly a sufficient reason, but it would be neither comprehensible to nor affirmable by our reflective consciousness.

The supreme aesthetic value precedes and conditions artistic development, even when art claims to oppose it; for art cannot do without it. Again the supreme aesthetic value stimulates and is present during the formation of the work. Present in the spectator as it was in the creator, this value will ultimately judge the work. The hermeneutic destiny of the work of art remains under its influence and that is why aesthetic criticism can and should be, as du Bos said, a creation in a creation. The hidden God who is the alpha is also the omega of the history of art: inspiration has an eschatological aspect, under various names it runs through the temporal series of participants who will be eternally submitted to the Last Judgment of Value.

16. This Value remains a hidden God for reasons which we have remarked above. (§ 13) But we can add another: God veils himself, because he only reveals himself to the artist in the call of the work. He shows himself to the artist only through this narrow channel. What indeed is a work? It is a creature which struggles to become a quasi-personal center. Like an unexpressed and autonomous monad, it crystallizes in its singularity a universalizing emotion and thought. A tragedy of Sophocles, a Bach fugue, a cathedral are essences worthy of existing as thinking and acting substances. But the artist, not being God, is only a procreator and he does not produce the animation which would detach his

children from himself. He is only inspired, not a creator ex nihilo, and he cannot meet God without a veil, just as he cannot establish the essence of his creatures in the plenitude of an autonomous or super-existence.

17. We should also understand that inspiration assists human subjects to go beyond themselves. While he is concentrating on the projected work he wishes to execute, the artist transforms his own being and is shaped in his turn by the work. The same must be said of those who contemplate and critique (in the noble sense of the term) his work.

However, this transcendence will also be specified and limited. For the work is a presence which offers itself, but promises nothing. Up to a certain point, it can wash a guilty soul of its stains, but it cannot efficaciously sustain its moral combat. It can be a path toward transcendence, but it cannot incorporate us into God himself. This explains the vast difference between the biography of a man as a man, and of a man as an artist.

Inspiration is an episode in personal development. It proves that one consciousness can awaken another, because art achieves inter-human communication. But inspiration also reveals a further development of consciousness; one which it owed to the work itself and which is a presentiment not merely of some limited liberating influence, but of a radical and divine impregnation.

Yet the impurity of inspiration is a fact. The greatest genius is not apt to receive infinite genius and he is apt to degrade his genius. The artist always lives in the shadow of a divine Value, a Value which is also immanent in him in proportion to his genius; but it is he who selects and determines both the degree and the form of the transformation which will affect his being, his work, and his values. [21] Thus, there will be an interdependence of these three transcendencies which he achieves: they will rise or fall together and the distinguishing characteristics of each will have repercussions on the others.

NOTES

1. Cited by G. Maire, **Les instants privilégiés**, Paris, 1962, p. 13.

2. R. Wellek and A. Warren, **Theory of Literature**, New York, 1956, p. 84ff.

3. An ample collection of testimony concerning the two types of artists is assembled in J. Berthelemy, **Traité d'esthétique**, Paris, 1964, pp. 95-130.

4. Cited by Wellek and Warren, op. cit., p. 82.

5. Charles Du Bos, **Du spirituel dans l'ordre littéraire**, Paris, 1967, pp. 7, 19. He applies the same type of reflection to art, the soul, and analogically to the words of Christ in the Gospel. See, among other texts, his **Journal** II, Paris, 1949, p. 211; VI, 1965, p. 167.

6. Ibid., **Journal** V, 1954, p. 203. Of course, the notion of genius will be demolished and vanish as does the notion of author from the theory of contemporary a-literature. Michel Foucault, during a meeting of the Societé Française de Philosophie, 22 February 1969, explained the criticism which dissolves the bond of appropriation and the attribution of the work to one individual whom we call the author . . . If one accepts such a perspective, is it not contradictory to propose a work as one's own? One does not really eliminate the personal subject: it retreats to remain itself in the discourse in which it pretends to deny itself.

7. Du Bos, **Du spirituel**, op. cit., pp. 16-17.

8. **Journal** VII, 1957, p. 74.

9. Ibid., II, 1948, p. 370.

10. J. Hoffman, **L'humanisme de Malraux**, Paris, 1963, pp. 314-320.

11. L. Pareyson, **Estetica, teoria della formatività**, Torino, 1954. See also the pages of Guzzo on poiein and prattein in his work **L'Arte**, 1, Torino, 1962, pp. CLVII ff.

12. J. Hoffman, op. cit., p. 377.

13. Schiller, **Poésie naïve et sentimentale**, trans. P. Laroux, Paris, 1947, pp. 83-87.

14. Cited by O. Poggeler, **La pensée de Martin Heidegger, un cheminement vers l'être**, trans. M. Simon, Paris, 1967, p. 299.

15. E. Souriau, **L'ombre de Dieu**, Paris, 1955, p. 261.

16. Ibid., p. 262.

17. Ibid., p. 333, 298, 319, 351.

18. Ibid., p. 372.

19. It would be interesting to single out in du Bos and Souriau similar experiences expressed in different words. Du Bos distinguishes "l'exaltation" (in the etymological sense of the term) from "l'élan" (which is a concomitant psychologi-

cal phenomenon without any ontological ramification). Souriau would surely see in the exaltation of du Bos both "orientation" and "anaphora"; he would call "enthusiasm" what Du Bos called "élan."

Another apparent difference in their basic agreement: "sublime" in Souriau is homologous to "spirituel" in du Bos.

20. **Entretiens sur H. Bremont,** under the direction of J. Dagens and M. Nédoncelle, Paris-La Haye, 1967, pp. 197, 202.

21. All value is perceived through evaluation and in the process of execution. Our achievements mirror our values without affecting the ontological foundation of ultimate Value, whether we act in concurrence with or in opposition to such Value. There are no values without a relation between beings and between beings and being, but there is diversity and a scale of values.

Chapter Fifteen

AMBIGUITIES IN RELIGIOUS LANGUAGE[*]

The Idea of Event and Time
In Religious Language: Some Ambiguities

The following analysis is concerned with the religious language most familiar to us, that of the Catholic Church. The first part will attempt to underline the most obvious ambiguities of this language from a phenomenological point of view. The second part will shed light on our previous reflection by means of examples drawn from common religious language, that of such prayers as the Our Father and the Creed. Finally, the third part will be devoted to the fundamental problems which surfaced during our reflections on these ambiguities.

I

I. Event

The principal meanings of event (in French événement) are as follows:

  a) a happening;

  b) among happenings, those which are apparent and are noticed;

  c) among those which are noticed, those which are noteworthy; that is to say, historically important.

Obviously, none of us can claim to know every event in sense "a" or even in sense "b."

---

[*]   Translated by Patrick T. Brannan

We should be modest as we use it in sense "c." Not only are the nature and significance of historical events relative, from the historian's viewpoint, but the mere act of singling out and isolating a dynamic event, as if it were a static fact, reveals the choice of a perspective and the risk of inaccuracy or extrapolation.

Theology of history chooses its perspective from revelation and faith. We should venture forth modestly, not remain mute, and there is great risk when God speaks. Everyone should take risks and perhaps a similar one . . . The philosophies of history take no less a risk, and the historian who has presumably been liberated from theology or philosophy perhaps takes the greatest. But, granted our choice, our first job is to sharpen our basic vocabulary. When we talk of an event--and of an event for the Church-- what do we mean?

1) It can be a reference to a past, present, or future divine action. Now such action is manifest on various levels and in various forms. For example, the creation of the world is imagined or even thought of as an event, but its typology is clearly different from that of the coming of Christ two thousand years ago or from a miracle at Lourdes or from the future parousia. Each paradigmatic occurrence "happens" in its own way and, in distancing itself more or less from the ordinary run of events, involves itself with faith and the language of faith.

2) It can be an allusion to developments within the Church, and these are quite diverse:

A) The existence and activity of each believer and especially of those thought to be most influential. The viewpoint which holds the believer's attention can vary: St. Augustine, Innocent III, Count Albert de Mun are remarkable for different reasons.

B) Dogma, in as much as it is lived and develops in time. The history of spirituality, and ultimately of institutions, can be linked to the history of doctrinal belief. Therefore, to avoid problems of nomenclature, we can group under one and the same heading the formulations of dogma (as expressed, for example, in the formulas of Chalcedon or Trent), the appearance of devotions (the Way of the Cross, the Rosary), and the establishment of formal institutions. Again, and most importantly on this last point, we recognize the great variety of "events" involved: the birth of the Episcopacy is more central than the appearance of a religious congregation and the latter affects the Church more intimately than the establishment of Catholic Boy Scouts.

C) Bio-social break-throughs, whether gradual or violent,

which put pressure on the life of the Church from within, and especially the internal upheavals which launch schisms or heresies (the contemporary crisis in Catholicism furnishes some examples).

3) Finally, it can be an allusion to extra-ecclesial worldly events which, for one reason or another, are a concern to the Church. Some of these occurrences have no effect on her structure, but merely on her missionary function; others, however, have at least an indirect impact on her internal development. The reaction can be conscious or unconscious, sudden or delayed; finally, external occurrences can spur negative reaction or imitation.

It is frequently very difficult to draw the line between what influences Christianity and what does not affect it either de jure or de facto. Thus, the malaise of the nobility of the long robes in the 17th century is thought to explain the "Hidden God" of Pascal and the Jansenists, but it could just as well explain the recruitment and ideology of the Jesuits, or even of the free-thinkers. Here the cause-and-effect relationship ultimately loses all significance. On the other hand, the French Revolution of 1789 was slowly but surely responsible for French Catholic support for the Republic, at the request of Leon XIII, in 1892.

The three categories of event distinguished above are rather confused in most religious discussion: they are introduced willy-nilly into a salvation history which is homogeneous and generally supports a view of the spiritual growth of the Church over the centuries. The theologian of history mobilizes all events in the organization of his fresco. But our preliminary distinctions have just shown that these disparate kairoi reflect three types of chronoi: the time of divine action or revelation; the time of the response of faith or the time of the Church properly so called; the time of the world, to the degree in which it is distinguished from the first two and constitutes a time that is secular or secularized. Thus our study should now turn to the idea of time.

II. Time

1) Duration, Rhythm and Time

We do not define duration; we recognize it as the very stuff of the person, if not of the world. If time is understood as a synonym for duration, it can be described only in terms of before and after, like a qualitative stream. But the continuity of duration, or of time which resembles it, is heterogeneous. This heterogeneity implies a plurality, thus we can form the concept of a time which is quantitative, anonymous, detachable in some way from consciousness. We are already able to discern rhythms of different tension in the description of each individual; they are all the more obvious in the encounter of consciousness.

What, we may ask, is a rhythm? The concept wavers between two extremes. On the one hand, it may be the qualitative individuality of some movement, analogous to that of a melody. If so, it will have an immanent beginning and end without any void between. On the other hand, it may be the repetition of some element in a series; when this repetition occurs at regular intervals, we have meter. In this case, repetition interrupts duration, but once again there is no absolute void, it is the product of abstraction, that is to say, of the intervention of an act of consciousness capable of free flight over other acts of consciousness.

A type of rhythm between these two extremes is worth considering. It is produced by the imposition or combination of the two tempos. Nothing else is required for passage from qualitative duration to discrete time; we do so through comparison of rhythms. We then establish a homogeneous and universal time, because we are able to integrate old rhythms indefinitely into the renewed rhythm of consciousness. The process begins with a heterogeneous quality, that is to say, with a virtually plural quality; the process ends with a number of motions according to before and after, that is to say, with a quantitative time which appears separated from qualitative content, but which makes no sense without its virtual presence. Time, thus conceived, is coextensive with beings; it is something derived from them and not something into which they are inserted.

When we speak of different times, we are concerned with different rhythms. This fact at once reveals the ambiguous character of time considered as the form which unites different rhythms into an ensemble. If a general judgment is applicable here, it is this: time sometimes breaks rhythms, sometimes recaptures it. It pulls us apart or pulls us together, depending on how we use it. This conceptual instability has an ontological foundation: it is linked to the contingencies of life and the choice of freedom. This is why we sometimes see it as the principle of dissolution of being and sometimes as the means of eternalizing development.

2) The Three Times of Christian Language

On this topic, the three distinctive rhythms mentioned above can be specified as follows:

A) By <u>God's Time</u> we mean the time of divine activity which is expressed in public revelation. It is the time of sacred history, of the Old and New Testaments. It has its center in Jesus Christ. •

B) By the <u>Church's Time</u> we mean the response to this divine activity in the faith of Christians. It could also be called the time of salvation. God entrusts this time to our liberty to be used with care.

C) By the <u>world's time</u> we could mean many types of secularism and secularization. For the moment, let us be content to proceed with the lowest common denominator and say that this is time as perceived by the believer and non-believer alike. Or let us even say that it is time as it would appear in a reading of history without faith, that is to say, a reading which denies revelation and the time of salvation. For example, all in Jerusalem witnessed Jesus; only a certain few saw in him the Christ; others denied that he was indeed the Christ. The latter go beyond the perception common to themselves and Christians in an affirmation contrary to that of the Christians. The indifferent see both ending in the unknown. But some partial rhythmic line of the life of Christ is commonly perceived by disciples, adversaries, and the indifferent: this is what we will call the world's time.

3) Relationship Between These Three Times

A) In a certain sense, God's time is always flowing into the time of faith, and the time of faith into the world's time. Or, if you prefer, the qualitative individuality of divine activity is manifested in the qualitative individuality of the attitude of faith, and this in its turn in the qualitative individualities of human acts.

Furthermore, every element of religious language has been borrowed, whether directly or indirectly, from worldly elements. Religion is but a part of creation.

But in the intentionality of the believing consciousness, faith is revealed to itself as a break-through which shatters the limits of common time, transforms its meaning, and, by a second shattering, goes beyond its own limits to attribute itself to an initiative of grace. Grace is thus <u>immixta ut imperet</u>. If God's action is always mediated, if it dies and is resurrected in our faith, then this happens so that we might personally acknowledge his immediacy and omnipresence.

B) This is why, in another sense, the three rhythms are superimposed and then interact. At the heart of creation, the rhythms can henceforth be complementary, but also juxtaposed, or they can be in opposition and at war.

A comparison is in order. When I take my place in the qualitative individuality which is the movement of the train which takes me from Strasbourg to Paris, I cannot perceive in this real rhythm the qualitative individuality which is the movement of the thought of Heidegger. And yet I can think of Heidegger, either to adjust the rhythm of my trip to the rhythm of his thought or to criticize his thought. Heidegger himself could be in the train and restate his thought, or expand it contrapuntally, or as a fugue, or in some free development . . . A train in motion contains the immense tangle of all the rhythms of consciousness which are the passengers; their impressions of other passengers blend with their memories and their plans. Every form of marriage and divorce is possible within these parameters of mental becoming.

There is all the more reason why we should find complexity in the relationships of revelation and humanity. The Creator's action not only makes possible and sheds light on the faith which it inspires; it also makes possible and sheds light on the neutrality or revolt which it respects. Still, God's voluntary abasement is radically different from the coexistence and interweaving of rhythms in the secular comparison mentioned just above. From the viewpoint of faith, at least, it is this: the activity of God is never absent from the life of the passengers or from the progress of the train, and nothing prevents us from beginning to know this here below. When we do know it, the finality and the sense of human rhythms are changed. It is not enough to say that the rhythm is changed in its very nature. Without annihilating its factual existence, it is the eschatological destiny of the face of history to be overwhelmed in the vision of the valley of Jehoshaphat.

II

The phenomenological investigation just sketched offers only principal highlights in superficial outline. It should be pursued in detail in the great flowering of formulas of faith and in manifestations of Christian life. We cannot dream of such a program! But we would at least like to give an example. Let us examine two fundamental liturgical documents: the prayer, Our Father, and the profession of faith, I Believe in God. [1]

1) Our Father

A) The time of divine activity in this prayer is considered to be future, whether in the first three petitions which relate to God, or in the last four related to man. Only once is mention made of a present disposition ("Your will be done") and there is no explicit mention of the gesta Dei of the past. But the beginning is an implicit recollection of this past time and of the eternity of God ("Our Father who are in heaven"); eternity makes an appearance again in the middle (" . . . on earth as it is heaven"), The final Amen gives this eternity an image of eternalized time.

B) The Church's time admits only a single mention of the past ("our offenses"); most of the other petitions look to the future (the sanctification of God's name, the kingdom, the accomplishment of His will, bread, pardon, assistance in temptation, deliverance from anticipated evil). But there are three mentions of the present: the believer confesses that he is a child of God, that he lives on bread which is ἐπιούσιος and especially that he forgives those who have offended him. Transcendence, "self-sufficiency" in heaven, is proper to God; proper to the Church are its progress in faith, its trespasses, the pardon which it gives and receives.

C) The world's time is not presented in its endless duration: it is shown only once in the past (those who have trespassed against us), it is never shown in the future, it is shown four times in the present (on earth as in heaven, our daily bread, the fact that we pardon others, the existence of evil).

Certain notions are obviously ambivalent and connected: the bread which is ἐπιούσιος (whatever may be the exegesis of this term) is at once religious and earthly; the religious pardon of others is fully intelligible in secular time; the πειρασμός and the πονηρός despite their partial obscurity, are also certainly connected.

The world's time shows the insertion of the Church into the common history of mankind. This total, surprising, scandalous and indispensable penetration is achieved only by pardoning offenses of others. This is the golden rule of the gospels: as you have done to others, so God will do to you. For the revelation of God's love is dependent on man's decision which is situated at the junction of the three rhythms: the divine, the Christian, the human.

If the golden rule were omitted from the Our Father, the Christian would be turned exclusively towards God. He would not act visibly as a Christian in the world's time, and the non-Christian would have no experience of the dynamism which, through the instrumentality of the Christian, comes from God.

2) I Believe in God

A) The time of divine activity. The eternity of God appears in the first lines concerning the Father, then in the mention of the two other persons of the Trinity, the only Son, and the Holy Spirit. There is only one reference to the future (he will come to judge the living and the dead) and only one to the present (he is seated at the right hand of God). All the rest is a recitation of the past, an exposé of the gesta Dei in Christ.

B) <u>The Church's Time</u>. It appears in the perpetuity of the relationship established with God (<u>Our</u> Lord, the communion of saints, everlasting life, the final amen). There is no mention of the past, but several of the present (the very act of the profession of faith before God and men; I believe . . . in the Father, and in Jesus Christ . . . I believe in the Holy Spirit; the existence of the Holy Church, the present remission of past sins). Finally, there is mention of the future (judgment, the resurrection of the body, life everlasting).

C) <u>The world's time</u>. It is concerned especially with the past: Jesus is born of Mary, suffered under Pontius Pilate, was crucified, died, and was raised. The present is represented only by the act of the profession of faith and by the existence of the Christian community, both of which are perceptible to all. Earthly behavior is not predictable. Affirmations about the future require faith; non-Christians can record only the psycho-social reality of Christian witness.

But these two are still connected: the notion of Church is at once interiorly religious and exteriorly earthly. Miracles involve a mix (born of the <u>Virgin</u> Mary, he <u>was raised</u> from the dead . . .). The <u>Our Father</u> does not, so to speak, present any problem of demythologizing. The <u>Creed</u> most certainly does and must produce a clash between believers and non-believers in the phenomenal order.

The overall impression is that predominance is given to God's time, but that there is firm insistence upon his insertion into common time: on the one hand, by the evident humanity of Jesus and, on the other, by the presence of the believing Church. Finally, the eschatological inclination of the Church, which is preparing for life everlasting, is a response to the summons of the <u>gesta Dei</u>.

Faced with the three rhythms found in the examples just surveyed and, indeed, in all Christian language, theologians do not adopt a uniform attitude. Some attempt to wrest divine revelation as much as possible out of time; others, on the contrary, thrust it into time in different ways even to the point, sometimes, of expecting that the only possible revelation of God must come from the totality of earthly becoming. [2]

It would be senseless to become involved in this debate before we review certain presuppositions of our argument, shift emphasis, and underline implications. In this process, our position will become self-evident.

III

I. Temporal Distance

We have admitted that events and times are known or knowable. But the distinction of the three rhythms forces us to ask under what conditions such knowledge takes place or could take place. Are we concerned with an intutition which leads us to interior participation in a reality or with a perception which always supposes our temporal distance from the reality? Further, is such a perception always possible? Asking these questions is enough to show us that the ambiguity lies not only in the object, but even more in the relationship between the subject and the object. Let us say that all the residents of Jerusalem could see Jesus, but that the disciples alone felt summoned by God in him and saw the Christ. The situation is still more complex for us after two thousand years and is much less simple than we may have imagined, before we were confronted with the rhythm of our own intimate development.

We must distinguish clearly between the living past which is organically linked to the present and the dead past which is composed of material fragments floating in a sea of oblivion. Actually, the living past is nothing more than the density of the lived presence whose moments are inseparable: we are aware of a before and an after, but of no gap between our memory and the present. We carry in our animated body and in our psyche the totality of our previous life; an attentive observer need only look at us to find in us a permanent source of information about what we have been. This information is not limited to our individuality, but also reveals something about our contacts with others and, consequently, something about the beings with whom we have associated, as well as about our bio-social roots. As he gets closer and closer, precisions and paradigms vanish; with the persistence of a thread of Ariadne, he will discover that the entire human past somehow lives in us. What is true of our persons is also revealed in our institutions; for they are an accumulated extension of what has already been involuntarily revealed in our psycho-physical appearance. A civilization is the complex rhythm of a series of individual actions and passions. We cannot grasp a moment in a rhythm without a general sense of the total rhythm; if we fail to do so, it ceases to be a rhythmic moment.

But as the radiance of the living past shifts away from its center or its personal centers, so the more gaps in and lapses of memory appear--the presence of the anti-presence. The death of the past has already started in our interior rhythms and is making us strangers to ourselves. What can we say of our massive forgetfulness which impedes our exterior efforts and must be brought to life again from the living past by laborious, methodical techniques or by the inspired jolt of a vision! The distancing which seems to precede the experience of rhythms in our consciousness is an ambiguous concept. Sometimes, it is only a qualitative heterogeneity in which each moment begets the next moments, in such a way that each re-echoes in all and none is separated from the others even though it proceeds from them. At other times, the thread of Ariadne is concealed by empty, black beaches which no longer let us be aware of it and which have effectively reduced the density of our experience to that of a broken outline. The distance between the past and us is then all too real. It invites us to achieve a reconstruction by means of interpretation. From the background of heterogeneous continuity which constitutes the unity of the temporal universe and which situates us at the very beginning of the developing game, emerges a special way of encountering rhythms, one which requires overcoming an obstacle. Our waning intuition should give birth to the perception that works.

II. Hermeneutics and Personality

Thus, let us now turn to the hermeneutic problem. When we speak of hermeneutics, we must speak of language, whether body language or verbal language. When we speak of language, we must speak of separate, personal consciousnesses. But it is absurd to speak of an absolute separation of personal consciousnesses. We must conclude, therefore, that an intersubjective unity pre-exists language and remains the underlying unity of language itself. This is one of the aspects of pre-comprehension. Yet in pre-comprehension resides, in point of fact, the most precious germ of comprehension--the living past. I actually believed for a long time that the task of the philosopher was to reach a definition or an explanation of such notions as presence, comprehension, and duration without getting involved in a vicious circle. But it is only possible to establish, enumerate, and analyze notions which are so primitive that they ought rather be called givens and, when they are conceptualized, categories of experience. The problem is not presence, but absence, not comprehension but incomprehension, not the communion of rhythms, but their partial incompatibility.

From this viewpoint, two types of hermeneutics may be distinguished. The first, which is based on the heterogeneous identity of consciousnesses, need not justify itself, but must justify everything else. For the person with his living past constitutes a capacity of understanding the other and of entering into reciprocal influences with the other. It is not true that the self is annoyed by the other on the level of budding knowledge. "The self knows the other" is the basic axiom of epistemology. "The self knows the self" is the axiom of ontic withdrawal and collapse, whose existence is derivative and whose breadth is limited. By maintaining that the most fundamental hermeneutics may easily open a rhythm of consciousness to another, we are merely recognizing what art reveals in a special way: Rembrandt's insight into the model whose portrait he is painting in no way diminishes Rembrandt's originality; both painter and model are simultaneously revealed in the language of the picture in keeping with the lines of force of their past, present, and future. Intersubjective ontology also concludes that there is no major reason why such an interpersonal relation cannot project itself in a work; for we have just acknowledged above that the living past transfuses the body itself, then the material environment of _artefacta_ and institutions.

Before leaving the first type of hermeneutics, let us add once again that encounter with otherness is not only interhuman; it is also axiological--even divine. The question which is raised by the dawning of the true, the beautiful, and the good within us and which will verbalize our indirect language is a revelation of altereity in the rhythm of our persons. The imagination succeeds in being creative only if it receives a transcendent act and is aware of it. Thus, all the more reason why, in sacred history, revelation, grace, and access have their origin in a supra-personal center! In the work, whether word or deed, which expresses the response of faith, we have no greater distance to cover, since the rhythm from on high descends even to our own, gives it meaning, transforms it, and makes us consious of it.

But it would be utopian to think that assent to this principle precludes a second hermeneutics, quite different from the first, one which should take into account forgetfulness and aim at remembrance. While the first hermeneutics cannot distort and personal prejudice is here synomymous with an intelligent veracity, the second is open to some fumbling and error. It corresponds to exegesis of the dead past, to the elements of dislocation and dispersion which burden time and language; it must bring the dead back to life and bridge the temporal distance between separate events. This is the type of hermeneutics most often discussed. But all too frequently people fail to observe that it is not the only hermeneutics and that it is subordinated to the other. They simplify their method: they assign it the task of demythologizing and disregard their obligation to remythologize which ought to follow their critical inquiry. Such an inquiry is a means: it never begins or ends of itself, but it should arise from a desire for presence and make the consciousness more capable of receiving or giving the presence. The interpreter, aware of the reality of the tradition in himself and in the text he is reading, should not be suspicious of the very fact of the tradition, which is inevitable and enriching, but of all that is not intersubjective and enriching in the tradition and which thus saps the tradition, hinders the revelation of altereity, and closes the minds instead of helping them to see.

To pass to that aspect of the theology of history which interests us most, let us say that the hermeneutics of the Bible demands renunciation of our ways of thinking in so far as they block the transmission of meaning and in as much as they conceal the event which gave rise to the transmission. We must achieve this renunciation for ourselves and for the intermediaries who would otherwise have obscured what they had to transmit to us. In short, cultural customs, theirs or ours, ought not to be substituted for, but should serve the truth. But there is no reason to renounce the perspective of our person or of any person, precisely as person; for the collegial aptitude unfolds the meaning of the initial event in the transmission which the event prompts. The mistake would lie in believing that the more the objective truth, the less the subjective originality. Originality of outlook is not suspect, but a defective way of seeing is. The initial event is human, that is to say, it has a meaning and this meaning itself grows with time in the transfer from one head to another. What starts with men, needs to mature in men, that is to say, in an active tradition, in order to achieve its own being and the progressive revelation of this being.

Historians and exegetes know only too well the delicate choice to be made between what respects unifying altereity and what compromises or destroys it. There is no need to stress the point here. Let us merely indicate the two main obstacles which may prevent the encounter and communion of rhythms. On the one hand, there is the rebellion and withdrawal of those who reject their universal vocation: this is a most serious obstacle, even if it cannot be as total an obstacle as some may wish. On the other hand, there is the isolation caused by our earthly condition which, in fragmenting communication (whose instrument is languages), at once makes its elements ambiguous, degrades exchanges into mutual showing off, reduces intuition to a perception that is not only retrograde but even disordered. Event then becomes equivocal by the mere fact that it results from a selection from the past and such a selection can be more or less unfaithful to the actual unfolding of the real. Time becomes equivocal by the mere fact that the demarcation of periods can result from the historian's ignorance or recourse to a fanciful Idéal-Typus.

III. Sacred Time, Secular Time

From these notions of distance and hermeneutics, we are finally led to the notions of sacred time and secular or secularized time. In our analysis of the Lord's Prayer and Credo, we defined the world's time as residual: something on which the language of the believer and non-believer could agree. Needless to say, this agreement is sometimes uneasy, but it does finally occur often enough, thanks to areas of personal or rather interpersonal pre-comprehension which guarantee the effective interplay of language and the substance of society. This minimum, by which we have designated the assertions common to believer and non-believer, seems a last resource, something neutral which draws wide recognition. Extreme minimal positivism usually preserves only what is insignificant and tends to become the form of time without content. But in this present devaluation it preserves one value, universality, and thus establishes within the framework of time a permanent passage from the sacred to the secular and vice versa. As noted in examples above, it also provides the Christian and non-Christian with an area for conversation and even with common ground. The secularity of time is, therefore, not radically exclusive; it is duly obliged to let the believer take his place in it and to baptize events acknowledged by believer and non-believer alike.

This analysis reveals how extremely difficult it is to remove the secular from the sacred. The apostles of secularization are very lucky: they believe that their basic concept is univocal and that they can dismiss the sacred without fear of seeing it return. Sometimes they are even naïve enough to claim that while Christianity has driven the gods and nymphs from nature, its dogma of creation simultaneously suppresses the mystery of creatures. These new barbarians substitute politics for theology and technology for poetry under pretext of "defatalizing" time and of establishing man's self-determination. But what does it mean to claim autonomy?

a) There is certainly a <u>secularizaiton of being</u>, if by this expression we mean the fact of individuality and finitude of being. Every form of the real (whether of person or thing) has its own proper being, every idea even has a kind of individuality; indeed every finite determination has an existential formality and even consequent structure, exigencies of internal organization and a corresponding auto-finality. God himself teaches us this secularization or creaturely right, because he is the Creator.

Thus understood, the secular is in no way opposed to the sacred. For we cannot absolutely isolate a physical or mental reality from the universe. Strict atomism is a mere abstraction. No one thing is defined, no one thing achieves the fullness of its being without a network of relationships with all other things. There is no autonomy for separate entities without an interconnection with other entities and with God. This fact reintroduces the sacred.

b) In another sense, there can be a <u>secularization of works</u>. All is secular that is or can be manipulated by man, that is destined to be dominated by man and to become the product of his hands: in short, the world of projects and operations, the world--however formidable--of technology.

Thus understood, the secular is distinguished from and can even tend to distance itself from the sacred: for it implies a free choice. But it never achieves complete separation; for man creates his work according to a certain spirit. Assumption of his responsibilities does not free him from the question of his destiny. He responds and takes sides. The subject's activity remains in itself a mysterious question and the response lies at the heart of the mystery.

c) Finally, secularization can conceal desecration. It can be an attempt to escape from and, essentially, to rebel against the sacred. But those concerned only with desecration cannot live without the sacred. Desecration must have the sacred, if it is to fight against it.

Whatever form of secularization we consider, we find that one idea necessarily implies the other; the impulse by which we discover one triggers the impulse by which we discover the other.

What orients us toward being beyond measure and suddenly reveals, at least virtually, the secret of our destiny is sacred. We experience not merely extraordinary vitality, but the disclosure of something beyond appearances, the revelation of a depth of being which had been hidden from us, the introduction to a world of constitutive relations with other beings and with their source. The sacred requires us to enter at once into the mystery of things, of the very subject, and of the reality which overshadows both subject and things.

However, the sacred is usually considered a species while it is a genus involving many species. A species of the sacred is found in what we accomplish and a species of the sacred is found in our transgressions. There is the Holy One of God and the Accursed One who encamps in the divine _aura_ to challenge God or to abandon himself to the joy of self-destruction. Not every form of the sacred deserves praise; for the demoniacal is sacred. But all forms imply the recognition of the mystery which they partially reveal in the adventure into which they thrust us.

Secularization is not desecration, but it has an eye open for secularization: desecration consists in wishing to lay violent hands on what is sacred and divine instead of receiving it as normative revelation. And here once again we have a metamorphosis of the equivocal with respect to event and time in Christian language. But is not our representation of revealing event and revealing time a desecration? Is not the conceptualization of rhythms the beginning of error and sacrilege? We aspire to decipher sacred history in the history of the world, but are not both histories the fraudulent magic of the theologian and philosopher respectively? These unavoidable questions make an issue of the very possibility of a theology or philosophy of history. Some supporters of secularization like to say that secularization is not secularism. But the worst form of secularism is not perhaps the secularization of faith, but the sacralization of a travesty of faith. We should reject on equal terms the idolaters of human evolution and of biblico-ecclesiastical Heilsgeschichte. Both offer only a naked faith which is open to everything, but knows nothing.

There is no reason for being less severe with the theologians who know everything than with the other conjurers of historical thought. But there is also no reason to grant baptism to the will and to deny it to the intellect, or to decide that God's summons is not concerned with both the knowledge of self and of God. Faith cannot avoid affirmation and carries within itself a theology of history: in other words, conceptual certitudes--even if they are paradoxical--concerning gesta Dei and gesta hominis. We have seen that the simplest of Christian prayers, the Our Father, cannot be entirely detached from the perspective of the past or from the sin which was then committed; it points us toward the future only by supporting us tacitly by the endless action of the Father who comprehends time. The other text on which we commented, the Apostle's Creed, presents temporal rhythms as truth inseparable from faith; it singles them out and weaves them into a scheme which extends through all ages.

The insertion of the divine into the human occurs in such a way, it is true, that there is no need for each portion of ecclesial rhythm--and a fortiori what we have called worldly rhythm—to correspond materially to some portion of the divine rhythm. In this sense, there is no bi-univocal correspondence which would justify slicing up events. The Creed is not an allegory and "secular" history cannot cover over all "sacred" history. It is even inevitable that these rhythms will go beyond their normal boundaries; otherwise we would have neither the transcendence of God's time nor the contingency of man's time. But these rhythms have areas of mutual tension and contact. The most strained relation of all is that of the miraculous event or of the miracle hidden in every event. The impulse of Christianity is to prolong the Revelation of the Cross and Resurrection by sacralizing human development with a somehow progressive measure of liberty while respecting the determinations which orient us towards God and which we have never fully accepted or understood in our language.

Everything happens as if the first response which God's grace permitted us to make was the power to discover progressively what God's time is by taking upon ourselves the world's time. In this way, the most extraordinary of all hermeneutical circles is verified--that of immanence and transcendence. There is no liberty without obedience, no obedience without liberty; there is no proper alignment of one event without the revelation of the meaning of events, which is manifested in its turn by the events. The interplay between plurality and unity had its beginning in the interhuman relationship of the I and the Thou, as well as the relationship of the we and nature. It achieves perfection in the collaboration of the secular and the sacred. In its basic form, secularization is but the vocation of the creature to be itself by becoming everything, but the creature reaches fulfillment either by secularizing God's time or by sacralizing the world's time. This is the source of the fluctuating and indefinite limits of events and of their loyalty according to our existential choices. This is the source of the dramatic character of every theology of history--legitimate in its origins, weak in its achievements.

In Christian language, event and time involve certain equivocations, but their use does not necessitate incoherence. The Amen which ends our prayers bears witness to promises of old and imposes hope which is a mixture of revealed certitude and ignorance. Physical time is the order of phenomena and we know neither their secrets nor their windings. What can we say about spiritual time, which is the order of beings, except that God alone brings about its precious synthesis? Nonetheless, we are asked to prepare this synthesis in the field of experience and to discover it in the forest of symbols; for in its effort to abolish the equivocal, the eternal synthesis passes through the maturing process of time.

NOTES

1. We shall respect the ordinary resonance of this text in contemporary Christian consciousness and, in general, shall leave aside the semantics of the first users of these formulae.

2. This two-fold development is divided on several sides. By exaggerating perhaps certain positions, a list might be had as follows:
a) Salvation and temporality. For the separation of salvation from time: Gottschalk and the supralapsarians, supporters of absolute predestination (cf. in another list, the non-temporality of revelation with certain scholastics); among our contemporaries: in certain respects, Bultmann and Tillich. For the immersion of salvation in time: Cullmann, Urs von Balthasar.

b) <u>Sacred history and the history of religions</u>. For the separation: Karl Barth, Kraemer. For the immersion: W. E. Hocking.

c) <u>Sacred history and the history of the world</u>. For the separation: E. Castelli, K. Löwith. For the immersion: Teilhard de Chardin and, in certain respects, Pannenberg.

The Augustinian tradition, which avoids extremes, is well presented in the recent work of H. I. Marrou, <u>Théologie de l'histoire</u>, Paris, 1968.

3. Or again, can we affirm that our "reflection on the plurality of times" is not "a consideration of unseasonable times," of apparent, false, illegitimate times? (E. Castelli, <u>Le temps invertébré</u>, Paris, 1970, p. 154).

Chapter Sixteen

AUTONOMY AND HETERONOMY

**Doubts Concerning Philosophic Autonomy
and Religious Heteronomy**

It is almost a commonplace to affirm that the philosopher is autonomous. Anyone who looks for the reason will not lack for answers. The philosopher's mind depends on nothing but itself. It is supposed to choose not only the subject of its reflection, but also the methodic principles which guide this reflection and finally the conclusions which emerge from its system of thought. On the other hand, the philosopher does not recognize any ground as out of bounds: any proposition, any form of being should be able to be submitted to his judgment, because he considers himself called to scrutinize everything without assistance. Somehow, everything should appear intelligible to him. Of course such an understanding is primarily <u>critical</u>, but this adjective makes even more evident how pretentious it would be to save or condemn without appeal what another might offer. For the philosopher also burdens himself with the kingdom of negation, he admits nothing which he is not prepared to verify by way of counter-proof, and he rejects without regret what gives way in the negative argument.

The price of such a kingdom is solitude. The philosopher constructs an edifice which is a monologue. But, in the sequence of disembodied discourse, this monologue transfers into itself the autonomy which was in the flesh-and-blood thinker. Monologue even reinforces autonomy. By the fact that it detaches itself from one specific person and becomes anonymous, it forms a perfect organism which henceforth draws its matter and form from its own depths. But the paradox is that at the moment when the worker achieves consumate solitude in his work and disappears in a self-sufficient monologue, he receives in return, hope of the universality of subjects, of thinkers, which he would seem to have sacrificed to pure objectivity. What indeed is this universality of subjects, if not the region of possible encounter of all minds? If the thinking individuality is willing to die according to the objective demands of its own creation, it deserves to be reborn in the virtual accord of thinking individualities which have made the same sacrifice and which will have been equally fruitful.

Thus it is true to say that the philosopher and philosophy are autonomous and cannot be otherwise.

*   *   *   *   *

In the face of philosophy, the believer seems heteronomous. Once again, there are abundant reasons for this statement. At the root of faith lies not a reflection, but a tradition. The religious man receives from his society both his élan and the objects of his belief. He can, of course, introduce reflective thought into his attitude, but it will always be grafted onto an authority which precedes it, which it cannot replace without destroying. In addition, reason, which calls into doubt--or even submits to a methodic doubt--the data of a religion, will always appear to be somewhat sacrilegious. Besides, if the obligation to believe is made known to the faithful by their Church, the Church claims to be only the vehicle of a superior authority, that of a divine absolute. But even when all human obligation is called into question, how does one call God into question? If there is a God, he can only be an authoritative being. To be a believer is to possess from him the norm which is imposed on us as the first and last appeal of our thought and conduct. God alone is autonomous; if we wish to be, we are at once absurd and criminal. That is why faith excludes philosophical judgment as an arbitrary act. We cannot choose fundamental religious values at our pleasure; we should receive them humbly, our only chance to understand them is to accept them as gifts. And our comprehension will always be partial; for we cannot oust the mystery which signals the presence of the Divine Other in us or imagine without blasphemy a situation which would falsify the being of God. God escapes the virtual negations of a radical challenge.

Faith is never solitary. Because it is prayer and thus breaks the monologue, it establishes us in a dialogue which is, furthermore, unique in type; for the anxious concern of God is too rapid and too lofty for us to be able to capture it without getting winded in the tangle of human discourse. As regards the meditation of the faith or on the faith, that is theology, it always attributes its intellectual source to a spiritual source. Just as philosophy transposes and condenses in itself the autonomy of the philosopher, so theology (if at least it does not betray the spirit of religion) proclaims with increasing force the heteronomy of the believer. The theological edifice appears complex and complicated like a cathedral. It is constructed by men on order from

God and according to divine plan; it is an effort to submit self to revelation. In the theological, as in the philosophical transposition, both anonymity and virtual encounter with other minds (in this case with all believers) are expressed; but the effacement of the individual subject is not the triumph of liberty and of reason. Those who here find themselves in accord do not do so because one of them has disappeared in his work as the philosopher in his philosophy or the sculptor in his statue. The paradox is much more profound. There is absolutely nothing constraining in the structure of the work: the constraint comes from heaven. Man seeks to efface himself before his God and his recompense would be to have been sufficiently pure and transparent to have mixed nothing from the depths of his being with the work of God. Philosophy tries to purify; theology to be pure.

* * * * *

Such are the appearances. But what is the reality? We will perhaps be helped to discover the truth, if we examine the fundamental problem, that is to say, resolve the ambiguities of the term "autonomous." Indeed, we may have played on the meanings of this word by slipping from one idea to another without warning.

1) In the biological sense, the living being is autonomous in the degree to which its specific structure renders it capable of assuring its essential functions. From this point of view, it is not possible to distinguish the autonomy of the living being from its individuality. But the individual receives its being and exercises its autonomy in a milieu which it cannot do without. Thus a distinction must be made between this autonomy and an independence properly so-called.

2) From a juridical point of view, an autonomous being is one that has the right to conduct its own affairs freely within the framework of existing laws. For example, we speak, above all, of budgetary autonomy. An individual or group may receive an allocated sum and be able to dispose of it as it wishes, as long as it respects the assigned objectives which specify and protect the legislation. Limited by source and destination, submitted even to administrative supervision or to official controls, autonomous management is thus primarily a liberty of execution, with a real but narrow field of action.

A metaphorical and picturesque derivation of this sense was applied by aviators when they got in the habit of using "autonomous" to mean the maximum time during which an aircraft could fly without refueling.

3) Autonomy can be more than all the above--the physical or juridical capacity to realize one's self by one's own means. There may be more to autonomy than liberty of execution: there may already be a liberty of invention. For example, we can formulate regulations and even statutes (as the French universities were asked to do within the framework of the recent laws of orientation).

It goes without saying that such an initiative also has all sorts of limits. But we see a new element surface in this notion, the desire not to be totally attached to an organization or not to be swallowed up in a crowd. This nuance is particularly clear in another example: an autonomous union is one which is not affiliated with a central union; it seeks to be free of authority which would be partially alien, derived as it is from several professional groups. By this very fact, this union ought to depend on itself alone, that is, on one homogeneous profession.

4) A more ambitious degree of autonomy is attained when we not only have the means to fulfill ourselves, but also intend to establish principles, laws, values. The will then becomes creative and integrates into this ideal the executive or inventive forms of autonomy, listed above. Juridically, we thus see grow the desire for independence, since we are moving toward the idea of sovereignty. Morally, it is the expression of an analogous desire: to obey self-imposed principles is to be simultaneously master and subject; it is to adopt a perfect and self-sufficient discipline which aspires to form freely its matter in its form.

5) Also, autonomy thus pursued is ultimately confused with personality: it is not a question of merely creating a law, but of being oneself the law and of being it for oneself and by oneself.

Absolute autonomy could thus be identified with sovereignty (the juridical aspect) and with independence (the moral and metaphysical aspect), in as much as independence excludes all subordination, if not all relation ad extra.

Earlier, autonomy consisted in the projection of principles by the self; now, the principle returns toward the self and rejoins pure subjectivity, from which it is no longer distinguishable.

6) To escape the mirage of a savage individualism, the great Kantian tradition, as we know, is careful to reach pure subjectivity by passing immediately from personality to rationality. That rationality is autonomous--and only that rationality--that has as a rule of action a proposition which can be universalized and that acts thereafter in accord with reason and not self-interest. Pure will would ultimately be the equivalent of pure practical reason.

A quick glance over the six usages listed above shows that autonomy is related to liberty. Such a relationship is already present, in a preparatory and approximate sense, in the biological order, but it becomes clearly established in the psychological and social orders. One need not repeat the evidence. But can autonomy be dissociated from the gift which brought it into being? Is it never anything more than a ratification? Even if someone denies his liberty, he still does so while recognizing that he was formed in liberty; he contradicts his contradiction. And if he maintains that his liberty excludes the necessity of the being through which his liberty is able to assert itself, he contradicts himself again; he fails to notice that he is a cause only in being caused.

For the most part, the forms of autonomy distinguished above explicitly suppose that autonomy is not independent: it is governed by a primordial statute, whether from a juridical or metaphysical point of view, over which it has no control. Only forms 4 and 5 seem to be exceptions. But such exceptions are only apparent. The moment autonomy asserts itself in the most pure and triumphant way, it discovers that it springs from a source other than itself that lies not outside itself, but within its very depths. Man's creation of values comes second: it is a re-creation or an approbation, since it presupposes the aptitude to create and the fact that we receive this aptitude before we use it. Finally, in the act by which we use it, even if we choose counter-values, we can only do so in conjunction with an authority which regulates the dialectic of our acts and of our being. The chronological priority of the gift is less startling than its ontological priority. By being itself, the I asserts itself, but in asserting itself it cannot not accept itself as it is: although this inevitable admission may be obscured and equivalently denied by the consciousness encumbered by and absorbed in superficial activities, the I can only be creator of itself and of its values or counter-values by accepting itself as a creature. If reflection on our actions leads us to the perception of our most intimate act, we will become aware that our liberty is only an I in being a we: in the most profound regions of our immanence, we discover the transcendent will which is the foundation of our will. We likewise see emerge from our person a norm for its growth and development which, unlike other norms, does not clash with and diminish external decision, but so constitutes it that the measure of our autonomy coincides with that of our dependence.

Uniting autonomy with dependence is indeed unusual and the concept of dependence is certainly not ambiguous; for it can designate either subordination of simple connection. Because of our transcendent source, we are in a total subordination which is the promise of total liberation. The creative source calls us to be ourselves and, in this sense, to unite ourselves with it and, ideally, to subordinate ourselves to it. But it is always in virtue of this call that the creative force imposes itself on us so effectively that it creates the paradox of an absolute authority which remains undiminished while giving itself. The creative all-powerful assumes a new appearance where we would not expect it--on the path of weakness and silence. It imposes itself according to its own norm on those who struggle against it; to those who receive it, it offers itself and is reborn in them to obey them. In both situations, autonomy and theonomy are in consort, although the type of harmony differs in each case and one of the two harmonies is dramatic. An image may help us to represent this human condition. In the Roman Empire, certain cities enjoyed imperial autonomy; they had full authority to coin money, but each coin bore two images: on one side, the emblem of the city; on the other, the portrait of the emperor. In truth, the free act and the creative influx are separated only epistemologically; the view (contuitus) of one which we apprehend from the other demands, on the metaphysical level, a kind of heterogeneous identity.

These general considerations have not drawn us away from our subject. For we easily see their application to the problem of philosophical autonomy and religious heteronomy. Contrary to the most popular opinion, we insist that, on this matter, the positions of the philosopher and believer are not far apart. Both are at once autonomous and heteronomous, or rather theonomous. The philosopher always yields to the Logos; but the reason by which he freely decides is divided--it is him and it is not him. The force of his critical or architectonic judgment certainly does not depend intrinsically on earthly objects and it is indeed his own, but it has its origin in a superior power the norm of which allows him to establish his own norms. The confused progression from the fifth to the sixth conception of autonomy is clarified and ceases to be confusing, if we become aware of the bond which links our spirits to the Spirit. No philosophy of liberty or reason has ever succeeded in cutting the umbilical cord which connects the thinker to something transcendent; it has only succeeded in obscuring such an annoyance. As for the apparent self-sufficiency of philosophy, it is also quite clear that the objectivity of the argument does not suppress the mystery which we find in the philosopher: its formal coherence is only conceivable in relation to a received gift and concomitant norm. It becomes independent only by divinization, that is to say, by incorporating into itself something more than itself, and also by forgetting that it originates in the concrete liberty or personality of the thinker.

The believer, on his side, easily takes his place in theonomy. But does he thus cease to be autonomous? A faith of any value is free and responsible. The gift should be ratified and even subjected to critical scrutiny; for faith also represents personal growth; it is a call to self-determination and purification. The first participation in the Logos, which is reason, is not abolished in this new stage of participation which is revelation; for the first article of faith is that the Logos of reason and of revelation is the same. In submitting himself to a church, the believing Christian (our primary consideration here) should submit himself freely and his adhesion signifies that he believes in a continuous procession which gives correlative witness to the fidelity of the divine act. Earthly authority is only a vehicle for divine work. The New Testament clearly shows that our respect for the "deposit of faith" and the outpouring of the Spirit are joined in the faith of the Christian; far from being incompatible, they appeal to each other.

Must we add that theology, in tandem with philosophy, will bear the double mark of autonomy and theonomy? The very multiplicity of its manifestations shows that it is a human endeavor and that hearing the Divine Word does not free it from continued choice of fields of inquiry, from formulating axioms, from submitting to reasons which it has explicitly accepted as valid and thus from abandoning arbitrary preferences for conclusions which it might wish to make universal.

* * * * *

How then are we to differentiate philosophy from theology? Most often, we do so only by distinguishing the levels of nature and grace. There is nothing wrong with having recourse to this distinction, as long as we maintain that there is simultaneously autonomy and theonomy on both levels. But--without being able to discuss the question in depth--we can prefer another distinction.

"Supernatural" can mean: (1) an intimacy with God (to think as he thinks, to love as he loves); in this sense, the gift of the supernatural appears inseparable from the creation of a personal being and the notion of supernatural creation does not inevitably demand two moments (the call of the creature to being and then its elevation to the supernatural); (2) something beyond this initial gift, freely and lovingly given by God to the already-constituted personal being. This meaning is the most frequent in theology and even, for some theologians, the only possible meaning.

In these two senses, the supernatural is by definition beyond the reach of the creature left to himself: in the first case, the creature does not yet exist; in the second, the created person cannot vie with God and take possession of Him, if God will not give Himself.

Why then can philosophy not, in fact, be supernatural

188

in the two senses thus distinguished? The only way to avoid confusing it with religion and theology is to show that it always has ideas for its object, while religion and theology (at least in Christianity) are directed in the first place to events and persons, and only in the second place to ideas which evolve from them.

Another difficulty which concerns only Christian religion and Christian theology should be addressed. Is not the descent of the Eternal into time in the Incarnation, according to Kierkegaard's famous remark, a break with all thought? Is it not in virtue of the absurd that the Christian believes in the God-Man, in an Eternal being who is born, grows, and dies? Are we not this time in pure theonomy, a theonomy cruelly heteronomous, when the Utterly Other thus reveals Himself to us? And has not the philosopher the right to be scandalized and to take refuge in an autonomy which banishes faith?

However, the philosopher can maintain this position only if he denies the analogy between the two domains, as if clarity were to be found entirely in one camp and obscurity in the other. In reality, the mystery of transcendence, together with the long line of rational perplexities and provisional contradictions which it involves, already exists in the briefest reflection on a piece of straw. The struggle of Jacob with the angel permeates all our knowledge and all our action. This is precisely what allows us to verify once again that the condition of both the philosopher and the believer inevitably involves autonomy and theonomy. The goal of comprehensive vision which is at the heart of both reason and faith condemns the two to this double orientation.

Fundamentally, to reserve autonomy for the philosopher and to vow the believer to heteronomy is a pragmatic stratagem intended to preserve the peace between two categories of persons in a society which is becoming more secular. The process is convenient: each can even change aprons like Maître Jacques according to the hours of the day. But only half-hearted reflection would not experience some reluctance to accept this artifice and would not seek some other criterion in order to distinguish and understand what it means to philosophize and what it means to be a religious being; he will feel obliged to unite what has been separated and to distinguish what has been confused, with the aid of keen reflection and not of some specious postulate.

Chapter Seventeen

THEOLOGY AND PHILOSOPHY

Philosophy, Handmaid of Theology? [*]

Before touching on the theoretical problem of the relationship between theology and philosophy, [1] it is good to recall that these sciences are man-made, and that men are possessed of varying temperaments.

We might even say that theologians and philosophers belong to two different races. If it were not for the danger of being irreverent, I would gladly compare them to cats and dogs who live under the same roof, but regard one another without affection. The philosopher--meaning here the Christian philosopher-- is afraid of the theologian. He thinks that the latter is often guilty of snap judgments, that he makes grand affirmations, and facile connections, under the pretext that divine revelation serves as a guarantee, between hypotheses that are neither certain nor verifiable. The philosopher always wants to arrest the winged flight of the theologian; to say to him, "Not so fast; do not confuse the line of argument as you so frequently do . . . " But what the philosopher fears most of all is that the theologian will not hesitate to force him to make incursions into his field, and that he will use philosophy for the benefit of his own Schwarmerei, enthusiasms. Accustomed as he is to go along step-by-step, he is mistrustful of anyone who seems to know everything, and who walks among the mysteries as if he had been party to the councils of the Eternal Father.

For his part, the theologian is not any happier with the philosopher's approach. Recently, a friend of mine who knows my propensity for philosophical works, and who is himself a real

---

[*] "Philosophy, Handmaid of Theology?" by Maurice Nédon- celle. Translated by Ruth Dowd. **The Church and the World** (Con- cilium, Theology in the Age of Renewal No. 6). New York, Paulist Press, 1965. Pp. 93-104. Reprinted by permission of the publisher.

theologian, sent me his latest book with an acknowledgment which gave evidence of characteristic timidity. He wrote, "The theologian trembles before the philosopher." These words seem to me worth thinking about. Why this fear?

First of all, the theologian fears that he is in the presence of someone who, as the saying goes, splits hairs, and submits the product of his reasoning to a pitiless critique. He quickly feels paralyzed by the intervention of the philosopher. Then, he registers the fact that this would not happen if the two fields had nothing in common. The fields and the language, too. Basis and form intersect. It is precisely in this middle ground that the theologian runs the risk of being ill at ease: his freedom is under observation. Finally, the theologian fears in the philosopher, even in the Christian philosopher, the virtual presence of a lay critic and an unbeliever. He is under the impression that the philosopher, who "does not believe" in the role of grace <u>as a philosopher,</u> only pays it lip service as a man; he suspects him of being one of the false brethren, always ready to sabotage his neat doctrinal arrangements, in spite of every possible protestation of good will.

This introduction, which I am afraid is a little long, was necessary in order to "situate" the problem concretely. It is difficult, even chimerical, to omit consideration of this diversity of characteristics, when we scrutinize the demands the theologian can make of the philosopher, and the response that the philosopher will make to his colleague.

I

Since I have to speak here of the demands of the theologian, let us come immediately to the best-known and the most controversial question. Does theology need philosophy as her handmaid, yes or no? According to the old axiom attributed to Peter Damien, the unhesitating answer must be <u>yes!</u> However, the medieval authors whom he has in mind put philosophy at the service of faith, rather than of theology, and the shade of meaning here should not be overlooked. Their conception of philosophy or of dialectic must also be recast: it is certainly not ours, nor is it strictly uniform.

The term <u>ancilla</u> is not very clear, and it can designate a whole range of quite different services. Is philosophy a <u>slave</u>? a <u>maid-of-all-work</u>? a <u>housekeeper</u>? or the <u>wife</u> in a more or less morganatic marriage? How many ways are there of "<u>coming-to-the-aid-of</u>"? How many different ways there are of being an auxiliary to theology! And even if it is a question of marriage, the status of a married woman is also a variable!

It has become fashionable today to recognize that philosophy has a real autonomy. We are a long way from the rather conventional style that is found, for example, in the **Confessio Philosophi** of Leibniz, where the theologian is reputed to say to the philosopher: "Laudo modestiam tuam; instrumentum in te habebo." [2] However, very recently a thesis at the Sorbonne, written by M. Tresmontant, is in certain respects not very far from resurrecting this way of speaking. [3] The author believes that all religion implies a metaphysical Einstellung, or attitude-- what he terms a "metaphysical gesture." Hinduism requires an immanentist metaphysics, while Judaism and/or Christianity simply cannot be brought into line with such a teaching. What I still have not grasped in the very fine book of M. Tresmontant is the exact place of this profound metaphysic: does it agree with religion, and nothing more? Is it its preliminary basis? or its expression? or a little of all this at the same time? Whatever it may be, Christians in the course of history would have made their choice among available schools of philosophy, in line with the radical orientation prescribed by their religion. Little by little, a specifically Christian philosophy was formed, in opposition to non-Christian thinkers. On this score, some questions remain to be asked: Did Christians arbitrarily choose certain of the theses presented to them by pagan thought, and reject others? Or did they really innovate, did they create original ideas? The examples given by the author are especially those which concern a choice between a Creator and a Demiurge, or between a soul which forms part of the divine substance, and a soul which is not so mingled, etc.

In the second interpretation, namely that of a radical novelty in the philosophical concepts proposed by Christians, philosophy would be very dependent on faith. Nevertheless, if one were to grant, like Gilson and like Tresmontant with him, that the philosopher should think on his own, one might argue that extreme dependence would not in any way hinder, but would rather promote autonomy. It would be as if faith, having whispered the answer in the philosopher's ear, the philosopher went on to discover by his own methods the demonstration without which there would be no philosophy. But isn't the theologian also autonomous in this sense? Must not every intellectual development be a personal reflection on what is "given"? The data can be of various kinds, but the method is always either hypothetical-deductive or hypothetical-connective. It receives the data and puts them into operation.

To describe what takes place, I will not say, therefore, that on the one side there is autonomy and on the other there is not. Rather I would say: the theologian asks the philosopher to ply his trade and to speak up, but he asks him to speak after he, the theologian, has spoken. The theologian encourages the philosopher to be positive and effective. Philosophy is somewhat like his child; a living child of whom he can be proud, because this child, this daughter, will be respectful and grateful. Laudo modestiam tuam; instrumentum in te habebo . . . A living instrument, this must be insisted upon; a glorious offspring, capable of walking by herself, and on the right path.

This is a consoling vision of things, and consequently, it is seductive; perhaps, even, it is inseparable from the Christian outlook. Let it be noted, however, that Leibniz's phrase is indeed subtle, and that theology does not always ask philosophy to speak up. Sometimes, rather, it asks her to keep quiet, to make an admission of indigence and even of uncertainty, to question and not to be questioned. Such is, perhaps, the conception of Blondel, who seems at first to present philosophic certitude, and then, little by little, cuts the ground away from under his feet. He questions, if not exactly what he began by stating, at least what he must end by exploring. If philosophy wishes to go all the way under its own steam, it ends both in apotheosis and in failure; it is inevitably condemned to posit on its own the problem of the supernatural and not be able to solve it. It is a philosophy of insufficiency, at least in the vertical sense.

Certain theologians--probably Protestant ones--would go still further; they require reason to be their enemy. Karl Barth demands that philosophy (at least religious philosophy) be erroneous, and he cannot do anything without this beloved enemy whose flattery seems to him a perfidy. He does not want a handmaid, and above all he does not intend to marry the handmaid; he files suit for divorce before the wedding ceremony takes place!

But in all these attitudes, seemingly contradictory, what always characterizes the theologian is that he determines with prophetic assurance what philosophy has to say and to do. He insists that she will be either for him or against him; he predicts how she will act and he judges this action. Instrumentum in te habebo . . . The formula is more difficult to get rid of than one would imagine. There is not much difference in this respect between the partisans of the direct power of theology and those of its indirect power, nor between our Catholic manuals and the **Dogmatik** of Karl Barth. Resting-place or taking-off point, philosophy is an indispensable subordinate.

The stranglehold of the theologian on philosophy is accentuated by pedagogy. For the teaching of theology demands the preliminary adoption of a widely accepted language and logic. P. Mesnard has shown--following, in this, certain German authors--how Luther was obliged to re-introduce philosophical teachings into the German universities, and that this movement, which began with a return to formal logic, ended by a return to ontology. With all the more reason then, does the Catholic tradition call for an underlying philosophy. Our professors of theology need students who have been trained in scholastic philosophy:

1. Because a uniform vocabulary is needed, an audience that will understand what one intends to say, e.g., they must know the meaning of <u>essence</u>, <u>substance</u>, <u>cause</u> . . .

2. Because dogma must be based on firm convictions, e.g., the fact that there is a God, a soul, etc., must be established.

The theologian, it is true, does not wish his students to be philosophers except within certain limits; for if they go beyond the propaedeutic, there is the risk that they will no longer be well disposed toward a theological calling. A little philosophy leads to theology; too much of it can interfere with the recruitment of theologians, who undergo a vocational crisis all the more marked in that within their own discipline they experience the brilliance of, and are challenged by, the competition offered by kerygma, liturgy, etc.

The pedagogical demand is a worthy one. If we could put ourselves once and for all into the ways of the 13th century, all would be well. Besides, as professors we always have a nostalgia for this kind of thing. But in the measure in which history has given birth to different ways of thinking, the whole situation becomes problematic. So much so, that theologians are obliged to oscillate between two attitudes. On the one hand, they cherish their scholastic foundations. These are essential to their vision of themselves as teachers. On the other hand, in spite of the confusion in philosophy which is the result of differences in culture developed through the centuries, they are interested in these attempts; they know that they find in them indispensable occasions for renewal; they need them for research. This free and new philosophy is not their <u>handmaid</u>, but their <u>sister</u>. She is not always well behaved; but if they do not take an interest in her, they run the risk of paralysis. They no longer dictate to her; they try to learn from contact with her, and, above all, to understand her.

II

This second attitude leads me to the second part of my argument. The theologian--not perhaps the professor, but the seeker--turns to philosophy as to a spectacle; he wants to read in it spiritual adventures different from his own, adventures that can teach him things he does not even suspect. Perhaps in reflecting on this material he will understand revelation better. His mental attitude is not different from the one he adopts toward exegetes and historians. Thus, he is brought to practice reflection in many different fields. Ricoeur, apropos of Nabert, [4] spoke recently of this phenomenon; its fecundity is derived precisely from the fact that it is not connected with a source or a principle in absolute isolation.

1. <u>Anthropology</u> is the first field in which interest or concern is manifested. Let us take some examples. If we are satisfied to describe death as a separation of body and soul, then the theology of the cross will remain for us paltry and dry. If, on the contrary, we attempt to gather and deepen human experience on this subject, as have, for example, in different senses, Landsberg, Karl Rahner, and Mouroux, then we inevitably throw an appreciable light on the meaning of the redemption. Meditation on the death of man, whatever his death and whoever this man may be, is a stimulus to meditation on the death of Christ, and can renew its meaning. All the more reason for this when the man is a Socrates and the death, the death of Socrates. And still greater reason if, over and above the exact experience which is being described, is added a reflection on the experience. [5]

Likewise, who will deny that a deeper knowledge of motherhood will contribute to a better theological grasp of certain aspects of Mariology?

The <u>gnôthi sauton</u> implied in a philosophical program not only throws light on the humanity of Christ or the humanity of Mary; it renders even greater services; it throws light on the being and the work of the incarnate Word. Thus, a deeper search for the meaning of human solidarity cannot but have repercussions on our exploration of the mystery of the incarnation. The Council of Quiersy in the 9th century declared: "Almighty God wishes that all men, without exception, be saved, although not all may be saved . . . Just as there is, was or will be no man whose nature Christ Jesus, our Lord, did not assume, so there is, was or will be no man for whom he has not suffered" (Denz. 318, 319).

Is it not evident that it will be an advantage for us to know how relationships are established between human beings in the so-called natural order, and that if we do understand them, we will understand better the conciliar statements we have just cited? For certain ones of the Fathers, <u>humanitas</u> was then <u>quasi unus homo</u>. Their background was perhaps neo-Platonic; they were probably disputing the subject of traducianism. Are their ideas valid for us, or not? Do they better express what we think of human intersubjectivity? The answer cannot be indifferent to those who wish to determine the relation of human beings to Christ and the effects of the work of the redemption on the salvation of men.

In the same manner, the whole treatise on the sacraments

is an offshoot of anthropology. It is so, first of all in general, for a concept of the spiritual act and of the sign is inherent in the meaning of the sacrament. The Scholastics, arguing about this in terms of matter and form, have sometimes ignored, or consigned to second place, the intentio, about which the Council of Trent is, however, more concerned. Would not the intentio be the very soul of the sacrament, insofar as it has a sign-character, that which binds matter and form together? Philosophers would have to say so. Intellect, which takes hold of the materiality of the sign, transforms it. It does so not only by the reflexive consciousness of intentionality, or by an associative pursuit of objecive symbols, but by an aptitude for discovering the transparency of the data in relation to a transcendence that operates in them and in us. A purely associative theory of signs--such as we find in our manuals--enables us to penetrate the nature of the sacrament in a far less satisfying way than does a theory of efficacy-through-transparence, which, by starting from the notion of intentio, is alone capable of giving new meaning to the notions of sacramental structure and of ex opere operato. And what is indeed instructive here is reflection on the co-existence, or influence, at the level of philosophic anthropology.

If we now study the sacraments in particular, the same facts are borne out. Is it not significant that the history of religions focuses the largest number of rites of access to the divinity on sacred meals and sexual unions? The meaning of this union seems to have more importance in this respect than what Pradines called the "sense of distance." In Christianity, these perspectives are not forgotten but are purified. The eucharist is indeed a sacred banquet. It is a sacrificial eating (manducation). Rooting it thus in the history of religions is not the essential thing, but it is bound up with the essential thing. Theologians have nothing to be afraid of here. St. John Chrysostom was not afraid of this fact: he prefaced his theology of the eucharist by a philosophy of repasts. And Bossuet strenuously insisted on the destruction of the species in the holy sacrifice. In addition, we again find the anthropological connection of death and of Calvary in this nucleus of Catholic teaching on the eucharist.

It would be easy to point out examples that pertain to the other sacraments. Thus it is not surprising that the supernatural understanding of marriage is aided by a philosophical meditation on love. Many modern thinkers have spared no efforts to show this. And it is not always in vain. In certain pages of Madinier, there are remarks on this theme which could never be found in the writings of St. Augustine.

But without further delay, let us come to a general conclusion. There is a philosophical teaching (both from a phenomenological and a metaphysical point of view) which is confused with an anthropology, and which is not a simple introduction to a theology of revelation, but which finds a place within it, a sort of "predestined" part of it. In this respect, the supernatural is, purely and simply, nature elevated. The Schools say that the supernatural is an accident and not a substance in us. This way of speaking is sometimes equivocal, but it seems here to be very much to the point. Who could have any objection to this status of anthropology <u>within</u> theology, this integration to an order of new relationships by a kind of simple transposition? The justification for it lies in the fact that Christ is man. The human element can be immediately adapted to a theological perspective by the fact that the humanity of Christ is not an illusion, but more really human than our own because it is more perfectly human than ours.

2. There is a second philosophical realm whose implication would be equally fruitful for theology. This is the supreme metaphysical realm, that of <u>the investigation of being,</u> of the problem of God. Again we find ourselves faced with an immense program of research. Let us limit ourselves to a single point. Is not the Thomistic proof of God's existence a definitive proof, much more than a deduction or an induction, a kind of reduction? The lamented M. Rabeau saw this very well. <u>Anankè stênai</u> . . . The abstracting mind is the term. There is an <u>ontological</u> dynamism of the mind, a deficiency of the world which is compensated for by the plenitude implicit in <u>mind</u>. Undoubtedly, this is what leads us to God himself, and what establishes his existence. This is the God of the philosophers. But is this Absolute incomplete <u>because</u> it is philosophical? Let us admit at least that it can be kept in its totality, and ennobled by revelation. Philosophy's mode of survival in the theological order does not differ essentially from what it was just now when we were speaking of anthropology.

3. However, there is a third region of theology where cooperation with philosophy is manifested in an entirely different way. I wish to speak here of theology as it was understood by the Fathers, of <u>the trinitarian life of God</u>. When the theologian treats of the place of the Word in the Trinity, are we not thrust beyond all borrowing and all analogy, even that of proportionality? Certainly, insofar as the theology of the incarnate Word offers us taking-off points within our human nature, just so far does the theology of the Word in heaven abruptly draw us far away from every region inhabited by creatures. We can no longer foresee anything. Our powers fail.

Nevertheless, perhaps this is true only in appearance. In any conversation with theologians, three tendencies can be observed. Some show themselves to be anti-psychological and even anti-philosophical in their trinitarian speculations. Unfortunately, they never cease to speculate, but they do so in a code, on data whose trans-rational nakedness they preserve. For them, trinitarian theology divorces understanding and explanation or explicitation.

But side by side with this tendency there is a second one. For this second type of theologian, the human intellect left to its own powers is able to find phenomenological and metaphysical indications which are capable of bringing about a better understanding of the data of faith. Gregory of Nazianzen said of the Son that he was from the Father, and that he was like the Father. Could these theses be unrelated to human sonship and human fatherhood? What is from below can serve for understanding what is from above.

And finally, there is a third group of theologians. For them, all theology must submit to a twofold and inevitable movement. On the one hand, our natural experience and reflection imply a supernatural apprehension; or, to put it more precisely, our concrete nature finds within itself the steppingstones which Blondel described, and which are related not only to the supernatural life in us, but to the inner life of God. Thus, it is useful for the theologian to listen to this witness. On the other hand, this movement would come to nought if our trans-natural reflection did not make us aware of the sacrificial offering which we ought to make of our nature and of our philosophy itself. Even more, it would not be anything at all unless a movement were produced by which light and strength descend through grace into our faculties, and if they were not the bearers of a revealed datum of the supernatural order which is the object of theological meditation.

Is not this third kind of theology the best? Not only is it useless to make an absolute separation between theology and oikonomia in the sense in which the Fathers use this term; but even taking the term of theology in its widest and most modern meaning, it cannot be isolated from philosophy, to which it is bound by a reciprocal osmosis, in use and even in specification.

But there are limits to this interpenetration or osmosis. The theologian has a much more interpellative attitude than the philosopher has. He thinks, so to speak, in the vocative case; he inclines to prayer; in any event, he thinks in the current of historical perception; revelation is event, and the dominant event is the coming of Christ. But philosophy is not concerned with proper names, and it takes a slanted view of events. It only examines ideas, and abstracts them from facts and/or persons, even when it is studying the ideas that radiate from persons and the history of those ideas. This is the reason why the two specialists will never become identified, will not always relish each other, and will often have difficulty in coming to a mutual understanding, although they will never cease to have the need of mutual consultation.

NOTES

1. The sole purpose of these observations is to open a debate. They are, in part, the result of a conversation with my two colleagues, MM. Plagnieux and Chavasse, whom I wish to thank here, while assuming full responsibility for the opinions expressed in this article.

2. G. W. Leibniz, **Confessio Philosophi.** Text, translation, and notes by Y. Belaval (Paris, 1961), p. 110.

3. Cf. Tresmontant, **La métaphysique du christianisme et la naissance de la philosophie chrétienne** (Paris, 1961).

4. E. Nabert, **Eléments pour une éthique.** Preface by P. Ricoeur. (Paris, 1962), p. 9.

5. It goes without saying that every caution must be used in facing the risks inherent in a given situation or experience, which I have used here just as an example, and which, by definition, is a presentiment, or a perception of another, not of a passage already realized by us, since we are still alive.

A Final Remark: The Two Forms of Relation

Lengthy additions should not encumber a collection of articles. Such material would often be repetitious of earlier works, while the articles are intended to explicate the theses and develop certain lines of previous studies.

But one possible objection should be answered briefly. You may say: "You have spoken primarily of the relation to others. But have you not used the term in two incompatible senses? On the one hand, you consider the relation as interior to beings: it almost defines the person. On the other hand, you make a character-istic of being, which you identify with its form of exteriority. How can these two conceptions be reconciled?"

There seems little point in answering in different words, in opposing the lived "relation" to the conceptual "connection"; for being is not only a representation, it also affects beings and, in this sense, is lived. Nor is this the place to comment on the distinction between _esse_ _ad_ and _esse_ _in_. This would draw us into certain disputes and make us appear to parody the historical formu-lation.

Rather, let me recall what I have suggested in the course of this volume, in the first paragraph of Chapter XI and in the thirteenth paragraph of Chapter XII. The human person is actually subjected to two forms of relation: one, which I called primordial, is that of being, that is to say of the exteriority into which we are born as creatures; this form of relation is reborn each moment; for creation is continuous and we cannot escape from this native condition or from the developments which constitute the history of renascent being. But this perpetually preliminary relation is perpetually oriented toward an interpersonal communion by the reciprocal genesis of consciousnesses. Yet this last form of relation is an otherness without exteriority, it is the We in its purity, it is constitutive of the beings it unites. Thus we must live the relation on a double level.

We certainly agree with Renouvier or Hamelin that the person cannot be understood without the relation and that the person is the most synthetic center of the relations. But we must first take into account the complex anatomy of the world of the relation and, second, we must avoid the trap which consists of thinking of interontic communion in terms of ontological communication. Were we to make this mistake, our conclusion would inevitably lead us to the classic logical difficulties of the Anglo-Saxon problem concerning the interiority or exteriority of relations; we would see the bonds which unite the terms or the terms which are united by these bonds vanish one by one. For we cannot make the communication absolute without renouncing the person, and the subsequent difficulties serve to warn us that the person is not a thing, but a vocation and a liberation.

In communion, we discover a love which actually fosters our personal oneness: it respects the contingency of our encounter and leads to successful attempts at communication. Communion is the most complex and highest relation, that which establishes us in the other and in God without reducing us to the rank of attributes or adjectives. I fear Bradley has pushed this relation too far into exteriority. But after some possible modifications, I would transpose and gladly apply to the We what he says of the one: "In such a unity the imperfect relational scheme and the imperfect whole of feeling are both included and absorbed." The We is "something which is positive and all-comprehending and not in principle unthinkable." [1] It is not unthinkable, but it is not explainable. Whatever bears the print of the absolute breeds and eludes explanations.

The We does not only unite the I and the Thou into a harmonious reciprocity, it can also bring together into its field the otherness and even the hostility of consciousness. Nothing can suppress it or cease to contribute to it, neither the scheme of being nor the violent forces of the world in which we struggle. On the contrary, this alteriety and, a fortiori, the impulses of negativity cannot reach the depths and destiny of personal beings as such. But in its ultimate source and ultimate auto-finality, the We clearly has the fullness of love and controls its own development. It reconciles the It as a third with the I and the Thou or the I and the You; its central value is not dimished by the qualitative worth of participants nor is its reality modified by the multitude of participants.

The relation which is the form of being and the relation which is interior to beings are compatible. One last consideration will help clarify this point. Instead of isolating the indefinite entirely from the finite, we have linked it to the infinite and condemned it to the finite. [2] Such is, of course, the profound explanation of our rational duality. Man is amphibious. We cannot free ourselves from the exteriority which limits every creature in and by being; that is why, for example, we cannot imagine a time before time without a regression which makes us cruelly aware that our thought is born and reborn outside of the infinite. But we are also even more aware that our destiny, because of its metaphysical beginning and end, transcends our birth and ontological rebirths. We are among those beings whose person feels the pull of the infinite and finds in interontic communion the constitutive finality of an eternity which is not specious. Thus the end which reveals the I and the We assumes and cures in both the infirmity of our earthly condition. Even though man is amphibious, his states are not irreconcilable.

Let us take a different approach to the distinction between the ontological relation and the ontic relation or, if you prefer, the contrast between being and personal or interpersonal being. This will help us to understand better their complementarity.

1) One aspect of the relation that defines being is the thrust into exteriority and the creation of a gap. Being is at the origin of the creaturely state and implies a sort of initial and recurrent fragmentation, a stepping aside from self toward self, toward the other, and toward God. Thus comes the inevitable distance between us and our works in the image of the distance between us and our Creator. This distancing from origin is renewed in every nascent state: it enlarges the community of beings and constitutes for each not only an intimate duality, but also a world which comes to the self as a third reality. Distance is the stigma of an imperfection in persons and between them. [3]

But we cannot reduce being to a chasm. Another of its aspects is a call to close this gap. Being which puts us apart is also the means which leads us toward "ipseity" and communion. It is appropriate here to recall Heraclitus' profound comment on the reversible (palintropic) unity of the bow which bends and relaxes: what is different can be reconciled. The being who reflects on being begins to close the gap and moves it from its natural state to a mental existence. The idea of being makes us discover the most elevated function of being itself--to be integrated by being into the final destiny of being. When, simultaneously with God, we ratify desire, evaluate being into which we are born and endlessly reborn, its form of exteriority changes character and becomes in some fashion glorified matter. From a chasm which prepares indirectly and asymptotically our personal vocation, we pass to an exteriority quite unlike exile; since it henceforth manifests our vocation in its content and in its realization. Art effects a return of this sort and helps us to understand the norm of our own development.

When being is antecedent to us, it separates us from ourselves and from all things: by the same token, it permits us to escape natural attractions and to progress freely and critically toward ourselves and toward all things. When being is consequent and has passed through our consciousness, it becomes a victory over the chasm and closes the vast circle of personal beings. Being has made the world arise as a third in the relation of the I to the Me and the I to the Thou, but the third, become articulated and objective, is not isolated; it is the meeting of reciprocal perspectives and if it never becomes the center of the We, it is for us a docile and transparent satellite. [4]

Being, whether abstract or concrete, is not the opposite (and a fortiori an obstacle) of beings. We should even say that being as being, not as a category, has no opposite, no contradictory. Its history does not include non-being or negation, even though it may be open to spatio-temporal growth. Such is not the case for a being in which it has engendered contingency; for birth and death surround us and touch us. We live in this world under the continual threat of annihilation, as does the world itself. We can observe the absence or disappearance of an earthly being, but the absence or disappearance of being makes no sense as long as there remains a being and a world.

In the conception of being just presented, nothingness has no place; being extends everywhere there are beings and is not touched by their tragedy. The representation of the nothingness of being could only result from the being's terror that it might be abandoned by God or from the being's vain revolt against God, or even from a hypothetical manner of expressing a non-creator God. The originality of being, in comparison with the values of truth, beauty, and goodness, is that it has no real counter-values, as they do in the false, the ugly, and the evil; because of this purity and it alone, being participates in the dignity of the absolute Being and reveals to us its design in creation. But it introduces in us the possibility of a negation that it is not and the possibility of suppressing the separation it initially imposed on us. But what is neither aporetic nor antinomic elicits aporia and antinomy in us when we conceive of the ontological relation as an isolatable and absolute reality which will not be subordinated to any being.

2) The relation that defines being is the constitutive element of the intersubjectivity of persons. The I and the Thou are revealed in this relation or, better yet, they there effect and realize their very essence. If this dynamic relation is truly constitutive, it is identified with a reciprocal genesis of consciousness. It is not different from the very singularity of persons in communion. Thus there is no need to subject it to radical analysis, "because it is him, because it is me" . . . Inevitably, the interpersonal ontic must end in an ambiance of intimacy which cannot be conceptualized.

But it does conceptualize. That is why it leads to the

articulation of the other and of others, with the progressive intervention of concrete partners into the universal form which has us expecting them and is rooted in the creative Thou of the I. In this form, it establishes the moments of intersubjective causality and the hierarchy of the We according to degrees of intimacy. Above all, the constitutive relation of intersubjective reciprocity is capable, because it is conceptualizing without being able to be conceptualized, of giving an account of the ontological relation. This relation discerns in being the fruitful ambiguity of the chasm and of the closing of this gap; this relation discerns in our indefinitude the interplay of the finite and infinite; finally, this relation gives meaning, in its very depths, to the scheme of being and thus becomes the bond which assumes the other bonds--in a word, the relation of the relation.

NOTES

1. F. H. Bradley, **Essays on Truth and Reality,** Oxford, 1944, p. 239.

2. See Chapter IX. On this point, we have not followed the much more "finitist" anthropology of Descartes' **Meditations.**

3. From this point of view, our "ontological relation" can find analogues in the most disparate contexts: from the Platonic chora to the "difference" of Derrida, and passing through a host of other concepts scattered throughout history: the diastema of the Stoics, the materia signata quantitate of the Scholastics, the sensorium divinum of Newton, Berkeley's principle of nature as language, the Leibnizian mediation, the Zwischen of M. Buber, or the intervalle of R. de Senne . . . Of course, we have no intention of confusing these systems nor even of adopting some of these notions, we merely wish to point out in all an element which corresponds to being conceived as primordial relation as we have explained it. We could say as much for M. Blondel's idea of vinculum, but it covers many things: it may designate either a finite and intermediate reality which is independent of personal beings while serving as an exterior support, or it may be a factor acting from within them, or finally the act of an infinite, eternal or incarnate Word.

4. In regard to the divinity, we would be tempted to see rather than a messenger, a "body of God" to adopt the expression of the Indian philosopher Ramanûja.